JEWISH LAW ASSOCIATION STUDIES I
The Touro Conference Volume

JEWISH LAW ASSOCIATION STUDIES I
The Touro Conference Volume

Edited by
B. S. Jackson

Scholars Press
Chico, California

JEWISH LAW ASSOCIATION STUDIES I
The Touro Conference Volume

Edited by
B. S. Jackson

©1985
Scholars Press

Library of Congress Cataloging in Publication Data
Main entry under title:

Jewish Law Association studies I.

Proceedings of the second International Congress of the Jewish Law Association, organized by the Touro College School of Law and held in New York in Dec. 1982.
1. Jewish law—Congresses. I. Jackson, Bernard S.
II. Jewish Law Association. International Congress (2nd : 1982 : New York, N.Y.) III. Series. IV. Title: Studies in Jewish law 1. V. Title: Studies in Jewish law one.
LAW   296.1'8   84-1329
ISBN 0-89130-732-X   (alk. paper)
ISBN 0-89130-868-7   (pbk.: alk. paper)

Printed in the United States of America
on acid-free paper

Table of Contents

Preface	vii
Reb Zadok Hakohen of Lublin on Prophecy in the Halakhic Process	
Yaakov Elman	1
The Corporate Status of *Heḳdesh* in Early Sefardic Responsa	
David Fink	17
Jewish Divorce in American Courts—The New York Experience	
Steven F. Friedell	25
A New/Old Look at the Fifth Amendment—Some Help from the Past	
Joseph B. Glaser	29
Participation of the Common People in Pharisaic and Rabbinic Legislative Processes	
Alexander Guttmann	41
The Use of a Sacred Object in the Administration of a Judicial Oath	
G. Libson	53
The Marital Status of Jews Married under Non-Jewish Auspices	
David Novak	61
The Use of Excessive Force by a Peace Officer: One Halakhic Opinion	
S. M. Passamaneck	79
Geṭ and *Geṭ Shiḥrur*	
Daniela Piattelli	93
Coercion in Conjugal Relations	
Nahum Rakover	101
Dina Demalkhuta Dina	
Sylvan Jay Schaffer	121
Extensive and Restrictive Interpretation of Terms in Rabbinic Hermeneutic	
Norman Solomon	125
Some Stock Arguments for the Magnanimity of the Law in Hellenistic Jewish Apologetics	
Abraham Terian	141
Abstracts	151

PREFACE

In December 1982, the Jewish Law Association held its second International Congress in New York, hosted and organized by the Touro College School of Law. The event was the first such international gathering to be held in the United States, and marks, along with the establishment of an Institute of Jewish Law at the Touro Law School and the initiation of a Jewish Law section in the American Association of Law Schools, the upsurge of interest in Jewish law which is presently to be observed in the United States, and among legal scholars in particular.

The Conference coincided with Chanuka of 5743, which made the central venue of the Conference, the Civic Center Synagogue, New York City, especially appropriate. Participants appreciated the opportunity to share in the festive seasonal atmosphere. Grateful thanks are due to the President of the Civic Center Synagogue, Judge Jerome Hornblass, and to Rabbi Joshua Hecht, for their hospitality and cooperation. The Association owes a considerable debt of gratitude to Touro College, and in particular to its President, Dr. Bernard Lander, the Dean of its Law School, Professor John Bainbridge, and especially to the then Director of the Institute of Jewish Law, Professor Dov I. Frimer, and his conference organising committee, for making the Conference the notable success it was.

Any ban which may once have existed upon the writing down of oral teaching has no application to modern scholarly discussions of Jewish law. In undertaking to sponsor the Conference, Touro College (while not associating itself with the views expressed herein, which remain those of the individual authors) also committed itself to secure the publication of the Conference proceedings. This volume is the result, and with it The Jewish Law Association is able to initiate its own publication programme. For this, too, the Association expresses its profound gratitude to President Lander.

The papers which follow illustrate the breadth of scholarly activity currently directed towards the Jewish legal tradition. Historical studies, ranging from the second commonwealth to the modern period, are matched by comparative, dogmatic, and philosophical treatments—the four "avenues" to the study of law which the late Boaz Cohen, who virtually founded the academic study of Jewish law in the United States, viewed as both essential and complementary. As Cohen remarked, "While the demarcations of these four points of view are sharply marked, a full and complete understanding of the law, in breadth and depth, would require a masterly acquisition of these four disciplines" (*Jewish and Roman Law*, I. viii). Today, we realise more than ever not only the wisdom of Cohen's remarks, but also the need for scholarly co-operation in order to achieve his objectives. Jewish law has become a truly inter-disciplinary field, encompassing not only distinctive approaches to Jewish law itself, but also contributions from the various outside disciplines to which these different approaches are related.

From the conception of The Jewish Law Association as a result of a conference organised by the Oxford Centre for Postgraduate Hebrew Studies in 1978 (see *Jewish Law in Legal History and the Modern World*, Leiden: E. J. Brill, 1980, The Jewish Law Annual Supplementary Series, II), such a broad approach to Jewish law has characterised its conferences and activities. The recent increase in interest in Jewish law in American law schools is to be unreservedly welcomed. But jurists alone cannot do full justice to the task: the Jewish legal tradition requires the attention equally of the various disciplines which make up the field of Jewish studies. The proceedings of The Jewish Law Association have been notable for the participation of both jurists and Judaica scholars, as is well represented by the contents of the present volume.

REB ZADOK HAKOHEN OF LUBLIN
ON PROPHECY IN THE HALAKHIC PROCESS

by

YAAKOV ELMAN*

I

The cultural discontinuity between the Biblical ("Israelite") and post-Biblical ("Jewish") periods in the religious history of Israel is one of the staples of modern scholarship, though it has never been recognized, except in the most limited way, by traditional Jewish thought. Y. H. Yerushalmi, in the recently published Stroum Lectures,[1] has most recently delineated the outlines of one crucial aspect of this discontinuity in contrasting the overwhelmingly negative attitude of all mainstream post-Biblical Jewish thought toward history and historiography—outside of Biblical "metahistory"—with the high value placed on it as a mode of discourse in the Bible.

In his third lecture, Yerushalmi investigates the astonishing efflorescence of Jewish historical writing in the sixteenth century, only to underscore its lack of influence in its own time, its lack of continuity with earlier trends—and the absence of a continuing historical school to carry on its work.[2] It is thus highly unusual, to say the least, to come upon a recognized, traditional thinker whose historical awareness penetrated to the very essence and center of his thought, and whose influence continues to grow. Such a thinker is the subject of this paper, the first of two, on the historical dimension in the theological system of Rabbi Zadok Hakohen Rabinowitz of Lublin. "Reb" Zadok (1823–1900) was born to a

---

*Ph.D. candidate, Department of Near Eastern Languages and Literatures, New York University. I wish to thank the following for discussing various aspects of R. Zadok's work with me: Profs. Dov. I. Frimer, Bernard S. Jackson, Bezalel Safran, Lawrence I. Schiffman, Rabbis Irwin Haut and Eliezer Weinstein, to Rabbi Israel Zalisky for the loan of *Tsidḳat Hatsadiḳ Hashalem*, and to Rivkah Haut and Rabbi Reuven Porcelan for obtaining for me several articles pertaining to R. Zadok. In particular, my thanks go to Prof. S. Z. Leiman, who not only took the time to read over an earlier draft of this paper, but has been a constant source of encouragement. None bears any responsibility for any mistakes or misinterpretations found therein.

[1] *Zakhor: Jewish History and Jewish Memory* (Seattle: University of Washington Press, 1982), esp. 36–38, 43–45.

[2] *Ibid.*, 66–67.

family of *mitnagdim* in Latvia, where his father served as a rabbi. He reportedly began the study of Talmud at age three and one-half, and completed it for the first time at eight. As a young man he joined the Hasidic movement, and became a follower of R. Mordechai Yosef Leiner, of Izhbitz, Poland, one of whose successors he eventually became. R. Zadok was incredibly prolific, but most of his books, none of which were published in his long lifetime, were lost in the destruction of the Lublin ghetto by the Nazis; what remains,[3] however, runs to thousands of closely-printed pages in a terse, elliptical style.

His interests were diverse, at least in terms of his time and place: his writings include commentaries on parts of the Bible,[4] Talmudic *novellae*,[5] responsa,[6] discourses on Hasidism and Kabbala[7]—and historiography.[8] His control of talmudic, midrashic and kabbalistic sources, within their traditional boundaries, was total, and his writings are composed of densely clustered collections of condensed references to those sources, interspersed with longer or shorter analyses of common themes. His thought, as noted, had a decided historical cast to it, similar in its concerns to that of Maharal, by whom he was greatly influenced, but his understanding of the Biblical period in particular was (and is) quite radical in the context of Orthodox thought.[9]

Traditionally, it is an article of faith that the entire system of *Halakhah* was revealed in minute detail to Moses and continued in force from then on to the present time, albeit with occasional losses which

---

[3] See the list of his known works, including (some of?) the lost ones, in A. I. Bromberg, *Haadmor Milublin* (Jerusalem: Beth Hillel, 5742), 174–76.

[4] Among his lost works are said to be commentaries on *Job* and *Jeremiah*.

[5] He occasionally quotes from his own notes and *novellae* on Talmud. These too are lost.

[6] *Tiferet Tsevi*, 2 volumes (Bilgoray, 5669, repr. Bnai Brak: Yahadut, 5727). Two other collections were lost.

[7] Chiefly *Pri Tsadik*, 5 volumes (Lublin 5661-94 [hereafter *PT*]); *Tsidkat Hatsadik* (Lublin, 5662, repr. Bnai Brak: Yahadut, 5733), but the best edition is *Tsidkat Hatsadik Hamale*, (Jerusalem: "A" Publishers, 5728 [hereafter *TH*]); *Resise Laylah* (Lublin, 5663, repr. Bnai Brak, Yahadut: 5727 [hereafter *RL*]); *Mahshevet Haruts* (Pietrikov, 5672, repr. Bnai Brak: Yahadut, 5727 [hereafter *MH*]); *Divre Soferim* (Lublin, 5673, repr. Bnai Brak: Yahadut, 5733 [hereafter *DS*]).

[8] *Zikaron Larishonim*, see n. 40. His catholicity of interest may be gathered from the fact that he refers to the Apocrypha more than casually. Also, *Shemot Baarets* (a play on Ps 46:9), whose publication history is similar to that of *Zikaron Larishonim* (see n. 40 below), indicates a lively and lifelong interest in historical problems.

[9] Despite that fact, or perhaps because of it, his work has become more influential in the last generation, chiefly through the efforts of the late Rabbi Yitzhak Hutner of Yeshivat Chaim Berlin, and the late Rabbi Gedaliah Shorr, of Yeshivat Torah Vadaat. The use made by the former is particularly of interest, and I hope to deal with the similarities and divergences on another occasion. Claims have also been made for R. Zadok's influence on Rabbi A. I. Kook, but see Y. Hadari, "Shir shel Yom Betorat R. Tsadok Hakohen," *Sinai* 53 (5723 [=1963]), n. 4.

were, in the main, restored. In the course of time additions to the system were made, in the form of specific judicial legislation, but on the whole, the *"Torah"* which the Rabbis possessed was essentially identical to that which existed in the Biblical period, with all its attendant techniques and values.[10] The Patriarchs were considered to have lived out their lives in voluntary compliance with norms which became compulsive only at Sinai.[11]

This doctrine raised a number of serious historical problems with whose symptoms the rabbis grappled, with varying degrees of awareness and success. The most pervasive was the relative lack of importance assigned to learning, in the Rabbinic sense, in the Bible. The solution was simple if not altogether convincing: the Rabbis depicted various Biblical personages as great scholars, and interpreted their political and personal conflicts as stemming from scholarly disagreement.[12] That in turn led to the need to explain the instances of un- or counter-halakhic acts attributed to those Biblical figures.

For example: David's use of the shew-bread for secular purposes in *I Sam.* 21:4–7;[13] Michal's reunion with David (*II Sam.* 3:13–16) after her marriage to Palti(el) b. Laish (*I Sam* 25:44)[14] in the light of *Deut.* 24:4 and *Yeb.* 11b, the latter of which prohibits such action even in the case of an *arusah*; and Tamar's statement to her brother Amnon, *II Sam.* 13:13) that King David, their father, would not withhold her from him, if asked in the proper manner,[15] all represent such un-*halakhic* acts.

The general rabbinic response has been to interpret each such situation as reflecting certain unusual circumstances, which can be dealt with by a special rule that allows the problematic act to be subsumed under the usual legal forms while accounting for the anomalous aspects of the particular incident.

R. Zadok provides a solution to the problems outlined above, though he never addressed himself, at least in just these terms, to them. But he does so at the cost of denying that religious continuity the rabbis posited in its essential aspect: the role of Oral Torah in the prophetic era.

---

[10] Y. *Peah* 2:6, "All that a mature disciple would in future times innovate [in Torah] before his master was already revealed to Moses at Sinai." An erudite defense of the traditional view may be found in Z. H. Ḥayut, *Torat Hanevi'im*, in *Kol Ṣifre Maharats Ḥayut* (Jerusalem: Divre Ḥakhamim, 5718), I, 1–135.

[11] *Yom.* 28b.

[12] This is so common as not to require proof; see *Sanh.* 101b–4a, for example.

[13] *Men.* 95b–96a; see also, *Rashi, ad loc.*, s.v. *mesukan*: David was in danger of death by starvation; moreover, he was at that moment faint from hunger.

[14] See *Radak, ad loc.*, and *Sanh.* 19b.

[15] See *Sanh.* 21a.

II

R. Zadok viewed the history of Biblical religion in terms of a continuing struggle between the allure of prophecy and the demands of the Oral Torah, the latter epitomised in talmudic dialectic. His basic prooftext is *Tanhuma's*[16] reinterpretation of the talmudic depiction of the acceptance of the Torah at Mount Sinai as having taken place under duress, with God suspending the mountain over the heads of the recalcitrant Israelites;[17] according to Tanhuma, their unwillingness was directed against the acceptance of the discipline required to master that dialectic[18] rather than to Scripture itself. Another consideration, which appears already in an early work,[19] and would seem to have been one of the motivating factors in the formation of his theory, was the inclusion of the prophets as a group, without the naming of individuals in the line of transmission of Torah in *Ab.* 1:1. According to R. Zadok, this lack of detail reflects the irrelevance of tradition in the training of the prophets, whose mission is validated from Above rather by an ordination grounded in a mastery of traditional lore. Though some degree of scholarship is necessary in a prophet according to the dictum that prophecy comes only to one who has some right to the title of scholar,[20] that is not its essential prerequisite. To place the prophets in the line of transmission of Oral Torah is, to R. Zadok, incongruous. Moreover, if the laying-out of a chain of transmission of a certain body of knowledge was intended in this mishnah-passage, details of that long history should have been provided. Finally, if the Mishnah's interest in the prophets is primarily for their scholarly attainments, why call them prophets?

For these reasons, R. Zadok interprets this mishnah as referring to something other than oral Torah; rather, what is traced here is the line of authoritative leadership from Moses to the Rabbis, and it is in this that the prophets constitute an important link.[21]

The struggle over acceptance of Oral Torah continued after Sinai. The ill-fated mission of the ten spies, sent initially by Moses and only reluctantly agreed to by God,[22] symbolizes Moses' wish to inaugurate the era of Oral Torah.[23] It is through mastery of the techniques of that Torah that human beings can in some measure acquire control over the workings of Torah, and use it as a basis for their own legislation.[24]

[16] *Tanhuma Noah* 3, *RL* 158b.
[17] *Shab.* 88a.
[18] Compare *Gitt.* 60b.
[19] *ZL*, 12.
[20] *Ned.* 38a.
[21] *RL*, 161a.
[22] *Num.* 13–14, compare *Deut.* 1:22–3, and see *LM*, 87–88.
[23] *LM*, 88a.
[24] *RL*, 158a–b.

In R. Zadok's system, the Land of Israel is the proper locale for Oral Torah, in contrast to the Written one, for it has a direct relevance to life within a natural economy.[25] The change-over to agricultural produce from reliance on the manna of the desert represents the attempt to pass, once again, from the regime of the Written Torah which obtained in the Wilderness to that of the oral one. Both efforts were abortive, but Moses' spiritual stature insured that his command to the spies would itself become part of Scripture.[26] His wish for the right to begin the era of the Oral Torah was granted in part by the form the Book of Deuteronomy took: a commentary on the earlier books of the Pentateuch, which, like the command to the spies, was composed by Moses with God's agreement.[27]

Again, the Book of Joshua symbolizes one of the sources of Oral Torah, since it was the first book to have been composed after the completion of the Pentateuch.[28] In some respects it is to be bracketed with the latter, however, since both were produced by men untouched by the sin of the Golden Calf, and thus more open to prophetic illumination than those involved in that apostasy or their descendants. Had Israel not sinned, the Pentateuch and the Book of Joshua alone would have sufficed as Scripture, according to the Rabbis; according to R. Zadok, the reason is that the mediation of Oral Torah would not have been necessary, and all *halakhah* could have been derived directly from Scripture.[29]

At any rate, it seems that despite Joshua's status as a prophet himself, the era of prophecy did not begin until later.[30] This may explain why, when with Moses' death, according to the Talmud, many *halakhot* were lost, Joshua is reported to have refused to resort to the *Urim Vetumim*. Eventually those lost *halakhot* were restored by Othniel b. Kenaz in a way that was paradigmatic for all future learning, and which prefigured the restoration—or, actually, in R. Zadok's terminology, the *establishment*, of Oral Torah in the Second Temple period; that is, he reclaimed them by use of his intellectual acuity (*pilpul*) guided by divine inspiration.[31] To be sure, this divine inspiration was not comparable either to that of Moses or to that of the prophets. But, in explaining Nahmanides' comments on *B.B.* 12a, wherein the latter concludes that the sage is superior to the prophet in that his intellectual endeavors are guided by an element of divine inspiration, R. Zadok declares the sages'

---

[25] *LM*, 84b.
[26] *LM*, 89a. See also *PT* 127a, and compare *LM* 85b.
[27] *PT* V, 21a, *RL* 128b, based on *Zohar* III 261a.
[28] *PT* II, 174a, *LM*, 72–89. I hope to discuss this theme of repeated beginnings in more detail on another occasion.
[29] *Ned.* 22b, see *PT* V, 54a.
[30] Prophecy began with Samuel, see *Komets Haminḥah*: (Lublin, n.d., repr. Bnai Brak: Yahadut, 5733), 80a and *ZL*, 2, based on *Midrash Tehillim* 90, *Sot.* 48b and *Y. Ḥag.* 2:1.
[31] *Tem.* 15b–16a.

understanding as greater than that of the prophets.[32] For that reason it can be applied to all ages and many cases, while that of the prophet cannot; on the other hand, the sages' knowledge is subject to doubt, while prophecy, which partakes of some of the features of Holy Writ even when not actually preserved in written form, provides knowledge which is absolutely true. As such, however, it is ultimately unsuited to this world of falsehood.[33] It is only by the union of these modes of acquiring knowledge that the development of a Torah more at home in this world, one mediated by the human intellect, is made possible. That union was not achieved until the end of the Biblical era.

To proceed: Othniel's work was not to continue. After his time, *pilpul*, that is, the extraction of Oral Torah from Scripture by intellectual effort, fell into disfavor,[34] for the same reason that its original acceptance was attended with difficulty. With the ready availability of prophecy and prophets from the time of Samuel—twice six hundred thousand[35]—it was far easier to bring one's legal, personal or theological problems to one's local seer than to seek the answer either by one's own endeavors or to seek out a sage who was likewise remote from absolute truth. R. Zadok reinterprets the criticism leveled by R. Jeremiah on Babylonian Amoraic methods of study—applying to them the verse "He sat me down in darkness"—as a reference not only the the nascent Babylonian Talmud, but to the uncertainty associated with all intellectual studies, which are symbolized by darkness.[36]

This emphasis on the limitations of human intellect is quite different from the same note as sounded by Maimonides. For the latter, intellect remains, despite its limitations on the human plane, the only common ground between the human and the divine; it is the only "quality," in the Aristotelian sense, which can be applied precisely and without ambiguity to the two; it is the one aspect of which it can truly be said that man is made in the "image of God."[37] But for R. Zadok, certain, clear, reliable knowledge comes not from the intellect, but from divine, prophetic or mystical, illumination. Intellectual methods are reliable only to the extent to which they are guided by divine inspiration; reason unaided is untrustworthy.[38]

After the prophet Samuel's time, people resorted to the prophets for guidance, *hanhagah*. But prophecy, though certain, is limited in other ways.

[32] *DS* 41b, see *RL* 158b.
[33] *RL*, 161b, *passim*.
[34] R. Zadok does not actually date this process, but it must precede Samuel's time.
[35] *Meg.* 14a.
[36] *RL*, 160b, based on *Sanh.* 24a.
[37] *Guide of the Perplexed*, I:1.
[38] See immediately below.

Prophecy, which is (after all) the word of God, is "garbed" in writing and is thus inevitably limited and restricted (both) by the means (of transmission, that is, the prophet) and the "garb" (language). The prophet can perceive only that which God wishes to show him by prophetic means. Nevertheless, even though they (the prophets) were sages as well, intellectual means of perception were considered as naught in comparison with the overwhelming plenitude of prophecy and revelation, inasmuch as intellectual activities lead to dimness and doubt.... (At that time) all guidance (of public and private affairs) was by prophecy.... All decisions for that time (*lesha'ah*, as opposed to *ledorot*, for future generations as well) were made by prophets....[39]

It is extremely instructive to compare the description here with R. Zadok's reconstruction of conditions in Biblical times given in an unfinished work, *Zikaron Larishonim*.[40] This work dates, according to the author himself in a short introduction, from shortly after his Bar Mitsvah, though his references to a work on prophecy named *Divre Hanevu'ah*, now lost, and also to a responsum (his word) which he composed on an ancillary problem, indicate either that he reworked it later, or that its composition extended over a long period, for his known and dated responsa date from his thirties,[41] though that fact is not an infallible guide; certainly his youthful work betrays the hand of a mature scholar.

In this early work, then, begun long before his conversion to Hasidism, he develops at great length the theme that the major teachers of Torah in the Biblical period were the kings and high priests in Judah, and the prophets in Israel. He investigates, based on Talmudic and Midrashic sources, the relative positions as teachers, of various contemporaries (David and Nathan, Hezekiah and Isaiah, and so on) on the basis of the number of their students and depth of knowledge.[42] Even more striking than the specifics of the inquiry is the "Lithuanian" atmosphere with which the discussion is permeated: what counts primarily is Torah

---

[39] *RL*, 160–61.

[40] Printed from a copy made by Rabbi David Alter, apparently in Lublin, which reached Palestine, where A. I. Bromberg published it in *Sinai*, 5707, 1–25, together with *Shemot Baarets*. Prof. S. Z. Leiman has kindly provided the following bibliographical information on its later publication history: it was reprinted in E. Garetenhaus, *Eshel Hagedolim* (New York, 1958) as an appendix, 1–25, and in H. Y. D. Azulai, *Shem Hagedolim Hashalem* (Jerusalem, 1979), II, Appendix, 2:25; see Hadari, *supra* n. 3. As to the question of extended composition, the somewhat inchoate state of his surviving works indicates that R. Zadok seldom returned to them once the initial inspiration which called them forth weakened, though he often returned to subjects of interest to him; hence the duplications to be found in his work. It is thus likely that the responsum he referred to dates from the same time as ZL.

[41] At least from the few dated ones published in *Tiferet Tsevi*. See I, 8, dated Sunday, (Parashat Shofetim, 5623 [=1863], when he was about 40; the earliest are II 14 and II 22, both from 5621 [=1860/1]).

[42] *ZL*, 8–9.

knowledge; prophecy, while important, is nonetheless secondary. The statement quoted above, that "intellectual means of perception were considered as naught in comparison with the overwhelming plenitude of prophecy and revelation," is inconceivable in the context of this youthful work. It is precisely this which distinguishes *Zikaron Larishonim* from the work of R. Zadok's Izhbitz period.

III

We have seen that R. Zadok allows the prophets an important role in the halakhic process, at least in his mature writings. The point is so important, and yet so controversial, that it behooves the present writer to pause to substantiate this interpretation of *hanhagah* in R. Zadok's works. What areas of public and private life came under their jurisdiction, as it were? What were the parameters of the "guidance" they provided?

> (Prophecy is limited) by the need to obtain a new decision in each instance. But the sage's perception is general and subsumes all cases under its rule; it applies to each individual in all times and epochs, inasmuch as (the sages) perceive the hidden parts of Torah and not only the outward "garb."[43]

Thus prophet and sage address themselves to the same problems; each approach has its advantages and disadvantages, but they are *comparable*, they relate to the same types of decision.

Another indication is the juxtaposition of "Divine Guidance" (*hanhagat Hashem*) and "legal exposition" (*perush hamitsvah*).[44] Since the Torah is the blueprint of creation,[45] parallel processes operate in each, creation and Torah; the sage who can innovate in Torah can create new worlds as well.[46] By the same token, "guidance" refers to both Torah and to the world. This is a roundabout way of saying that the prophet could make *halakhic decisions*.

Nevertheless, since it is not by virtue of his learning that the prophet is allowed this right, the prophet as prophet is not to be counted among the authorized transmitters of Torah; the passage in *Abot* discussed above refers not to the transmission of Torah, but to the regime under which *hanhagah* would be delivered. What was handed over was the authority to interpret Torah in particular circumstances, for societal and individual guidance. The phrase R. Zadok employs is *meṣirat hanhagah*,

---

[43] *RL*, 162a.
[44] *RL*, 160b; see Maimonides' Introduction to *Mishneh Torah*. It should be noted that R. Zadok's interest in Maimonides was life-long, as could be expected; one of his youthful works, *Otsar Hamelekh*, (Lodz 5699), composed at age 16, was on *Sefer Hamada*. His use of Maimonidean terminology is not fortuitous.
[45] *Genesis Rabba*, beginning.
[46] *TH*, n. 4.

"transfer of leadership"; to R. Zadok the passage is a listing of successive spiritual regimes.[47]

The prophets exercised authority (*hanhagat hanevu'ah*) by virtue of their abilities, not tradition; nevertheless, prophecy, which may in some cases be written down, is an extension of, and relates to, Written Torah. We can better understand the prophetic role by contrast to that of the Elders, who preceded them. The functions of the latter were *hanhagah* and *limmud*—leadership and teaching (perhaps: interpretation, the derivation of law from Scripture).[48] These teachings or interpretations the Elders received from Moses, and, according to R. Zadok, it is for that reason that they are called "Elders": their claim to leadership proceeded from their personal contact with Moses. The prophets could not make that claim; that is, their status as disciples of other prophets counted as nothing unless validated in a very concrete way from Above. But the prophet also hands down decisions regarding the precise application of Scripture: the content is similar, the means divergent; the requisite knowledge came to them through revelation and not intellection.[49]

> As long as (the Israelites) did not accept (the Oral Torah) willingly, it was not yet handed over to them entirely (*legamre*), and they conducted themselves in accordance with the (decisions of the) prophets—all in "writing from God" (based on *I Chron.* 29:19).[50]

We may understand the one side of the coin from the other. With the end of prophecy, the sage finally came into his own, and the Men of the Great Assembly gained the right to legislate—to erect "fences" around the Law—by virtue of their mastery of Oral Torah.[51] They could lay down guidelines, set precedents. The prophets could only make decisions on a case by case basis—but decide they did, and in the very same areas of law!

What then of the Oral Torah in the prophetic era, if not in terms of techniques of reaching decisions, of dialectic, at least in the sense of a body of knowledge which must be preserved, if not extended? It would seem likely that R. Zadok would allow for the transmission of what Maimonides refers to as the Oral Torah in the narrow sense, *perush hamitsvot*, the minimum required interpretation of Scripture which would enable us to comprehend what is demanded of us. It is scarcely conceivable that Scripture could have had any place at all in Israelite society without that modicum of Oral Torah.

---

[47] *RL*, 161a.
[48] *Idem.*
[49] *Idem.*
[50] *RL*, 158b.
[51] See *Y. Sheq.* 5:1, cited in *RL*, 158b, and see *PT* V, 38b–39a.

> It is clear to all, *now* that Oral Torah has been revealed to *all*, that it is impossible to attain a correct understanding of any *mitsvah* (*perush shum mitsvah*) or warning in the Written Torah (without reference to Oral Torah). It is impossible to know anything of it; therefore it is impossible to understand Divine governance (*hanhagat Hashem*) of the world, which is in accordance with Torah, since (Written) Torah is itself also hidden (without mediation).[52]

Now, in the era of Oral Torah, *hanhagah, perush hamitsvah*, and Oral Torah are inextricably bound together; in the prophetic era this was not the case, and prophecy could in some cases serve as a substitute for Oral Torah.

A clue to this problem of the Oral Torah in the age of prophecy, and simultaneously to R. Zadok's own solution to the halakhic problem posed by prophetic input in the halakhic process, may be found in *Zikaron Larishonim, to which* we now turn.

IV

R. Zadok's theory, which allows for direct prophetic intervention in the *Halakhah*, runs counter to those Talmudic rules which place strict limits on it. "[The Torah] is not in Heaven, [therefore] innovation through prophecy in now forbidden [*i.e.*, from the completion of the Pentateuch described in *Deut.* 31:26]."[53]

> (At that point) the revelation of Torah innovations by prophecy was suspended; from (then) on (the Torah was) no (longer) "in Heaven"; there would no longer be a heavenly revelation of "words of Torah" in this world, and all the prophecies of the prophets "thereafter" were intended only to warn, encourage . . . , and predict. . . .[54]

Here R. Zadok appears to draw back a step from the position outlined above. It is possible to account for this discrepancy either by limiting the semantic range of "guidance" in the passages from *Resise Laylah* quoted above, or by extending the range of "to warn" (*lehazhir*) to include legislative authority in the passage from *Maḥshevet Ḥaruts* quoted immediately above. But if we take this latter formulation literally, R. Zadok's scheme, as set forth in *Resise Laylah* and elsewhere, which culminates in the flowering of Oral Torah in the Tannaitic and Amoraic periods, loses its cogency and force. If the prophetic role is to be understood in traditional terms, there is no need for people to turn to the prophet for any specific prophetic insight in Torah. He may serve as

---

[52] *RL*, 160b.
[53] *Meg.* 2a, *Shab.* 64a, also *Yom.* 80a, *Tem.* 16a, *Y. Meg.* 1:5.
[54] *MH*, 141b (bottom).

clairvoyant (*I Sam.* 9:6f.), and double as a sage in determining *halakhah*, but not as prophet. These were certainly not the terms in which R. Zadok cast his discussion in *Resise Laylah*.

Luckily, however, we may have, in fragmentary form at least, R. Zadok's own solution to this problem. In *Zikaron Larishonim*, which predates in some form his conversion to Hasidism, his discussion of the role of the Great Assembly is understood quite traditionally.[55] There is no mention of them as originators, or founders, of the Oral Torah as we find in his later work (*Resise Laylah*, *Likute Ma'amarim*, *Mahshevet Haruts* and *Pri Tsadik*); we nonetheless find here the kernel of his later views on the history of prophecy in Israel, though, as noted, the resistance of Israel to Oral Torah has not yet entered the system as an essential element. There is, though, his unique interpretation of the *Abot* passage, with its denial of a chain of tradition which included the prophets, and the idea, taken from midrashic sources (and not the Zohar, as later), that Samuel was the first of the prophets.

Since it is important to understand the exact relationship of *Zikaron Larishonim* to his later works, we should list some of the salient differences in his understanding of the history of Oral Torah between the two periods of his intellectual development. The non-role of the Great Assembly has already been mentioned. Coupled with this is the idea of progressive revelation,[56] which will be discussed, D.v., elsewhere. In the earlier work, R. Zadok explicitly attributes the learning of the Great Assembly to traditions *received* from the exiled scholars in Babylon, that is, those exiled before the destruction of the temple. In *Resise Laylah*, Torah is seen as completely lost during the Babylonian Exile, and it is the Great Assembly which restored it by the *quasi*-prophetic intellection of the sages.[57]

Despite these differences of approach, a fair amount of continuity in his thinking on this matter may be observed, and his later writings may in this case be supplemented by his comments on the role of the prophets in this early work, at least in the absence of a fuller discussion of this point elsewhere.

Here R. Zadok deals with the multitudinous Talmudic references to a functioning apparatus of Oral Torah, courts and oral transmission, in Biblical times. Withal, he assigns the prophets an important role in *Halakhah*. Based in part on *Deut.* 18:15 and *Yeb.* 90b: "'him shall you obey'—even if he tells you to transgress a command of the Torah, as (did) Elijah at Mount Carmel—all *lefi sha'ah*, according to the situation

---

[55] ZL, 9–10.
[56] RL, n. 13, esp. 14b.
[57] RL, 130a. Strictly speaking, Torah may have been forgotten by the common people (*hamon*), but preserved by the sages.

and only for a time—obey him!"[58] Prophetic power he limits, however, to questions, or decisions, whose force is only temporary (*lesha'ah*), and not *ledorot*, for future generations, as he did in the passage in *Resise Laylah*, quoted above. He also distinguishes between the general law and the details of its performance in light of the exigencies of the time.

> All the days of the prophets . . . there was no need to obey the sages. It seems likely that, even though it is true that there is no place for prophecy as far as the study and knowledge of Torah (*ḥokhmat Hatorah viyediyato*), as it is written: "[The Torah] is not in Heaven, etc." (*Deut.* 31:26), as it is quoted in *Tem.* 16a. . . . . (This rule) applies to knowledge of the laws of the Torah and its general rules (*mishpaṭeha hakelaliyim*), but there is ample room (for knowledge acquired by means of) prophecy (as far as) the details of their performance at any particular time (*behoveh*), as Maimonides describes at length in his *Introduction (to the Commentary on the Mishnah)*: as a temporary expedient (*lefi sha'ah*) the prophet has the power to suspend the commands of the Torah (*Sanh.* 90a).[59]

The translation of *lefi sha'ah* as "temporary expedient" is not quite accurate, for R. Zadok intends it as equivalent to *hora'at sha'ah*: in halakhic terms, Torah law, which includes matters of public policy (see below), was *all* extra-legal during the prophetic era, as far as the application of general rules to concrete cases was concerned. On the one hand, decisions were made by prophetic means in particular cases; on the other, no general principles could be derived from such decisions; thus, *all halakhic decisions fell under the category of hora'at sha'ah*;[60] no precedents were set, no norms established, the "normal" operation of Oral Torah, as understood by the Rabbis, was, as it were, suspended. If the Sanhedrin did meet to consider an issue, it did have authority, as will be seen below, but most of its members were *themselves* prophets; and the Sanhedrin seldom met.

> It goes without saying that in doubtful instances they (the prople and the sages) were required to obey the prophet, and many prophets arose (in) Israel (to) command action in particular situations (*hagadat hanhagat hahoveh*) at all times. . . . Therefore *the general leadership of the(se) generations was in the hands of the prophets*, who were the leaders (*roshe*) of the(se) generations as far as the affairs of (each) generation (were concerned).[61]

He notes that although King David was prepared to build the Temple in consonance with the Torah's command to do so, he desisted at Nathan's command.[62]

---

[58] ZL, 8–12; see *Tosafot Sanh.* 89b s.v. Eliyahu.
[59] ZL, 11.
[60] I owe the full awareness of this important insight to Prof. B. S. Jackson.
[61] ZL, 11.
[62] *II Sam.* 7:5–7, 12–13; *I Chron.* 17:4.

On the other hand, the Sanhedrin did have the authority to review the legitimacy of each prophet. "But in cases on which [the prophet] and Sanhedrin agreed [that the man in question was indeed an 'authorized prophet'] . . . , it is true that *even the Sanhedrin [itself] was required to obey him* [in his extra-legal pronouncements]."[63]

However, the Sanhedrin too could act on the need for an *hora'at sha'ah, but, on the* basis of *Tosafot Yeb.* 88a s.v. *mitokh*, and a number of other sources, he distinguishes between the extraordinary powers of court and those of the prophet by the requirement that the court not act without an explicit reason (*ta'am*).

With due regard for the different emphases apparent in these earlier and later works, especially in the radically lessened status accorded human reason (in the wake of his study of Kabbalah and conversion to Hasidism?), we may understand the halakhic nexus between *halakhah* and prophecy as inhering in a type of *hora'at sha'ah* principle. Since R. Zadok returned repeatedly to the theme of prophet vis à vis sage in his voluminous writings, without however going beyond the position outlined in *Zikaron Larishonim*, it seems likely that he viewed the latter (together with the lost *Divre Hanevua'ah* and the lost responsum on the subject) as representing his last thoughts on this matter. Certainly, the contexts in which we now find expositions of his understanding of the role of prophecy do not lend themselves to that kind of treatment, though, were he so minded by the necessity to set down a new position he most probably would have. Presumably the change of emphasis between *Zikaron Larishonim* and *Resise Laylah* did not appear to him radical enough to require additional justification, though an argument from silence is always a hazardous undertaking.

So, *mutatis mutandis*, we may say that it was only in those matters regarding which no prophecy was received that the advice of the sages of the time was solicited; given the numbers of prophets on hand—twice six hundred thousand—this must indeed have been a rare occasion!

The Talmudic dictum regarding the huge number of prophets whose prophecies were not relevant to later times and were thus not recorded,[64] and so, subsequently lost, may now be seen in a new light. Many prophets served as the religious leaders of their time, but rendered decisions valid only for their contemporaries. This would explain why so little material of an halakhic nature survives from that time.

Having said all that, it must be admitted that the exact role allotted to the Sanhedrin and the judicial system as a whole remains unclear; the statement referred to several times in this paper, that "although they [the prophets] were sages as well, intellectual means of perception were

---

[63] ZL, 11.
[64] *Meg.* 14a.

considered as naught in comparison with . . . prophecy and revelation," and the comparatively active role given the courts in *Zikaron Larishonim* cannot be squared without doing violence to one or the other.

Prof. Bezalel Safran suggests[65] that the tension between prophet and sage in R. Zadok's mature system reflects the gulf between Lithuanian scholars and Hasidic rebbes of his own time, a gulf which he himself bridged in his own person. Wherever the truth may lie, it is certain that *Resise Laylah* represents his later view of the matter in general; whether he himself ever resolved the question of the exact place of the Sanhedrin in a context which so devalued Oral Torah and its commitment to human reason must for the time being remain open.

For those who wish to see it, the tension between prophet and sage is prefigured in the Biblical text itself. *Deut.* 17:8f. ordains the establishment of a court-system, but it also promises the availability of prophets "like" Moses (*Deut.* 18:15). While the verse preceding, which prohibits resort to soothsayers and augurs, who were employed by the Canaanites, would seem to stress the clairvoyant functions of the prophet and his mission as God's spokesman, Scripture refers, in v. 16, to halakhic matters as being within the prophet's competence. The tension thus set up was resolved only with the cessation of prophecy and the final victory of the sage in the Second Temple period.

V

As already noted, a considerable portion of R. Zadok's writings was lost in the destruction of the Lublin ghetto; although the beginnings of a commentary on Joshua, apparently never completed, survives,[66] there is no evidence to suggest that he ever completed a work on all of Early Prophets, or even contemplated one. Nonetheless, we may sketch out, in the light of the foregoing, the lines of his probable understanding of those incidents in which halakhic norms seem to have been disregarded.

The image of Elijah at Mount Carmel, which served both the Talmud and the Tosafists as the paradigmatic example of the prophetic suspension of "due process," served R. Zadok equally well.[67] But for him the suspension was more thoroughgoing and more pointed. While, *de jure*, an apparatus for the application of human reason to the Divine Law existed, *de facto*, the human element was absent by default. Two contradictory elements precluded a state of stable equilibrium: a code of sorts existed in Scripture, but its application was largely in the hands of the prophets, who lacked legislative authority. This was not the Divine intent, which preferred to leave such decisions in properly-trained, human hands.

---

[65] In a discussion during the winter of 1983.
[66] *LM*, 77–98.
[67] *Sanh.* 90a s.v. *Eliyahu*. See also the sources cited in ZL, II.

How well does this explain the instances of unhalakhic actions listed in Section I? Of the three cases considered, the first, that of secular use of the shew-bread by David and his men, is perhaps the easiest with which to deal, for David and his band were indeed fugitives in danger of their lives, as the Talmud states.[68] If we add to that David's status as a minor prophet, the problem becomes still easier. Finally, Scripture itself in the person of the priest Ahimelekh comes to our aid by elliptically stating his reservations in *I Sam.* 21:5. However, his reluctance is based on grounds or ritual purity, and not the non-priestly status of the eventual consumers. To that extent, we must fall back on either the Talmud's answer, which applies only to the case at hand, or to R. Zadok's more general answer.

In the case of Michal, no word of protest (except, naturally, for that of Palti[el] b. Laish) is raised. No notice is taken by anyone, even Nathan, of the grave halakhic problems involved. The solutions proposed by the Talmud[69] either invalidate her earlier marriage to David; or, alternatively, her divorce by David (of which no hint is contained in the text) is posited, which divorce is rescinded by David, unknown to Michal, who then marries Palti(el) in innocence, thus sparing her the rigors enumerated for similar cases in *Yeb.* 87b. Or, the suggestion is made that the marriage to Palti was never consummated, thus freeing her for David. R. Zadok's solution would have the virtue of simplicity, not a small gain in the present instance. However, the fact that David's proposal to build the Temple, which occurred about the same time, is narrated in some detail, while this prophetic permission to remarry Michal goes unmentioned, is certainly surprising.

Finally, Tamar's statement[70] is in one respect the most difficult of all, for it raises the specter of the existence of a whole system of *Halakhah* quite different from the rabbinic one, for Tamar here apparently appeals to a law known to all, and not an on-the-spur-of-the-moment *hora'at sha'ah*, which she was in no position to obtain at that moment! Perhaps Ibn Caspi's remark *ad loc.*, that no halakhic significance is to be attached to her appeal in these circumstances inasmuch as it is likely that Tamar was attempting to delay Amnon, either until help arrived or Amnon regained his senses, is the simplest solution in this case.

It is important to note that this exegetical scrutiny of R. Zadok's thesis, while a legitimate exercise in its own right, is in a sense false to the spirit in which the theory was offered. First and foremost, R. Zadok provides an historiosophical doctrine rather than an exegetical rule; it arises from a highly individual conception of Jewish history, based on

---

[68] *Men.* 95b–96a.
[69] See n. 14.
[70] See n. 15. The Talmud suggests that she was only his half-sister.

talmudic and midrashic sources, in the main, and not the Biblical text itself. It is thus no closer to the plain sense of the text, or should be expected to be, than the Rabbinic expositions on which it is in part based; its advantage is, however, that it is not *ad hoc*, and provides a *general* solution to a certain type of exegetical problem.

It is in its own way as forced and artificial in its perhaps overschematic views, but it does serve admirably to bring into sharp focus a sense of the historical distance which the Rabbinic system as a whole lacks.

An additional talmudic objection to R. Zadok's limits on prophetic legislation, which is after all just a restatement of the old rule of "not in Heaven," should be mentioned. It is an objection not directed solely at R. Zadok's reconstruction, but a true inner-talmudic contradiction. Enough talmudic references to customs instituted by the prophets exist to allow us to state that the "Talmudic" view, insofar as one exists, is less absolute than the narrative in *Tem.* 16a allows. Elsewhere in the Talmud,[71] the objection of "not in Heaven" is never allowed to go unanswered; the rejoinder is usually: such was the *halakhah* or custom of old, and the prophet(s) merely restored what had fallen into disuse or been forgotten, which in a sense is the reverse of our supposition regarding R. Zadok's system. But that *itself* is the precise measure of the divergence of these two systems. R. Zadok's theory turns the Talmud's extraordinary circumstance to the daily reality of nearly six centuries. It is only upon the return of the Jews from the Babylonian Exile, bereft of any knowledge of Torah[72]—R. Zadok takes *Neh.* 8:14–18, which describes the returned exiles' discovery and celebration of the Biblical holiday of Sukkot, for the first time since the days of Joshua, quite literally—that Oral Torah at last began to function. It is from this low ebb that the Oral Torah reached its flowering. But of that, more later.

---

[71] For a discussion of this point, see E. E. Urbach, *"Halakah Unevu'ah," Tarbiz* 18 (5607), 1–27, esp. 10–12; also, Y. Englard, *"Tanur shel Akhnai—Perusha shel Agada,"* in *Shenaton Hamishpaṭ Ha'ivri* I, 45–56. My thanks to Dr. Ronny Warburg for the latter reference.

[72] *RL*, 130a.

THE CORPORATE STATUS OF *HEKDESH* IN EARLY SEFARDIC RESPONSA

by

DAVID FINK*

A corporation is a body of men or property which the law treats as an artificial person distinct from its component parts. This concept lies at the foundation of the classical Roman *universitas*[1] and has become vital in contemporary law.

A corporation may bring suit or be sued independently of the persons who are members of the corporation.[2] A corporation may bring suit or be sued independently of its members. It is a typical characteristic of corporations that their owners need not be identical with their managers, who represent the interests of the corporation.

The contemporary law of corporations has been largely influenced by the historical development of religious and community institutions which the law began to recognize as legal persons before the advent of the modern joint-stock corporation.[3] The conceptual roots of modern legal persons originate in the older corporations sole, which typically consisted of a bishop or other ecclesiastic administering church property, or the Roman foundations *piae causae*,[4] which consisted of orphanages, poor houses, hospitals, or similar religious or pious institutions.

Charitable and other community or religious institutions have always been strongly supported in traditional Jewish society.[5] It is therefore not surprising that these institutions were the first to evolve into legal persons under Jewish law as well.[6]

---

*Assistant Professor of Hebrew, University of Maryland, College Park.

[1] See A. Berger, *Encyclopedic Dictionary of Roman Law* (Philadelphia: American Philosophical Society, 1953), 750f.

[2] See P. J. Fitzgerald, *Salmond on Jurisprudence* (London: Sweet and Maxwell, 1966), 66f., for a survey of the characteristics of the modern corporation.

[3] See J. P. Davis, *Corporations: A Study of the Origin and Development of Great Business Combinations and their Relation to the Authority of the State* (New York: G. P. Putnam's Sons, 1905), vol. 1, especially 35–87 and 92–129, for the early history of religious and community institutions in Europe.

[4] Berger, *supra* n. 1, at 629.

[5] See Y. Bergman, *Hatsedakah beyisra'el* (Jerusalem: Reuben Mass, 5735).

[6] A. Gulak, *Yesode hamishpat ha'ivri* (Tel Aviv: Dvir, 5727), vol. 1, 50–52, and

The main adumbration of the concept of legal persons in the Talmudic period was *hekdesh*,[7] the property and money donated to the Temple in Jerusalem to finance its upkeep and its sacrificial cult.[8] *Hekdesh* was administered by a *gizbar* (*i.e.*, treasurer), who was empowered to acquire and alienate *hekdesh* property and who would represent the interests of *hekdesh* in litigation.

Even though the legal personality of *hekdesh* was indeed distinct from that of the *gizbar*, there are two clear indications that it did not possess true artificial personality of its own. First, the Talmud explicitly considered God (Hebrew *gavoah* or *shamayim*) to be the owner of all *hekdesh* property. Second, the property of *hekdesh* was largely governed by rules very different from those governing ordinary private property. The principles of consecration and redemption of *hekdesh* property differed from the ordinary laws of acquisition and sale. Nor was theft of *hekdesh* property subject to the same penalties as theft of private property. For example, mere oral consecration was sufficient to transfer title to *hekdesh* without any of the formal requirements which normally govern the alienation of private property.[9]

The charity funds (Hebrew *kuppot*) of the Talmudic period were structured in a way somewhat similar to *hekdesh*. They were administered by *gabbayim* (*i.e.* collectors, *viz.* of communal assessments), who functioned somewhat like the *gizbarim* of *hekdesh*.[10] But according to the Talmudic law the *gabbay* was merely an agent of the poor people, who actually owned the property in the fund.[11] This meant that the *gabbay* could not represent the poor in litigation unless the specific interest of individual poor persons in the fund's assets had first been determined.[12] Thus the Talmudic charity fund did not possess the status of a legal person in the law courts of that period.

The initial stages of the evolution of personal status of the charity fund into that of a quasi-corporation occurred in the eleventh and twelfth centuries. Using methods of legal analogy, the Sefardic rabbis of that period gradually endowed the charity funds with artificial personality creating a new legal status for them.

The first of the great Sefardic scholars to deal with this issue was

---

Encyclopaedia Judaica (Jerusalem: Keter Publishing House, 1972), vol. 10, 1569.

[7] See *Talmudic Encyclopedia* (Jerusalem: Talmudic Encyclopedia Institute, 5707–) vol. 5, 335–38, and vol. 10, 352–442, for a survey of laws governing *hekdesh* and *gizbar*.

[8] It has been suggested that the Qumran community was also structured as a legal person. See E. Koffmahn, "Rechtsstellung und Struktur des יחד von Qumran," *Biblica* 42 (1961), 433–42, and compare her "Die Staatsrechtliche Stellung der essenischen Vereinigungen in der griechisch–römischen Periode," *Biblica* 44 (1963), 46–61.

[9] See Talmudic Encyclopedia, *supra* n. 8, at vol. 2, 40–42.

[10] See Talmudic Encyclopedia, *supra* n. 8, at vol. 5, 51–68.

[11] *B.K.* 36b.

[12] *B.K.* 93a.

R. Isaac Alfasi (1013–1103). In a number of his responsa, he began to broaden the status of the community fund by enabling an agent to represent the fund in litigation.[13] His responsum No. 135 revolves around a case where someone had willed his estate to *hekdesh* (*i.e.* community fund).[14] After the testator died, his family wanted to challenge the validity of the bequest to *hekdesh* and R. Isaac Alfasi was asked how to proceed. Among other issues the questioner who posed the problem to R. Alfasi was not sure whether all the members of the community ought to be considered joint litigants, thus requiring them all to be present during the trial.

R. Alfasi replied that the community had to appoint an agent (Hebrew *mursheh*) who would be authorized to represent the community in litigation and that the action should be brought to a court outside of the community itself.

There are two interesting points here. First, R. Alfasi makes it clear that an agent can represent the community in court. Second, the relationship between the fund and the members of the community is such

---

[13] I follow the numbering of the responsa in the Leghorn edition (1781) and have compared the editions of Z. Byednowitz (Bilgore, 1934), W. Leiter (New York, 1954), and D. Rothstein (New York, 5735).

[14] In medieval Hebrew *hekdesh* acquired a new meaning. In Talmudic usage it had exclusively denoted Temple property. But in the Middle Ages it referred to all forms of communal funds as well (*cf.* E. Ben Yehuda, *A Complete Dictionary of Ancient and Modern Hebrew* [New York: Thomas Yoseloff, 1960]), vol. 2, 1171b). This form of semantic change, whereby technical terms whose original meaning is no longer relevant acquire new, more useful meanings, was fairly common in the medieval Hebrew lexicon in the field of community funds (*cf.* Th. Lewandowski, *Linguistisches Wörterbuch* [Heidelburg: Quelle und Meyer, 1973], vol. 1, 103–6).

In the Talmud, for example, the terms *terumot* and *maʿasrot* referred to holy offerings or tithes associated with the Temple cult in Jerusalem. The Bible required the donation of these tithes and there was a sizable body of law dealing with them. After the destruction of the Temple the Jewish diaspora no longer found the strict meanings of these terms to be relevant and they began to apply them to all manner of charitable donations.

Thus, in the fourth century Epiphanius spoke about a Jewish fund raiser who collected *epidekata* (=*maʿaser*) and *aparxas* (=*terumah*) from the Jews in the diaspora (see Epiphanius, *Panarion* in *Die griechischen christlichen Schriftsteller der ersten drei Jahrhunderte*, ed. K. Holl [Leipzig: J. C. Heinrichs, 1915], vol. 25, 344).

The Targum on *Song* 7:3 also refers to charitable contributions as *maʿaser*. Similarly eleventh century Geniza fragments use *maʿaser* to refer to charitable contributions (see J. Mann, *The Jews in Egypt and Palestine under the Fatimid Caliphs* [Oxford: Oxford University Press, 1922], vol. 2, 206).

A further example of this kind of semantic change is the medieval Hebrew term *albitkah*, which referred to the communal tax record (see R. Shelomo b. Aderet, *Responsa*, vol. 4, Nos. 312–3). This term is derived from the Greek *pittakion*, which originally designated a document used in the administration of food supplies for the army (see Berger, *supra* n. 1, at 632). This Greek term entered Talmudic Hebrew in the form *petek* or *pitkah* and in Arabic it became *biṭaka*, which was the basis of the medieval Hebrew form appearing in the responsa. These are a few examples of semantic change in the field of medieval community funds.

that an outside court is required to adjudicate the case. The reason for disqualifying the local court is evident in a parallel responsum,[15] where R. Alfasi observes that all the members of the community have an interest in the community fund thus disqualifying them both as witnesses and judges.

The significant innovation here is the role of the agent. The Talmud considered the community residents to be joint owners of community property and required the active participation of the whole community to execute community matters.[16] Following this principle of Talmudic law, the questioner asked whether all of the community members must themselves participate in the litigation. R. Alfasi responded that the community agent could represent the community interest before the court.

R. Alfasi's introduction of the agent representing the community in litigation represents a small, but significant, development in the direction of corporate status for medieval *hekdesh*. There are two main factors which enabled R. Alfasi to take this step toward corporate status. First, although the Talmud had discussed joint ownership of community property as well as the requirement of active community participation to execute a sale of community property[17] it had never explicitly discussed the issue of procedure in litigating community fund actions. Thus R. Alfasi was free to introduce the agent, agency being a well known concept of Talmudic law in other areas.

Second, the semantic shift[18] in the meaning of *hekdesh* allowed R. Alfasi to some extent to equate the status of the medieval community fund with the status of Temple property. In responsum No. 247, for example, he insisted that the classical procedures governing acquisition by Temple *hekdesh* should be equally applicable to acquisitions by medieval community synagogues. Once the equation between the classical and the medieval *hekdesh* was made, he was well on the way toward viewing the community fund as an artificial person which could be represented by an agent.

The differences between classical and medieval *hekdesh* also played a role in allowing the Sefardic rabbis to begin to view medieval *hekdesh* as a corporate entity. First, God was the owner of classical *hekdesh*. Medieval *hekdesh*, on the other hand, was never imbued with the sanctity of the holy property of the Temple. Since medieval *hekdesh* was the property of the community, and not of God, the rabbis began to develop

---

[15] Resp. 247; *cf.* A. Schreiber (= Sofer), *Responsa of the Sages of Provence* (Jerusalem, 5727), 456, for variant readings on this text.
[16] See *Meg.* 26a; Gulak, *supra* n. 6, at vol. 1, 53; and Sh. Albeck, *The Laws of Property and Contract in the Talmud* (Tel Aviv: Dvir, 1976), 490 (Heb.).
[17] *Meg.* 26a.
[18] See *supra* n. 14.

their own approach to the relationship between the community members and the property of *hekdesh*.

In addition, it was clear that many of the unique laws of classical *hekdesh* could not be applied to the medieval community funds. For example, ordinary laws of theft, rather than the classical *hekdesh* laws of sacrilege (Hebrew *meilah*), were applied to the community funds. These distinctions between classical and medieval *hekdesh* allowed the medieval rabbis to develop the rudimentary adumbrations of legal personality inherent in classical *hekdesh* and apply the concept to their community funds, while simultaneously ignoring those aspects of classical *hekdesh* which distinguished it from legal persons.

Rabbi Joseph ibn Migash (1077-1141) was the leading disciple of R. Alfasi.[19] In one of his responsa (No. 153) he speaks of the mechanics of a private person incurring a financial obligation to the community fund for ransoming captives.[20] There are two possible approaches according to R. ibn Migash. Either one can formulate an obligation to the fund in accord with all the formal requirements for valid contractual obligations under Jewish law or one can use the method of vow, whereby the simple statement that one will support the fund is sufficient to create an obligation to pay.[21]

Of these two possible methods of creating a valid obligation, the first illustrates a further development in the corporate status of the community fund. The contractual obligation actually under analysis in this responsum is invalid for certain minor technical reasons. But if the contract had been more precisely formulated, R. ibn Migash would have indeed considered it valid, thus creating an actionable obligation, one party to which would have been the community fund. This was a clear advance for the personal status of the community fund in the law of obligations.

The second method, utilizing the mechanics of vows, represents a continuation of the position of R. Alfasi. R. Alfasi had held that the main principles governing acquisition by medieval *hekdesh* were identical to the classical *hekdesh* procedures of oral consecration from the Second Temple period. The questioner who formulated the problem presented to R. ibn Migash was aware that at the turn of the twelfth century not all scholars concurred that acquisition by classical and medieval *hekdesh* were to be treated identically. Here, and especially in responsum No. 136, R. ibn Migash makes it clear that he accepts the position of his teacher. Mere oral consecration of one's property is sufficient to transfer title to the community fund, even without observing the formal requirements of normal alienation of private property.

---

[19] I consulted the Warsaw edition (5630) of R. ibn Migash's responsa.
[20] On the ransoming of captives see *Encyclopaedia Judaica*, supra n. 6, vol. 6, 154f.
[21] *R.Sh.* 6a.

R. Alfasi had begun to endow *hekdesh* with some of the rudiments of legal personality. Building on this basis, his disciple broadened his approach to the corporate status of *hekdesh* by continuing his teacher's innovations and adding his own in the realm of the law of obligations. From the time of R. ibn Migash, *hekdesh* could be a party to a contract.

R. Maimon b. Joseph (d. 1165/70) was a disciple of R. ibn Migash. In addition to being a noted scholar in his own right, R. Maimon formed a link between R. ibn Migash and his own son, Maimonides. Of the few known responsa by R. Maimon, one fragment deals with medieval *hekdesh*.[22] As one would expect, this responsum accurately reflects the approach of Rabbis Alfasi and ibn Migash. According to the responsum mere oral consecration of books is sufficient to create a family trust. Once the books were consecrated to the family trust, they could no longer be sold nor redeemed and they would remain in the possession of the family in perpetuity.

The equation of medieval *hekdesh* and its classical predecessor was firmly established by the time of R. Maimon. At this stage R. Maimon broadened the application of the consecration principle to include an essentially private trust designed to enable the members of a specific family to study Torah. In the generations preceding R. Maimon we saw the beginning of the corporate status for coummunity funds. Now R. Maimon has applied the same concept to a private family fund.

Maimonides (1135–1204) was the heir to the legal theory developed in the previous three generations.[23] In a number of his responsa he discussed the status of medieval *hekdesh*.[24] The most interesting of these responsa is No. 209, which deals with books stolen from a synagogue. The thief subsequently sold the stolen books to a bona fide purchaser and the questioner wanted to know how to proceed.

Maimonides' response covers two possibilities. First, Maimonides observed, it is possible that the books were stolen by order of the Sultan, in which case the act of plunder would extinguish the *hekdesh* status of the books and vest title in the thief, who could then lawfully sell the books to a third party. This line of reasoning is based on the Talmudic interpretation of *Ezek.* 7:22: Robbers shall enter [the Temple] and profane it. On the basis of this verse the rabbis concluded that plundering Temple property (*i.e.*, classical *hekdesh*) profanes the property, meaning that the Temple forfeited its interest in the property.[25]

---

[22] See A. Freimann, "*Teshuvot R. Maimon hadayyan avi harambam*," *Tarbiz* 6 (1936), 418–20.

[23] For the responsa of Maimonides I consulted the edition of Y. Blau (Jerusalem: Mekize Nirdamim, 1960).

[24] Nos. 32, 54, 206, 209, 210, 257, and 341.

[25] See *Ned.* 62a, *A.Zar.* 52b, *Bekh.* 50a, Maimonides, *Mishneh Torah, Gezelah,* 5:13f., and Sh. Shilo, *Dina de-Malkhuta Dina* (Jerusalem: Jerusalem Academic Press, 1974), 277f.

Since the equation of classical and medieval *hekdesh* had been well established, Maimonides simply applied the Talmudic law of classical *hekdesh* to his case and concluded that officially sanctioned plundering of medieval *hekdesh* books would "profane" the books, meaning that the community forfeited its interest in them. They would then lawfully belong to the plunderer, who was free to sell them.

The second possibility analysed by Maimonides deals with a situation of a private thief operating without the Sultan's authorization. In this case the Law of the Market (Hebrew *takkanat hashuk*) applied.[26] According to this law a bona fide purchaser of stolen goods is obliged to return the goods to the aggrieved party. The bona fide purchaser is then reimbursed by the rightful owner of the property, who may then pursue the thief to recover his disbursement to the bona fide purchaser.

When Maimonides applied the Law of the Market in the case of the stolen *hekdesh* books, he meant that the bona fide purchaser was to be reimbursed by the community fund. This opinion of Maimonides represents another significant step toward formalizing the status of medieval *hekdesh*. According to this responsum of Maimonides the role of *hekdesh* in the Law of the Market is identical with that of any private person.

This position of Maimonides corresponds with the prevailing practice in the Jewish society of the period. Thus Cairo Geniza documents refer to the community fund as a party to contracts and orders of payment could be issued on a community fund.

Even though *hekdesh* was largely viewed as an artificial person by the middle of the twelfth century, one major impediment lay in the way of completing its quasi-corporate status. Those legal procedures requiring an oath could not be applied to artificial persons. Maimonidean responsum No. 32 deals with an inheritance problem where *hekdesh*, the plaintiff in the case, would prevail if it could state its claim under oath. *Hekdesh*, being an artificial person, could not utter an oath and therefore forfeited its claim to the inheritance.

Similarly in Maimonides' responsum No. 257 *hekdesh* is plaintiff. But, since it is only an artificial person, it cannot utter the claim (Hebrew *ta'anah*) which is required to impose an oath on the defendant. Nonetheless, if *hekdesh* can present proper testimony, it can still prevail, even though it cannot speak in court when Jewish law procedure requires speech.

This disability to speak in court is the basis of Maimonides' interpretation of the Talmudic statement that the poor fund cannot plead (*B.K.* 93a). *Hekdesh* is blocked from any procedure requiring it to utter specific claims or oaths in court. But *hekdesh* can be plaintiff and can prevail if its case is based on other procedures (such as testimony of

[26] *B.K.* 115a.

witnesses) not requiring actual speech of the plaintiff.

In conclusion, the legal status of medieval community funds was significantly more developed than that of the Talmudic charity funds. In the course of the four generations between R. Alfasi and Maimonides, the Sefardic rabbis slowly formalized their approach to medieval *hekdesh*. Beginning with the rudimentary concepts of quasi-corporate status inherent in classical *hekdesh*, they gradually applied the concept of artificial personality in more and more areas. By the twelfth century *hekdesh* was for most purposes treated as a quasi-corporation.

JEWISH DIVORCE IN AMERICAN COURTS—
THE NEW YORK EXPERIENCE

by

STEVEN F. FRIEDELL*

The state of the law in New York on the right of a woman divorced under state law to compel her ex-husband to give her a *get* is uncertain and very confused.

A New York trial court held in 1954 that it would not violate a man's right to the free exercise of religion to order him to comply with his written agreement to give a *get* if that were "necessary."[1] Although execution and delivery of the *get* might take two and a half hours, the court said that this was a small price to pay to bring "peace of mind and conscience to one whom defendant must at one time have loved." In later proceedings, however, the court dismissed the woman's action, and the appellate decision affirmed because the contract was indefinite.[2] The trial record demonstrated that the woman had remarried in a Jewish ceremony, so that it was unclear if a *get* was necessary.

Fifteen years later, in a case not involving a *get*, the appellate division cast doubt on the constitutionality of ordering a Jew to comply with an agreement to observe Jewish law. In *Wener* v. *Wener*[3] the trial court held a husband liable for child support based on the common law and based on the Jewish law incorporated in the parties' *ketubah*. The appellate division affirmed, but only on the former ground, saying that a court cannot require one to do something dictated by the tenets of the parties' religion. "Application of religious law would raise grave constitutional problems of equal protection and separation of church and state."

The confused state of the law was reflected in *Margulies* v. *Margulies*.[4] The husband failed to live up to his stipulation made in open court as a part of a settlement that he would give a *get*. The court held that he could not be incarcerated but that he could be ordered to

---

*Professor of Law, Rutgers University, Camden, NJ.

[1] *Koeppel* v. *Koeppel*, 138 N.Y.S.2d 366 (Sup. Ct. 1954).

[2] *Koeppel* v. *Koeppel*, 3 App. Div. 2d 853, 161 N.Y.S.2d 694 (1957).

[3] 35 App. Div. 2d 50, 312 N.Y.S.2d 815 (1970), *aff'g* 59 Misc. 2d 957, 301 N.Y.S.2d 237 (Sup. Ct. 1969).

[4] 42 App. Div. 2d 517, 344 N.Y.S.2d 482 (1973).

pay fines. The husband did not object in the lower court to the fines, and the court characterized his "[use] of the court for his own ulterior motives" as "contumacious." The court did not explain how its decision was required by the first amendment and did not explain why a court could fine but not incarcerate the defendant.

One New York court distinguished *Margulies* and held that a court can withhold relief from a party who refuses to cooperate in obtaining a *get*. In *Rubin* v. *Rubin*,[5] an Alabama court had ordered the husband to pay the wife a sum of money and ordered the wife to observe her earlier written agreement to cooperate in obtaining a *get*. The wife brought suit in New York to obtain the money, but she had failed to cooperate in obtaining the *get*. The court held that the wife's right to obtain the money could constitutionally be conditioned on her performance or her agreement to cooperate in obtaining a *get*.

In *Pal* v. *Pal*,[6] a divided court held that a court has no power to "in effect convene a rabbinical tribunal." The lower court appointed a rabbi as the husband's "designee" and directed the rabbi and the rabbi designated by the wife to appoint a third rabbi. The three rabbis were to determine whether the husband must grant a *get*. The court took a similar attitude to that taken in *Margulies*, however, in holding that the court would not grant the husband's motion to punish the wife for violation of his visitation rights. Since he did not live up to his agreement to give a *get* he could not demand relief for the wife's breach.

In *Waxstein* v. *Waxstein*,[7] the husband refused to deliver a *get* in breach of a separation agreement. The trial court held that its 1954 decision, *Koeppel* v. *Koeppel*, was still good law and that *Margulies* and *Pal* merely hold that a court cannot imprison a husband who fails to give a *get* and that a court cannot convene a rabbinical tribunal. The court ordered the husband to give a *get* and conditioned the wife's delivery of stock and real estate to him on his delivering a *get*. The appellate division affirmed saying only, "Under the peculiar circumstances revealed by this record, the determination of Special Term was correct."

A few years ago in *Stern* v. *Stern*,[8] a trial court ordered a man to give his ex-wife a *get* based on the finding that the *ketubah* of the parties obligated the man under the circumstances to give a *get*. The court swept aside the objection that it was enforcing religious law in violation of the first amendment. It observed that only those parts of Jewish law that define the relationship between man and God are religious whereas

---

[5] 75 Misc. 2d 776, 348 N.Y.S.2d 61 (Fam. Ct. 1973).

[6] 45 App. Div. 2d 738, 356 N.Y.S.2d 672 (1974).

[7] 90 Misc. 2d 784, 395 N.Y.S.2d 877 (Sup. Ct. 1976), *aff'd per curiam*, 57 App. Div. 2d 394 N.Y.S.2d 253 (1977).

[8] N.Y.L.J., Aug. 8, 1979, at 13 (Sup. Ct. 1979).

those rules of Jewish law governing the relationship between man and man are secular. It therefore ruled that because the writing, execution and delivery of a *get* are secular acts, the court's order to give a *get* does not violate the first amendment.

By a 4–3 vote, the Court of Appeals, the highest court in New York, has recently ordered a man to comply with a clause in the *ketubah* used by many Conservative rabbis that he appear before the *Bet Din* of the Rabbinical Assembly and the Jewish Theological Seminary. In *Avitzur* v. *Avitzur*,[9] the court viewed the matter of Jewish divorce differently from the *Stern* court. The Court of Appeals referred to a Jewish divorce as a "religious" divorce, not a secular act. It viewed the provision relied on in the *ketubah*, however, as "nothing more than an agreement to refer the matter of a religious divorce to a nonjudicial forum," and it viewed that obligation as being secular.

It is difficult to say how the Court of Appeals would have ruled on the *Stern* case, but it is probable that it would have reversed. In *Avitzur* the court stressed that the ex-wife was "not attempting to compel the defendant to obtain a Get or to enforce a religious practice arising solely out of principles of religious law. She merely seeks to enforce an agreement made by defendant to appear before and accept the decision of a designated tribunal." Since the *ketubah* used in Orthodox ceremonies does not designate a particular tribunal, the court might not be willing to imply an agreement in such a *ketubah* to appear before a *Bet Din* that would be acceptable to both parties.

As I have suggested elsewhere,[10] the first amendment ought not to prevent courts from ordering a man to give a *get* if a *Bet Din* determines that a *get* should be given. The Supreme Court has held that state action does not violate the first amendment's ban on establishment of religion even though it has religious motivations and effects, if it has a secular primary purpose and effect and if it does not result in excessive entanglement with religious bodies.[11] Ordering a man to give a *get* has the secular purpose and effect of preventing the intentional infliction of severe emotional distress. Without a *get* the woman would not feel free to remarry without suffering the distress of violating her deep beliefs. Also, no excessive entanglement occurs since the court does not continuously monitor the *Bet Din*. Further, ordering a man to give a *get* does not violate the first amendment's free exercise clause because the act of giving a *get* is devoid of religious consent. It contains no prayer or expression of religious faith.

---

[9] 58 N.Y.2d 108, 446 N.E.2d 136, 459 N.Y.S.2d 572, *cert. denied*, 104 S.Ct. 76 (1983).
[10] "The First Amendment and Jewish Divorce: A Comment on *Stern* v. *Stern*," *Journal of Family Law* 18 (1980), 525–35.
[11] *Lemon* v. *Kurtzman*, 403 U.S. 602 (1971).

In August, 1983, New York enacted a statute generally requiring plaintiffs in divorce actions to stipulate that they have "taken or will take, prior to the entry of final judgment, all steps in [their] power to remove any barrier to the defendant's remarriage." The statute requires defendants to uncontested divorces to make the same declaration. The statute defines "barriers to remarriage" as "[including] any religious . . . inhibition . . . under the principles of the clergyman . . . who has solemnized the marriage." The statute has sparked a sharp debate within the Jewish community. Many reform Jews have claimed that it is unconstitutional. The statute's effect will be limited because it will not assist a woman who sues for divorce if her husband contests it. It should not impose an obligation on most Reform Jews to give a "*get*" because Reform rabbis do not generally require a "*get*" to dissolve a marriage.

A NEW/OLD LOOK AT THE FIFTH AMENDMENT— SOME HELP FROM THE PAST

by

JOSEPH B. GLASER*

Eyn adam mesim atsmo rasha
Nemo tenetur seipsum prodere
"No person shall be compelled in any criminal case to be a witness against himself."

These are the formulations of three legal systems regarding the subject of self incrimination. The origins of the three maxims are strikingly similar, historiographically speaking. There is vagueness about the sources and reasons, the origins, the dating and the application. In all three, there appears to be a distinct difference between what we can make out to have been an original intent, if indeed discernible, and later thrust. To this day, legal scholars and jurists differ sharply. Extensions and regressions alternate back and forth through the histories of the development of the concept, especially in Jewish and American jurisprudence, with the British being quite less passionate, at least in modern times, on the subject, although recently there has been a flurry of interest due to some dramatic cases of late, and a BBC documentary.[1] But during the summer of 1978, when I was pursuing this study at the Oxford Centre for Post-Graduate Hebrew Studies, I could not find "Self Incrimination" or anything like it in the card catalogue at the University Law Library, nor had three librarians ever heard of it. One of them was resourceful enough to go upstairs and ask a visiting barrister, who told her to give me a copy of "Moriarty's Police Law," a paperback distributed to police officers instructing them what to inform suspects and how to restrain themselves in questioning same.[2] Nonetheless, although much of what I eventually discovered was written by visiting Jewish scholars from abroad, there is no question that the English law on self incrimination is vigorous, is owed a great deal by American law, and can further inform it, as we shall see.

---

*Executive Vice President, Central Conference of American Rabbis.

[1] B. Susser, "Worthless Confessions: The Torah Approach," *New Law Journal* (November 13, 1980), 1056–57.

[2] *Moriarty's Police Law* (London: Butterworths, 1976), 67.

With the Jewish law, there is general agreement that the prohibition against self-incrimination was established by the Second Century, though perhaps only for capital cases. There is no specific *mishnah* on it, though it is clearly proscribed in *Tosephta* and *Sifre*,[3] and easily derivable from Scripture. There is disagreement among scholars on the question of presumption of innocence and its effect upon the doctrine, and on the right of an accused to testify on his own behalf, a matter which brings up the difference between pleading and testifying. Rava's Fourth Century syllogism, which gave rise to the maxim, *Eyn adam mesim atsmo rasha*,[4] is often called upon to state the law, but as Arnold Enker has pointed out, it really was meant to deal with unwilling witnesses trying to avoid getting involved in someone else's litigation, and, ironically, compels testimony which, of course, a prohibition against self incrimination seeks to avoid.[5] Finally, we have the problem of the well-known medieval exceptions due to Spanish admixture and the fear of losing jurisdiction and the whole *mesirah* problem.

The history of the English law on self incrimination is similar in its rather jagged course of development and the almost mystery in which its origins are shrouded. As far as we can discover, it starts as a prohibition against the administration of the notorious Oath Ex Officio by the ecclesiastical courts, although there is a fascinating reference by Sir Henry Maine to a case involving St. Patrick's chariot driver which may indicate a much more ancient orgin.[6] The prohibition was extended to the infamous Court of the Star Chamber, where treason and sedition cases were tried, and then "seeped" into the common law courts in colorful cases involving Selden, Lilburne and William Penn in the Seventeenth Century, where prior to that there had been no such privilege. There are about four different Latin formulations of the maxim, which is indicative of the general vagueness with which the English treat the concept. There are also some tantalizing references to the "ancient law" and the "laws of God" during the early argumentation in establishing the prohibition, which have led some scholars to believe that Jewish law had something to do with it. These may have been references to the time of St. Patrick, but there may have been a connection to Jewish law there too. It is not likely that direct Jewish influence was effected through the law of the Hansa, since that was commercial law, but it is worthwhile to consider the theory that the Court of Star Chamber did not derive its

---

[3] *T. Sanh.* 9:4; *T. Shebu.* 3:7 and 5:4; *Sifre Shofṭim* on *Deut.* 19:15.

[4] *Sanh.* 9b.

[5] A. Enker, "Self Incrimination in Jewish Law," *Dine Israel* 4 (1973), cviii–cxxiv; A. Kirschenbaum, *Self-Incrimination in Jewish Law* (New York: The Burning Bush Press, 1970).

[6] Sir Henry Maine, *Lectures on the Early History of Institutions* (3d ed.; London: John Murray, 1880), 21f.

name from the stars that are alleged to have been on its ceiling, but rather from the fact that, originally, the room was used by the Jews to record *shtarot*, documents such as bills and notes.

In American law, the privilege against self incrimination came in with the common law, although there were dramatic exceptions such as the Salem witch trials. Not all states specifically provided for the privilege in their respective constitutions, although eventually the Fifth Amendment was applied to the states by the Supreme Court.[7] There is virtually no historical background to the passage of the self incrimination clause of the Fifth Amendment, which has made it quite difficult to plumb the legislative intent, leaving American jurists and scholars with the same unease as those attempting to divine the purpose of the Jewish and English traditions on this subject. Similarly, we find exertion of the privilege confined to the actual trial, until the late nineteenth century, when *Counselman* v. *Hitchcock*[8] extended it to the grand jury proceeding. There was not much action in the American law on the subject until the Nineteenth Century, altogether, as defendants were not called to testify in any event, until then. Great controversy has surrounded the privilege, as we shall see, for a variety of reasons, not the least of which is the rather general, elastic formulation of the wording in the Fifth Amendment: "No person shall be compelled in any criminal case to be a witness against himself." Ironically, the controversy pits Brandeis and Frankfurter against Cardozo, the latter having stated:

> Justice, however, would not perish if the accused were subject to a duty to respond to orderly inquiry.[9]

Frankfurter retorts:

> ... society carries the burden of proving the charge against the accused not out of his own mouth. It must establish its case, not by interpretation of the accused even under judicial safeguards, but by evidence independently secured through skillful investigation.[10]

To this day, the battle rages, backed by a jagged history of limited application, then extensions and then, again, regressions, similar to the Jewish development. Indeed, as can be seen, there are many historical similarities.

In all three legal systems, there is a common conflict between the interest of the state in acquiring information and a deep seated revulsion against forcing anyone, guilty or not, to condemn himself. It is not, as sometimes posited, the state versus the individual, which is too simplistic a view. The accused could be guilty, or could be an innocent ensnared,

---

[7] *Malloy* v. *Hogan*, 378 US 1 (1964).
[8] *Counselman* v. *Hitchcock*, 142 US 547 (1892).
[9] *Palko* v. *Connecticut*, 302 US 319 (1937).
[10] *Watts* v. *Indiana*, 338 US 49, 54 (1849).

or could be Maimonides' famous masochist. The partisans of the privilege, or prohibition, maintain that it is in the interest of society in general, in terms of an overall view of criminal justice, of the maintenance of the accusatorial system as opposed to the fishing expeditions of the inquisitorial system. The state must be spurred to do a thorough investigation, and must be restrained from using torture and exerting undue pressure. Also common to all three national contexts appears to be a visceral sense of sportsmanship. Guilty or not, the hunter is not permitted to shoot a sitting duck. There is also a general eschewal of oath and trial by ordeal and a common recognition of the vagueness of the respective origins of the prohibitions, summed up rather well by Judge Jerome Frank, who said: "A noble principle often transcends its origins."[11] There is one other point of interest in this brief historiographical review worth noting. At least two references are found in American writings to the "religious" attitude it is felt is manifested by supporters of the privilege in American law, one writer referring to the use of Norman Lamm's article on Maimonides[12] in a Supreme Court opinion.[13] While the word "religious" in both cases was used pejoratively,[14] let us now see if, indeed, the religious law of the Jews can shed some light on the problems vexing American legal scholars and jurists with respect to the law of self incrimination in the United States.

The problems surrounding the American law of self incrimination are many and complex. Chief among them is the natural tendency to assume guilt on the part of the person asserting the Fifth Amendment privilege. An innocent should have nothing to hide, pontificate the critics of the privilege who would actually like to do away with the privilege altogether, or at least rigidly restrict it.[15] They do not take into account the zeal and ambition of prosecutors who come into court like gladiators intent on destroying their opponent in order to save their own political or professional lives, for, unfortunately, prosecutors tend to be judged on the number of convictions they achieve over against the acquittals they suffer. Much the same can be said of the police, who also could incur liability for false arrest, but in any event tend to look foolish and to feel frustrated when someone slips through their net. There is also the factor of the questionable caliber of juries, both naive in the face of horrendous trickeries perpetrated by clever prosecutors, and drawn from the pool of what is left when the professional and business people have mangaged to

---

[11] *United States v. Grunewald*, 233 F2^d 566, 581 (1956).
[12] N. Lamm, "The Fifth Amendment and Its Equivalent in Jewish Law," *Decalogue Journal* 17 (1967), 1, 10.
[13] *Garrity v. New Jersey*, 385 US 493, footnote 5 (1967), Frank, J., dissenting.
[14] C. D. Williams, "Problems of the Fifth Amendment," *Fordham Law Review* 24 (1955), 19–52; R. Kaus, note 15, *infra*.
[15] R. Kaus, "Abolish the Fifth Amendment," *The Washington Monthly* 12 (1980), 12–19.

The Fifth Amendment—Some Help From the Past 33

squirm out of jury service in the variety of sophisticated ways open to them. In addition, increasing attention has been called to the inadequacy of defense attorneys. They are not all Clarence Darrows or Perry Masons. While some able young men and women do go into the practice of criminal law out of altruism, it is a pretty sordid experience, and it is only natural that the best and the brightest would incline toward the handsome offers of money and prestige offered by the fine firms dealing in the business world. Add to this an overworked, and not uniformly competent judiciary, and we have a set of circumstances which spells reason enough not only to retain the Fifth Amendment, but to find new ways to honor it. For, when all is said and done, the worthy commentators referred to above can feel totally secure and confident in their innocence while writing what they do in the august atmosphere of their oak-panelled studies; it is quite a different situation when even a pure innocent is perspiring in a police station, a grand jury room or a forbidding law court.

Turning to specifics, one problem encountered has to do with whether or not the Fifth Amendment is applicable to legislative hearings. It has been established that it is.[16] But much mischief resulted in the process, particularly during the 1940s and 50s when the House Unamerican Activities Committee and Senator Joseph McCarthy were conducting their infamous investigations into subversive behavior. Early on, witnesses hauled before these committees attempted to assert their First Amendment rights of freedom of expression and association. This was denied them,[17] wrongly, I think, and they had to fall back on the Fifth. There is a whole sad story there which we do not have the time to go into in this paper. Suffice to say that witnesses, who were being treated more as defendants, fearful of being trapped in a net of incriminating possibilities stemming from vicious, publicity seeking fishing expeditions and informers, some of whom were later exposed as liars, fearful of such possibilities as perjury indictments, and denied the appropriate safeguard of the First Amendment, took the Fifth. This gave rise to such indignant nonsense as Sidney Hook's outburst that "those who are the foes of intelligence are the foes of freedom, too," an allusion to what he and so many others felt was the unjustified stoppage of information about the alleged communist conspiracy undermining America.[18] After all, he opined, all the poor committees wanted was information. This confusion, plus the increasing use of the Fifth Amendment by notorious members of organized crime, brought the prestige of the Fifth Amendment to a low ebb, and created a mood against it which found its way into the attitude of

---

[16] *Watkins v. United States*, 354 US 178 (1957).
[17] *Branzburg v. Hayes*, 408 US 665 (1972).
[18] S. Hook, *Common Sense and the Fifth Amendment* (New York: Critereon, 1957).

jurists as well as the general public. The investigating committees did more to undermine freedom and respect for the American Constitution than the paltry conspiracy ever could have. The results are still with us in many ways. The contempt proceedings, black lists and other penalties suffered in those days amounted to bills of attainder. Now it is all part of the history of the law of self incrimination.

To do justice to any discussion of self incrimination, we must explore the psychology surrounding it. O. J. Rogge in his book *Why Men Confess*[19] concludes that a skillful interrogator or prosecutor, under the right conditions, can get anyone to confess to anything. It is a work well worth reading for anyone involved in the criminal law. An illuminating article in the *Yale Law Journal*[20] reports on FBI interrogations of Yale University law students who engaged in a public draft protest. Law students should know better than to answer questions from FBI agents who visited them in their homes. But most of them sang like birds, until the dean and faculty, learning of what was going on, advised them as to their rights as if they were miscreants off the streets. Why did they talk, asked researchers? They, law students, explained that they lacked an understanding of the ramifications. Some admitted nervousness, which made them sort of babble. Some, interrogated in their homes, said that it was a "social situation, after all," and they were embarrassed to refuse, and feared they would embarrass their "guest." Yet another responded, "I had to talk—say something." While under such disabilities, the article concludes, they could not make rational decisions even though they were law students.

The famous Scarsdale Diet Doctor murder trial is another case in point.[21] The defense, concerned that if he did not put his well-educated-society-lady-wronged-woman on the stand, people would wonder why an innocent woman could not speak for herself, presented her for testimony. She was, predictably, hyperpassionate, self destructive, desperate and ornery on the witness stand, as she had proved herself to be previously. She was found guilty, and when one of the jurors was interviewed on television that evening, she said, "She just wasn't believable." A yente from Yonkers, operating out of who knows what response to the defendant and conditioning which we cannot begin to fathom without putting the juror on the psychiatrist's couch, made that judgment!

A basic problem in the American law, perhaps the most basic, is the problem of the adverse inference which arises when an accused utilizes the privilege against self incrimination. While, generally, it is forbidden for any comment to be made, there is what Norman Lamm refers to as a

---

[19] O. J. Rogge, *Why Men Confess* (New York: Nelson, 1959), 67–209.
[20] Note, "FBI Interrogation of Draft Protestors," *Yale Law Journal* 78 (1967), 300–320.
[21] *People v. Jean Harris*, Westchester, N.Y., County Court, 1981.

The Fifth Amendment—Some Help From the Past   35

"natural presumption of guilt."[22] Yet, utilization inevitably raises, however mutely, the thought: "What's he hiding?" or "Where there's smoke, there's fire," and, as in the case of the legislative inquiry, "Birds of a feather flock together." While Professor Mark Berger, in his excellent, recent book, *Taking the Fifth*,[23] asserts: "The Fifth Amendment should stand as a presumptive barrier to the imposition of adverse consequences for its exercize," this high minded standard all too often is not operative in the musings of a juror. This issue is also involved, although somewhat tangentially, in the conflict between the Federal rule, which limits cross-examination to direct testimony only, and the so-called Massachusetts rule, which opens cross-examination to all relevant phases of the case.

Another problem in the American law has to do with the oath an accused, or a so-called "witness" in a legislative investigation, is required to take. All people who testify inaccurately do not do so intentionally. I recently observed a criminal trial where almost all of the witnesses for the State changed testimony previously given under oaths two or three times before, in what struck me as a rather questionable pattern, by the way. But memory can be a tricky thing in and of itself, and when one considers the possibilities of perjury penalties—and who can prove that he was not lying?—there is a tendency to take the Fifth because of real uncertainty as to facts. This inhibits not only the judicial process, but even more importantly, the process of legislative inquiry, which, in spite of its notorious abuses, is an important democratic function. Linked to this is the responsibility of public trust issue, wherein public employees are subject to statutory dismissal if they refuse to testify, such dismissal having been held not to be a violation of their Fifth Amendment right,[24] wrongly, some think.

Flowing from this is a consideration of the balancing theory currently in use by the Supreme Court, wherein the Court balances the rights of the individual under the Fifth Amendment against the needs of the State and, sometimes, between different Constitutional provisions. An example of such an issue would be dismissal of a public employee for failure to testify, or the disbarment of an attorney. Another example would be the Ohio unitary trial rule,[25] wherein the verdict not only establishes innocence or guilt, but also the sentence, forcing the accused either to remain silent when he could be pleading for leniency by virtue of extenuating circumstances or the like, or to forfeit his privilege against self incrimination in order to modify the sentence. Thus, in Ohio,

---

[22] *Supra* note 12.
[23] M. Berger, *Taking the Fifth* (Lexington: D. C. Heath, 1980), 216.
[24] *Gardner v. Broderick*, 392 US 273 (1968), where a distinction is made between a simple assertion of the privilege and a legislative requirement to waive immunity.
[25] *Crampton v. Ohio*, 402 US 183 (1971).

the classic "cruel trilemma" of self-accusation, perjury or contempt becomes a "quadlemma." The possible judicial vagaries resulting from the whole balancing approach are considered by some to burden the Fifth Amendment to such a point as to seriously vitiate, if not invalidate, its primary and historic purpose.[26]

The question of waiver of the privilege perhaps goes to the very heart of the problem of how to deal with self incrimination in America. In most jurisdictions, once the accused takes the stand to testify for the defense, he is considered as having waived the privilege, and becomes the object of ripping cross-examination by the prosecution. He must answer all questions truthfully—"the truth, the whole truth and nothing but the truth." This, of course, is the primary reason for the decision not to testify at all. It also accounts for the early balks at legislative investigations. By comparison, the English system and some jurisdictions in the United States do not consider testimony as waiver until the witness reveals a fact that subjects him to penalty, at which time the waiver becomes irrevocable. Until that time, he can pick and choose which questions to answer and which questions to which to assert the privilege. The results of the American approach are to frustrate the process of gathering information, both in the courtroom and the legislative site, and to subject the willing witness to all of the traps described above.

In the matter of the necessity for gathering information, whether for the orderly conduct of a trial, or for the illumination of a legislative purpose, the subject of immunity grants come up. There are British experiences with it, and although it really did not become a subject as such until 1857 in America, there is an analog in the famous proceedings against Aaron Burr, in Chief Justice Marshall's reference to a "link in the chain."[27] In the middle of the Nineteenth Century, Congress, eager to have information, enacted transactional immunity statutes which were so protective, that all sorts of wrong doers came forward to take immunity "baths" which would forever shield them from prosecution for their crimes. Attempts to modify down to what is called "use immunity" were frustrated by findings that this was not enough protection insofar as evidence could still be derived from the admissions given under the use immunity statutes, which could then be used for prosecution. So "use-derivative-use" statutes have become the norm, and it has been decided that these, which are applied reciprocally between federal and state and state and state, are about equal to the protection of the Fifth Amendment[28] save for two problems, at least. One problem is evidenced by the hesitancy of prosecutors to utilize the statutes, for fear of getting little in return for dropping the prosecution, for

---

[26] M. Berger, *Taking the Fifth, supra* note 23, at 214–19.
[27] *In Re Willie*, 25 F. Cas. 38, 40 (C.C. Va. 1807) (No. 14, 692e).
[28] *Kastigar* v. *United States/Zicarelli* v. *New Jersey*, 406 US 441/472 (1972).

they can never be certain of the extent or the worth of the testimony bargained for. The other problem is a bizarre development in a 1976 case where the target of immunized testimony subsequently pleaded guilty and turned around and testified against the use-derivative-use witness who had testified against him. Was this use or derivative use of the former, immunized testimony? The Circuit Court held no, in a troubling and perhaps irrelevant discussion of motive.[29]

In this already lamentably sketchy review of the state of the law on self incrimination in America, it is not possible because of the limitations of time to go into several other problem areas, such as the more recent tendency to treat the privilege more as a rule of evidence than as a substantive right, pretrial matters and personalization questions involving organizations and documents in the custody of attorneys and accountants. Suffice to say that there are plenty of problems, exposing the privilege and the Fifth Amendment itself, to erosion, attack, and even calls for abolition,[30] which should not be taken lightly in a regressive society, no longer awash with idealism and rationalism, but increasingly crowded and intrusive. The rise of fundamentalism and right wing reaction and intolerance, the generally parlous economy and the uneasy condition of foreign relations giving rise to the ominous echoes of the 1940s and 1950s emanating from high levels of government, and the possibilities of one disaster or another could bring on oppressive government. A Constitutional Convention could be around the corner, at which all of these forces could converge to change radically the American system. The First and the Fifth Amendments might be the easiest victims. Fueling all this is rampant crime, both street and organized, as well as public corruption, what will probably be an increase in the terrorism which has plagued Europe and the Middle East, and the excesses to which purveyors of pornography have gone. All of this amounts to an increasing frustration, on the part of the public in general, but shared by officialdom at all levels and in all functions. The trend back to capital punishment is a good indication of the prevailing mood.

The Supreme Court, in the landmark opinion of *Miranda* v. *Arizona*,[31] recognizing that the last word on self incrimination could not have been yet said, if ever, commented: "We encourage Congress and the States to continue their laudable search for increasingly effective ways of protecting the rights of the individual while promoting efficient enforcement of our criminal laws." Let us now see if new light can be shed from an ancient law.

Let us start with the psychological aspects of self incrimination, and

---

[29] *United States* v. *Kurzer*, 534 2^d Fed 511 (1976).
[30] R. Kaus, *supra* note 15.
[31] 384 US 436 (1966).

Maimonides' classic treatment of it, however *post facto* it may appear to have been. Rambam is speaking of the clear-cut case of the masochist, the unbearably guilt-ridden who, "disturbed, melancholy, depressed," seeking any means at hand to suicide, "comes forward so as to be put to death."[32] While there are those who maintain that Maimonides was reading into the *halakhah* the fruits of medieval medical enlightenment, one should not be so hasty to deny such wisdom, sensitivity and power of observation to the earlier authorities or, for that matter, to the Torah, particularly in view of similar concerns found in other cultures and legal systems. But there are gradations of Rambam's self-destructive volunteer. Coupling the nervousness which besets almost all of us even when accused falsely, and the justifiable fear when confronted by the awesome power of public authority, with the varying degrees of guilt complex instilled at tender age, we can all become the subject of the theory of O. J. Rogge referred to above.[33] Thus, Norman Lamm, in his comment on Rambam, now enshrined in US Supreme Court opinions, asserts that the prohibition in Jewish law against self incrimination—a prohibition, not a privilege to be waived—is to "ensure the total victory of the life instinct over its omnipresent antagonist."[34] Surely, this Jewish approach could be utilized in the American consideration of the subject to stand hard by the spirit of the Fifth Amendment, if not, indeed, to go back to the prevailing practice of most of the Nineteenth Century, and simply not call the accused at all, with the possible modification found in *Sanh.* 40a., 42b which allows the accused to plead, as opposed to testify, in his own defense. It is possible to interpret the word "compelled" which is found in the Fifth Amendment in such a way as to turn what has been deemed a privilege into a prohibition by very virtue of the attacks upon it from legal quarters which have almost invariably followed the line that one who took the Fifth had some guilt to hide, indicating that asserting the privilege is an exercise in futility, anyway, and thus the compulsion. As Lamm has pointed out, there is an inherent flaw in the Fifth Amendment. Asserting the privilege seems to raise a natural presumption of guilt. Mark Berger's attempt to find in the Fifth Amendment an *ipso facto* presumptive barrier[35] may be more than the human mind, at this stage of evolution, can handle.

As we know, in the context of this paper, the oath is not exacted in Jewish law. The rabbis wanted to establish total respect for the courts and for legal procedure and, especially, for testimony. It was felt that anyone who would lie in a court of law would lie under oath. One of the

---

[32] *Code,* Judges, *Sanh.* 18:6.
[33] *Supra* note 19.
[34] *Supra* note 12.
[35] *Supra* note 26.

reasons people take the Fifth, particularly in legislative hearings, is that they fear that they will stumble into inadvertant perjury. They are not sure of their facts, and/or they are aware that an overzealous, unscrupulous prosecutor or legislator will confuse and trick them, or present lying witnesses to demolish their testimony. So they take the Fifth or risk contempt—the "cruel trilemma." Within the oath as it is usually administered lies yet another problem in the words, "the whole truth." There may be some things which are really not relevant to the trial cause or the legislative search, and yet, matters which the witness would rather not be known publicly. However, once the fishing expedition begins, he has "the whole truth" staring him in the face. All of this is especially pertinent to the legislative hearing which, after all, is not supposed to be punitive but rather fact gathering. Dropping the oath could be a way of enhancing the effectiveness of those investigations. Witnesses would have at least one less reason for invoking the Fifth Amendment.

Turning now to our final consideration, we take up the Jewish legal concept of "split testimony," which goes to the heart of the matter of self incrimination, and beyond. There are a number of cases illustrative of this, but the one dealing with the *agunah* should suffice to make the point.[36] An *agunah* comes into court, asserting that her husband is dead. She produces a witness who claims he killed him. The court accepts his testimony with regard to the widowed status of the *agunah* but in terms of his own criminality, they say: "We do not hear him." This provides a societal benefit by inducing testimony crucial to the well being of a third party, yet not violating the prohibition against self incrimination. Elsewhere, we find that someone can confess to a crime, thereby becoming liable for the civil damages involved while avoiding criminal penalties. The talmudic theory there is that he is only admitting to a civil obligation which is already there, while if the court were to accept the criminal part of the confession, he creates a liability and thus violates the prohibition.[37]

Thus, we find a greater emphasis in the Jewish law on restitution than on retribution. American law would do well to consider the possibility of moving from punishment to rectification. The effects would be many. It certainly would tend to reduce the current court backlog. It would make whole people who have been victimized. It could even act as a rehabilitative agent for a criminal to make good the damage he has done, instead of fuming and embittering himself in already hopelessly overcrowded, and very expensive, prisons, and cut down on recidivism.

---

[36] *Yeb.* 25ab; see also *Sanh.* 96, *B.M.* 3b, *Ket.* 18b.
[37] H. Cohn, "The Privilege Against Self Incrimination Under Foreign Law. E. Israel," *The Journal of Criminal Law, Criminology and Police Science* 51 (1960), 175–78, quoting *Levush Mordechai* (Mordechai Epstein—19th Century).

Already, American courts are beginning to move modestly in this direction. Quincy, Massachusetts has instituted what it calls a restitution-diversion program for youthful criminals who work off the damage they have done while undergoing an education process.[38] Other jurisdictions have similar programs for adults. In Los Angeles, a movie producer convicted of possessing cocaine was sentenced to produce a movie on the evils of drug use. An overzealous proponent of the Equal Rights Amendment for women, convicted of bribing a state legislator, was given a similar assignment. How good it would have been had the judge in the Scarsdale Diet Doctor murder case "sentenced" Jean Harris, an accomplished and skillful educator, to seven years of directing the educational program in a correctional institution for young women.

Certainly, the intent of the Founding Fathers with respect to the Fifth Amendment would be preserved against the current attempts to whittle it down, if not obliterate it altogether. Well worth preserving, it is a noble principle, protecting the frightened and confused threatened by the awesome power of the state, placing practical limits on governmental power which make it fruitless to try to torture or connive admissions, preserving respect for the legal process, frustrating bad laws and procedures, especially in the political and religious area, standing as a bulwark against the fishing expeditions of inquisitorial legal systems, spurring competent investigation by the authorities, forcing them to prove their case, and finally, requiring govenment to leave the individual alone unless it has a good, independent case. Brandeis said it well when he said that a responsibility of government is to be as "examplar in keeping the law."[39]

The *Miranda* opinion rationalizes its extension of the privilege by quoting Judge Frank: "A noble principle often transcends its origins."[40] Whatever the exact intentions of the framers of the Fifth Amendment were, and we may never know, the new light which ancient Jewish law can shed could well dispel some of the darkness we have attempted to describe here, if we are to follow the approach of Justice Frankfurter who, in *Ullman* v. *United States*,[41] observed that the history of the privilege demonstrates that "it is not to be interpreted literally . . ." nor ". . . in a hostile or niggardly spirit."

[38] *Juvenile Diversion Program*, Norfolk County District Attorney, Massachusetts.
[39] *Olmstead* v. *United States*, 277 US 438, 478 (1928), Brandeis, J., dissenting.
[40] *Miranda* v. *Arizona*, 384 US 436 (1966).
[41] 350 US 422, 438, 426 (1956).

PARTICIPATION OF THE COMMON PEOPLE IN PHARISAIC AND RABBINIC LEGISLATIVE PROCESSES

by

ALEXANDER GUTTMANN*

The important role of laymen in the history of the *halakhah* shaping Jewish law and Custom is as old as the Torah itself. The instance of the daughters of Tselafḥad[1] constitutes a case in point.

Josephus maintains that the Pharisees prevailed because they had the support of the masses,[2] as do Talmudic (Tannaitic) sources.

According to *T. Sukk.* 3:1 the Boethosians, a Sadducean group, placed big stones on the willow branches before the Sabbath of the Sukkoth festival lest they be used on the Sabbath of Sukkoth. The common people (*amme ha'arets*) removed the stones so enabling the Pharisees to observe the ritual which called for the willow branch ceremony even on the Sabbath of Sukkoth.

Sukk. 48ab relates an incident in which the people pelted King Alexander Jannaeus with citrons (*etrogim*) because he violated the ritual Water Libation which, according to the Pharisees, was mandatory.

These incidents reflect the strength of the lay people in opposing priestly and other non-Pharisaic official leadership. Needless to say, the opposition of the people was stimulated by their teachers and "unofficial" leaders, the Pharisees. They were able to interfere successfully in matters of religious observance.

The power of the people, however, went much further. Indeed some essential elements of the applied *halakhah* have been decided in the past as well as in the present by the laymen, the ordinary people. The rabbis' activities, more than those of the priests, were focused on the realistic spiritual and material needs of the people. Therefore, they often had to react positively to the wishes of the people, accept and approve of many of their customs. Moreover, in several instances, rabbis had to accept

---

*Professor of Talmud and Rabbinics, Hebrew Union College–Jewish Institute of Religion, Cincinnati.
[1] *Num.* 36.
[2] *Ant.* XVI. II x.6.

their ways of executing laws, biblical (toraitic) and rabbinical, as legitimate parts of Judaism.

The Laymen's Role in the Realm of Customs

The broadest area of the lay people's contribution to the strengthening of vigorous Jewish life has been that of the *minhag*, custom. According to a dictum of the Talmud: *haminhag mevatel et hahalakhah*, "Custom nullifies the Law." This dictum, found twice in the Palestinian Talmud but not once in the Babylonian Talmud, has often been misunderstood. This dictum should neither be taken generally as a valid legal principle, nor even in the given context does it mean that the *minhag* nullifies an existing *halakhah*. The passages, when read in context, are unequivocal in telling us the following:

(1) Y.Yeb. 12:1, 11c:

> Rabbi Ba, Rav Yehuda said in the name of Rav: 'Should Elijah come and say that the *halitsah* ritual can be performed with a shoe, we ("they") listen to him. [Should he, however, say that] the *halitsah* cannot be performed with a sandal, we do not listen to him, because the custom of the people is to use the sandal for the *halitsah*, and the custom nullifies the law.'

We see that this case is not one in which a custom nullifies an existing *halakhah*. "*Halakhah*" here designates a *potential future ruling* by the Prophet Elijah seeking to abolish the using of the sandal for the *halitsah* ritual. The ruling (dictum) in this instance may be considered, at best, a legal opinion: no new *halakhah* or practice may be introduced which abolishes an existing custom or halakhic practice of the people. Hence in our case the method of carrying out the *halitsah* ritual with a sandal cannot be changed even by the Prophet Elijah.

The accord between the Palestinian and Babylonian Talmudim is noteworthy. To this end, I refer to *Yeb.* 102a, *Men.* 32a. The principal difference between the Babylonian and Palestinian Talmudim is that the Babylonian Talmud does not cite the rule, "The custom nullifies the law," as does the Yerushalmi.

(2) The second Talmudic passage in which the dictum "The custom nullifies the law" occurs is in *Y. B. M.* 7:1, 11b. The Mishnah *B.M.* rules:

> If a man hired laborers and said to them to work early or to work late, he has no right to compel them to do so where the custom is not to work early or not to work late. . . . Everything should follow local custom.

The Talmud comments:

> Rav Hoshaiah states, 'This Mishnah tells us that the custom nullifies the law.' Rabbi Immi adds that in every instance, except in this one,

the principle *hamotsi meḥavero alav har'ayah* (the burden of proof rests on the person who makes a [financial] claim against another one) is valid, but here it does not apply because it conflicts with the legalized custom which is the custom of the people (*i.e.*, the custom required by law).

Briefly, this case assumes the following situation: In order to prevent the employer from taking advantage of a specific legal principle by disregarding a custom, the Talmud rules that the custom prevails. The implication of this case is that the rule that the custom nullifies the law which is applied here, in a special case due to exceptional circumstances, has no validity in cases where no circumstances are present warranting an exception.[3]

Custom versus Law: Various Aspects

Since according to both, Babylonian and Palestinian, Talmudim, the law is, in principle, superior to the custom, why do we find a number of cases where, as above, the custom seems to, or actually does, override the law, even the law of the Torah? In these cases is there always a special reason present? Close scrutiny of the respective instances leads to the conclusion that this, indeed, is the case, even where the reasons are not readily apparent. A few illustrations will confirm this point:

Regarding the law in *Deut*. 18:3 stating that "They shall give unto the *Kohanim* the shoulder, and the two cheeks, and the maw," Maimonides says:[4] "This commandment is valid for all times, at the time of the Temple (of Jerusalem) and *not* (only) at the time of Jerusalem (*i.e.*, after the destruction of the Temple, meaning for all times), and in every place, in the Land (of Israel) and abroad. It applies to secular animals but not to sacrificial animals." However, the *Shulḥan Arukh*[5] states: "Someone says that this law does *not* apply abroad, and such has been the custom of the people."

The validity of the toraitic laws about the *matnot kehunah*, "the priests' dues," became controversial already in medieval times. In all fairness, the *Kohanim* no longer deserved the dues since they performed no major tasks as they had in the days of the sacrificial cult. Still, authorities of the *halakhah* could not simply abrogate laws of the Torah. They had to find other ways, and they did. The procedure was the following. In the *Shulḥan Arukh*,[6] Isserles states: "Some say that you do not give (lit. 'You do not make eat') *ḥallah* to any *Kohen*."[7] On this opinion,

---

[3] See a detailed analysis of the above cases and implications for the history of the *halakhah*: A. Guttmann, "*Lishe'lat Hayaḥas: Minhag—Halakhah Bitekufat Hatalmud*," *Bitsaron* 8 (1946), 95–103 and 9 (1946), 192–98.
[4] *Sefer Zera'im, Bikkurim*, 9:11.
[5] *Yoreh De'ah*, 61:21 (end).
[6] *Oraḥ Ḥayyim*, 452:2.
[7] Source: Rabbi Jacob Weil (Erfurt, first half of 15th century).

Magen Avraham (Abraham Gumbinner 1635–1683: Eastern Europe, note 9), comments: "Because we do not consider him to be a definite *Kohen.* It is possible that one of his female ancestors became a *halalah*, 'a defiled one',[8] and therefore her descendants are no longer *Kohanim.*" *Magen Avraham* cites several older sources.[9]

While the rabbis of all times looked mostly favorably upon the numerous *minhagim*, customs, abolishing or modifying some of them also was proposed. Among the critics of certain customs is Rabbi Ben Zion Uzi'el (1881–1953), the late Sefardic Chief rabbi of Israel. He strongly criticizes the custom of breaking the glass at the wedding ceremony as practiced by the Ashkenazim of our time.[10] People do not know its original meaning and purpose. They consider it a heroic deed on the part of the groom. They believe it to be an essential and joyous part of the wedding ritual.

At the same time, Rabbi Uziel praises the Sefardim who recite after the breaking of the glass the verse[11] "If I forget you, O Jerusalem, let my right hand wither." Therefore, it would be better to abolish this custom altogether than change its character. However, he does not suggest this only because of the advice of our sages: "It is a *mitsvah* not to say something that would not be heard."[12] Then he continues: "Our sages say of such customs: '*minhag* has the same letters (consonants) as *gehinnom.*' Whenever the original form and intent of a *minhag* is changed, it changes into the gates of *gehinnom.*"

However, due to the emergence of liberal Judaism, the abolishing of customs became a serious issue with traditional Judaism. Thus, for example, Rabbi Ezekiel Landau says:[13] "No custom, no matter how baseless, may be abolished without the consent of the sages." This warning by an outstanding halakhic authority shows that the abolishing of customs was a weighty issue in the eighteenth century. In the eyes of the traditional rabbis it constituted a sin. In this light we have to understand the statement in *Sha'ar Efrayim* (Aryeh Yehudah Leib ben Efrayim Hakohen 1658–1720, born in Moravia, died in Safed) that "a custom must not be abolished, and we are not responsible for harmful consequences even if

---

[8] *Lev.* 21:7.

[9] Judah Eisenstein, citing the above passage from *Magen Avraham*, refers to the view that the *Kohanim* (of later times) do not possess their *sefer hayahas*, document of genealogy, that proves their priestly descent. In other words, the law of the Torah is not abrogated or ignored. It is not carried out due to adverse circumstances. (*Otsar Yisra'el*, V, p. 259.) He then adds that the fact that the *Kohen* is called to the Torah first is merely a custom.

[10] B. Z. M. H. Uziel, *Mishpete Uziel* (Jerusalem, Mosad Harav Kuk, 1964), *Even Ha'ezer*, 431–32.

[11] *Ps.* 137:5.

[12] *Yeb.* 45b, *Y.Ter.* (end of chap. 4).

[13] Ezekiel Landau, *Noda Biyehudah Tinyana, Yoreh De'ah*, responsum 54 (ed. Israel Beer Jaiteles; Prague, 1776).

it contradicts a law of the Torah."[14]

The important, often decisive role of custom in making halakhic decisions includes, at times, customs practiced also by *non-Jews*. (See, e.g., Responsa of *Ḥatam Sofer* [Moshe Sofer, Moshe Schreiber 1762–1839, Frankfurt–Pressburg]). The case, in brief: While Jidel Kohen was out of town, non-Jewish burglars entered his house. After they left, the wife of Jidel Kohen claimed that the burglars had raped her. After she heard that, being the wife of a *kohen*, divorce was mandatory, she said that she was not raped. All that the burglars did was to lie on her quietly lest she scream. The question is now: Should we believe her first testimony or the second one? Ḥatam Sofer decided that her second testimony was the true one. Among his reasons was the importance of the *custom*. The custom of burglars is not to rape women lest they scream and alarm the neighbors. The burglars were arrested and gladly agreed with the woman's second story and Ḥatam Sofer's decision. Thus Ḥatem Sofer saved the marriage.

The Rabbis Had to Consider the Laymen's Negative Reactions

At times, the rabbis were compelled to consider the possibly negative reaction of the people to their intended legal measures. An example: "... And was not that year proper for intercalation? (*i.e.*, should it not have been made a leap year by adding an extra Adar to it)? And why did Elisha not intercalate it? Because it was a year of famine, and all the people were running to the threshing floors."[15] In other words, the year was not made a leap year in that year because Elisha realized that, due to the famine, the people would disregard the intercalation. Had they accepted it, they would have been forced to wait and eat from the new crop a month later. Consequently, many people would have sinned by eating from the new crop before the second day of Passover which, because of intercalation, it observed a month later.

An example from the *Shulḥan Arukh* involving *haminhag mevaṭel et hahalakhah* ("The custom nullifies the law"): "The sale of eggs that are bad, unfit for consumption, is a *mikkah ta'ut*, an erroneous transaction (purchase), therefore halakhically invalid. However, this law is presently not observed, and the *minhag* overrides the law."[16] This is so in spite of the fact that normally a *mikkah ta'ut* invalidates the sale as a matter of principle. The obvious reason for making an exception here is that it is very difficult to prove when and where the eggs became putrid. The court, therefore, would not be able to decide the case in unquestionable fairness.

---

[14] Moshe Sofer, *Responsa Ḥatam Sofer, Even Ha'ezer*, resp. 78 (6 parts in 4 vols.; Jerusalem: Makor, 1969/70, Pt. 7, Makhon Ḥatam Sofer, 1971/72).
[15] *T. San.* 2:9.
[16] *Ḥoshen Mishpaṭ* 232:19.

In some instances, the dictum *minhag avoteynu torah hi*, "The custom of our fathers is (like) Torah," is cited when the *minhag* of the people is stricter than the law to which it is related and for which it constitutes a *seyag*, a fence, without using the term *seyag*.

A case in point: "Rav Ḥisda said that a fast that is not observed until the sun sets is no fast."[17] *Toṣafot* in *Men.* 20b, s.v. *nifsal* quotes this passage and comments: "And the custom of our fathers is (like the law of the) Torah, and everybody's custom is to fast until the stars appear (in the sky)."[18]

The reactions, and even the possible reactions, of the people were considered by the legislating rabbis in many instances. Thus, for example, the prohibition against using the oil of the gentiles was revoked by Judah II and his court, because this prohibition was not widely accepted by the people.[19] Moreover, according to a dictum in both Talmudim, no prohibition must be ordained unless the majority of the people will be able to observe it.[20]

A noteworthy statement in this context is found in the Talmud: "... Ulla said, 'When a *gezerah* (a negative ordinance or prohibition) is ordained in Palestine, its reason is not revealed for twelve months, a whole year, because (knowing the reason) some people might disagree and will give little consideration to it.'"[21] In other words, the people may reject an ordinance of the rabbis if they know why it was issued. After a *gezerah* has been observed for a full year a negative option is not admissible because it has become an established part of authentic Jewish life.

Abrogation of a Court's Decision

According to a Tannaitic ruling, a smaller court cannot void the decision of a major (*i.e.*, higher) court.[22] According to a later *halakhah*, however, there is an exception. If the decree of the higher court was not accepted all over Israel (*i.e.*, by the Jewish people), then a lower court had the authority to abrogate it.[23] This instance shows that the power of the lay community increased with the passage of time as circumstances warranted a change, as in our case. This Maimonidean decision is based on a realistic assessment of the intent of the Jewish Law and is shared by other rabbinic authorities.

---

[17] *Taan.* 12a.
[18] See also *A. Zar.* 34a, *Toṣafot* s.v. *mit'annin* for different explanations of the above custom.
[19] *A. Zar.* 35b–36.
[20] *B.K.* 79b; *B.B.* 60b; *Y.Shebi.* 4:2; 35b.
[21] *A. Zar.* 35a.
[22] *M. Eduy.* 1:5.
[23] Maimonides, *Mishneh Torah, Mamrim*, 2:7.

The People's Voice in Historical and Theological Halakhah

According to the sages the reaction of the people has to be considered, as it had been taken into account in the past, also in the realm of historical and theological *halakhah*, that is in some areas of the *halakhah* of the hoary past and the distant future.

Revival of the Sacrificial Cult

A case in point is the revival of the sacrificial cult. According to some halakhists, the re-introduction of the sacrificial cult, even if circumstances indicate a possibility, will not be automatic. It will need the consent of the majority of the Jewish people all over the world. If many Jews will not consent to it, the resumption of public sacrifices will not be possible: "The consent of the majority of the Jewish people will be necessary. However, if many of the Jewish people do not agree, and even more so, if many have a negative attitude toward such a cult, it cannot be reintroduced. In addition, the *Shekalim* to be used for (purchasing) the sacrifical animals would have to be collected from all the Jews all over the world. This would be needed in addition to the consent of the majority of the Jews. Moreover, the majority must have the desire to introduce the sacrificial cult."[24]

The question of private sacrifices is also raised. The difficulty here is that the private sacrifices do not override the law of defilement (*i.e.*, defilement precludes the offering of private sacrifices). However, according to Tsvi Hirsch Kalisher (1795–1874 Eastern Europe), *Avodah Tamma* 7a and 38, the reintroduction of the sacrificial cult does not depend on the will of the majority of the people but on the *Bet Din Hagodol*, The Great (Jewish) Court. This rule applies to all other commandments which are not practiced today as well.[25] This instance, in which the rabbis assign an important right to the laymen in future times, parallels a case in which they ascribe to them a right with respect to the past.

Conquest of the Land of Israel

Maimonides states:[26] "The Land of Israel, wherever mentioned, are the territories which were conquered by a king of Israel, or by a prophet, with the *consent* of the majority of [the people of] Israel. This is called

---

[24] Israel Sokolov, (*Sefer*) *Har Hakodesh al Pe'at Hashulḥan, Perek* 3, *Hilkhot Yerushalayim Vehamikdash Ve-3 Sefarim bo Niftaḥim Panim Me'irot, Panim Masbirot, Panim Ḥadashot* (Moshe Naḥum Spira with the assistance of *Midrash Bene Tsiyyon*; Jerusalem, 1977), particularly the section *Panim Masbirot*, 179.

[25] *Avodah Tamma* 7a and 38, cited in *Panim Masbirot* (see note 24), 179.

[26] *Hilkhot Terumot*, 1:2.

public conquest."[27] Shemariahu Arieli says:[28] "See particularly *Ḳiryat Sefer, Hilkhot Terumot, loc. cit.*, where it is stated: 'It appears that the rule that for the conquest of the Land of Israel a king or a prophet and *the consensus* of the majority of the people are required holds true only for the *original* conquest of the Land (of Israel). However, for the second occupation ('conquest') by Ezra the consent of the majority was no longer needed, because Israel was holy already. Maimonides also requires the consent of the (highest) court. Consent of the court is needed only for an optional war.[29] Therefore, in *Hilkhot Terumot* where he speaks about a *Mitsvah* war (conquest of Cana'an), he does not mention the requirement of the consent of a court as he does in *Hilkhot Melakhim*."

Special Halakhic Problems, Controversial or Not, Were Decided by the People

Cases in this category include:[30]

> Rabba, the son of Rav Ḥanan, asked Abayye, according to another tradition he asked Rav Josef: What should be the law?[31] He said: Go and see what the practice (custom) of the people is.

That is, the practice of the people which, in this case, agreed with the first, anonymous opinion in the Mishnah, determined the *halakhah*. This category includes the significant incident in *Pes.* 66a where the people's method (custom) of transporting their knives on the Sabbath for the slaughter of the paschal sacrifices reminded Hillel of a forgotten *halakhah*. A similar incident with respect to another halakhic controversy is found in *Erub.* 14b.

In another case, the question was raised whether torn straps of *tefillin*, phylacteries, may be sewn together.[32] The problem was not controversial, but had to be resolved. Rav Ashi tells Rav Aḥa son of Rav Josef, "Go and see what the people do." Again, whatever the people do in this case is deemed halakhically proper.

Significant Role of the People in Halakhic Decisions of Recent Times

In modern times, traditional rabbinic authorities often ignored, and sometimes even abolished (though the term is not used) talmudic and later

---

[27] Cp. N. Roth, "Hagolan vehabashan le'or hahalakhah," *Shanah Beshanah*, 1971, 162ff.
[28] *Mishpaṭ Hamilḥamah* (Jerusalem: R. Mass, 1971), 173–74.
[29] *Op. cit.*, 175, on Maimonides, *Mishneh Torah, Hilkhot Terumot* 1:5 and *Hilkhot Melakhim* 5:2.
[30] *Ber.* 45a.
[31] In the controversy of the Mishnah, *ibid.* 44a, pertaining to the blessing over drinking water.
[32] *Men.* 35b.

halakhot, citing as justification the custom of the people. After the period of the emergence of the liberal-reform movement in the eighteenth century, traditional rabbis did not want to be accused of introducing changes, lenient practices or of abolishing old ones lest they be called "Reformers." Therefore, a reference to an established practice of the people was a welcome support and justification for their lenient halakhic rulings in special cases that warranted or necessitated such rulings due to circumstances that had changed. Two examples will illustrate:

(1) Ezekiel Landau (1713–1793, Prague) discusses the present day validity of the law in *M. Taan.* Chapter 1, ordaining fasts to induce rainfall after a certain length of drought.[33] In spite of the fact that Maimonides[34] and the Shulhan Arukh[35] uphold the law, in a somewhat modified form, even for the lands outside of Palestine, Rabbi Landau does not do so. He says: "We never heard that the series of the thirteen fasts was observed (*i.e.*, by the people, the farmers who need the rainfall) in our time. Our way is to say various prayers of supplication and also to ordain one or two fasts according to the need." After citing a few sources, he continues: "Nowadays, in these lands (*e.g.*, Europe) we are not experts in determining when the rainy season begins to know that the rain has not come down at its proper time. Therefore, we do not follow the order (*i.e.*, law) of the Mishnah." After claiming support from Maimonides, he continues, "In my humble opinion, this seems to be the proper way." And he adds in conclusion: "And go see how the people act." But "Go and see" is not a serious argument here. He very well knew that the people did not and would not fast for rain because, according to the law, the fasts would have to be ordained by leading rabbis and he, Rabbi Landau, would be one of them. Citing the dictum here is but an apologetic means, lest he be accused of having rendered a lenient decision contradicting a codified *halakhah* of the Talmud.

(2) Rabbi Jacob Briesh (1896–) discusses the question whether the sons of Jews who desecrate the Sabbath publicly may be circumcised on a Sabbath.[36] After a lengthy discussion, he renders a lenient decision. In conclusion, he cites a responsum by Simon Sofer (1820–1883) who also arrives

---

[33] E. Landau, *Noda Biyehudah Kamma, Orah Hayyim*, Responsum 31.
[34] *Mishneh Torah, Ta'aniyyot*, chap. 3.
[35] *Orah Hayyim*, chap. 575, *Hilkhot Ta'anit*.
[36] J. Reischer (ed. *Mahzike Hadat*, 2d ed.; Bne Brak, 1968–69), Part One, 47, 99–101.

at a lenient decision, in which he concludes with the words: "Go and see how the people act."[37]

Judaism and the Jewish People Saved by the Laymen from Sectarian Division

While the rabbis have clarified, taught and watched over the observance of law and custom, the people have not always cooperated and, by doing so, have saved the Jewish people from sectarian division and, perhaps, the disintegration of the basic unity of *Klal Yisrael*. Most rabbis, moreover, welcomed the people's resistance to the divisive rulings of their colleagues. This was the case already in Tannaitic times (ending about 200 C.E.).

A case in point is *M. Eduy*. 4:8 which states that, although Bet Hillel and Bet Shammai disagree in many *Halakhot* pertaining to marriage and related matters, their families would not refrain from marrying men and women from the opposite School. In other words, they intermarried without hesitation. Had they not done so, the Jewish people would have split into two sects at that time.

Did the sages object to the people's transgressions of some of their laws? On the contrary, they *praised* them for doing so even quoting Zech. 8:19 "Love (here: "They loved") truth and peace."[38] In this respect, history repeated itself in modern times. Outstanding Orthodox rabbinical authorities of the last century, among them Rabbi Moshe Shik (1807–1879, Hungary), declared reform marriages null and void, prohibiting Orthodox Jews from marrying children born of reform marriages. They may be *mamzerim*, bastards, as they do not adhere to the code of the Orthodox, the *Shulḥan Arukh*.[39]

As in Talmudic times, most Jews of our day disregard the warnings and prohibitions of their Orthodox rabbis, no matter how great, and intermarry with Jews of their personal choice, irrespective of their religious affiliation. Today's Orthodox rabbis no longer sound warnings, and often co-officiate with liberal and reform colleagues.

Again, the lay people saved the unity of the Jewish people by disregarding the divisive rulings of their teachers in modern times as they did in the time of the Mishnah.

---

[37] Simon Sofer, *Responsa*, vol. 2, chap. 156.
[38] *T. Yeb*. 1:10 (*Yeb*. 14b).
[39] M. Shik, *Responsa, Oraḥ Ḥayyim*, resp. 305. See also resp. 304 (ed. J. Shik, 3 vols.; Munkacs: P. Blayer, 1880–83).

Another Instance:
The Minyan, Quorum of Ten Jewish Men

Somewhat similar in its effect is the institution of the *minyan*, the quorum of Jewish men needed by traditional Judaism for public religious services. In the last century, we hear strong warnings by Orthodox rabbis against including liberal (reform) Jews in an Orthodox *Minyan*, because they do not follow the traditional pattern of life and thought of the Orthodox Jews. Thus Moshe Shik rules: Reformers are not members of the *Minyan*.[40]

However, Orthodox authorities of the twentieth century realized that his strict ruling was not workable. If Reform Jews were to be excluded from the *minyan* because they do not observe the laws, the same ought to be the case with non-observant Orthodox Jews. If done, it would render public worship service in most smaller Orthodox congregations impossible. Therefore, Orthodox congregations, with very few exceptions, admit non-Orthodox and non-observant "Orthodox" Jews as members of their *minyan* at the services and even call them to the Torah.

Needless to say, the non-observant Orthodox and Reform Jews of the *minyan* in traditional services are laymen. Their inclusion is so essential that Orthodox authorities seek and find halakhic justification for their inclusion. Thus David Hoffmann (1843–1921, Berlin) cites halakhic authorities and gives reasons of his own why transgressors of the Jewish law should be included in the *minyan*, meaning in context, the *minyan* of the Orthodox.[41]

Josef Jakobovits (father of Britain's Chief Rabbi Immanuel Jakobovits), a former Orthodox rabbi in Berlin, also justifies the inclusion of non-observant Jews in the *minyan*.[42]

No matter what the justifications for the inclusion of non-observant Jews, mostly laymen, in the *minyan* of traditional services, they are secondary to the decision dictated by the laymen, without whom the institution of the *minyan* would fall in most synagogues.

In conclusion we may say that rabbinic legislation, in some crucial areas, which might have resulted in sectarian divisions within the Jewish people, was disregarded by the people, thus preserving the basic unity of *Klal Yisrael*, the Jewish peopole and Judaism itself.

---

[40] M. Shik, op. cit., resp. 305.
[41] D. Hoffmann, *Melammed Leho'il* (3 vols.; Frankfurt/Main: Hermon Press, 1925–26), *Oraḥ Hayyim*, resp. 29, pp. 28–29.
[42] See A. Guttmann, *The Struggle over Reform in Rabbinic Literature During the Last Century and a Half* (Jerusalem and New York: The World Union for Progressive Judaism, 1977), 111.

THE USE OF A SACRED OBJECT IN THE ADMINISTRATION OF A JUDICIAL OATH

by

G. LIBSON*

During the Mishnaic and Talmudic periods, holding sacred literature while taking a judicial oath was common practice in the Christian church as well as in Roman courts.[1] We find a similar practice in Jewish courts. In the present article we shall endeavor to discover when this practice began in Jewish courts and how widely it was used. Our sources are meager, for there is little on this topic in either Palestinian or Babylonian sources. This also makes it more difficult to point to differences which may have existed between Palestinian and Babylonian practice during the Tannaitic and Amoraic periods.

The little we really know about this practice in Jewish courts during the aforementioned periods really stems from a relatively later time. The only Tannaitic source which possibly might have bearing on the subject is the phrase in *T. Ned.* 1:14, "One who takes a vow by the Torah" (*hanoder baTorah*).[2] This, however, does not refer to a vow taken while holding a Torah, but simply to one who says he takes a vow "sacred as the Torah."[3]

---

*Lecturer, Faculty of Law, Hebrew University of Jeruslem.

[1] See Boaz Cohen, *Jewish and Roman Law* (New York: Jewish Theological Seminary of America, 1966), II, 725; S. Lieberman, *Tosefta Ki-Fshuṭa* (New York: Jewish Theological Seminary of America, 1967), Part VII, Nedarim, 402, n. 34. The same practice existed in Islamic law; see, for example, I. Goldziher, *The Zahiris* (Leiden: E. J. Brill, 1971), 109.

[2] The correct reading, as found in the Erfurt MS. See *Tosefta Kifshuta*, *Ned*, 402.

[3] This is indicated clearly in the discussion of *Ned.* I, 3, 37a, as explained by S. Lieberman in *Tosefta Kifshuṭa*, *ibid*. "One who takes a vow by the Torah" means no more than a vow "sacred as the Torah," in contrast to the phrase "as written therein." This is the reading of the Palestinian Talmud as corrected by Lieberman (*ibid*., n. 31): "By the Torah," he is permitted. "By what is written therein," he is prohibited. "By the Torah," he is permitted (because this refers) to the "holiness of the Torah." There is no taking of a sacred object; only the statement "I swear by the holiness of the Torah." In the continuation of the *sugya* in the Palestinian Talmud, a *baraita* is quoted which teaches that even a vow "by the Torah and by what is written therein" has the same law as a vow "by the Torah," neither entailing prohibition. This is in contrast to the Tosefta. Lieberman explains that the Amora R. Jose takes "by what is written therein" to mean "by the holiness of the writing," since he includes "by the Torah," which means "the holiness of the

54   The Touro Conference Volume

The earliest Palestinian source which mentions the holding of a sacred object during the administration of a judicial oath is the aggadic midrash *Vayikra Rabbah* (Leviticus) 6:3: "Rabbi Simon said,[4] Why do we give an oath with a Scroll of the Torah and place before him blown-up wine-skins?"[5] Rabbi Simon is a third-generation Amora, although the editing of Leviticus Rabbah itself is post-Talmudic. It may indeed be that this relatively early attribution to the custom of using a Scroll of the Torah is authentic, although it may well be that the Midrash here may be attributing fifth century custom (the earliest possible dating for the Midrash) to an earlier period. Another more or less contemporary source to Leviticus Rabbah is the *Pesikta* (129, b)[6] which depicts the way Nebudchadnezzar forced Zedekiah to swear: "Nebudchadnezzar said to him, 'I shall not adjure you except by the Torah which was given on Mount Sinai.' What did Nebudchadnezzar do? He brought a Scroll of the Torah, placed it upon the lap of Zedekiah and made him take an oath."

In Palestinian literature generally, as well as in that of Palestinian influence in the post-Talmudic period, the impresssion obtained is that an oath was taken while holding a Scroll of the Torah. This is indicated by the story told in the *Sefer Ma'aseh HaGeonim*, the source of which is almost certainly the Palestinian *Sefer HaMa'asim*.[7] Here a maiden is

---

Torah." In the same context, therefore, we must conclude that he wishes to refer to the "holiness of the writing." Although the Tosefta uses the phrase "who takes a vow by the Torah," "vow" can also mean "oath," as is the view of Maimonides in *Shevuot* 12:4-5. See *Tosefta Kifshuṭa*, n. 34 and n. 415. Both the Talmud (see Lieberman, *Greek in Jewish Palestine* [Hebrew edition, Jerusalem, 1963], 119) and the early authorities generally very frequently use the term "vow" as a substitute for "oath."

[4] This is the reading in *Pesikta Rabbati* 113b, as well as in the *Midrash Hagadol* to Ex. 20:7. The readings of the printed editions and of the *Yalkut* are corrupt (see Margolis to *Vayikra R.*, 131). See also Boaz Cohen, *Jewish and Roman Law*, supra n. 1, at II, 726, n. 65.

[5] The parallel in *Pesikta Rabbati* (113b) omits "Scroll of the Torah" and adds "blowing of the *shofar*": "Rabbi Simon said: Why do we place blown-up wine skins before one taking an oath and blow the *shofar*?" This variant reading is quoted by A. Aptowitzer (*Mehkarim Besifrut Hageonim* [Jerusalem, 1941], 82), and in "Untersuchungen Zur Gaonäischen Literatur" (*Hebrew Union College Annual* VIII-X, 402-3), and he takes this as an indication that the *Pesikta* reflects Babylonian custom, whereas the Midrash reflects Palestinian custom. However, there is no proof that the *Pesikta* represents Babylonian custom. Moreover, he is not correct in asserting that a Scroll of the Law was not Babylonian usage, for if the *Pesikta* reflects the period of R. Simon, this is contemporary to that of R. Nahman and Raba in Babylonia. During this period in Babylonia a Scroll of the Law was used in the administration of an oath. Even if the *Pesikta* should reflect later usage, the Scroll of the Law continued to be used during the Gaonic period as well, although the oath was now only an imprecation (*alah*).

[6] See L. Ginzberg, *Legends of the Jews* (Hebrew edition), Vol. 6, 83, 228 (n. 2), with reference to other views as to how Zedekiah took his oath.

[7] Quoted also in *Pardes* (ed. Constantinople, 22; ed. Warsaw, 301). The book *Ma'aseh*

forced to take an oath with a Scroll of the Law to clarify an incident of betrothal. From the same first-mentioned source there is a quotation in one of the gaonic responsa, which may also refer to the taking of a Scroll of the Law when being asked by the court to take an oath:[8] "And with reference to your question, regarding one who was found with the mother-in-law of his betrothed, he is to be given stripes by the court and is to be required to take an oath 'by the Torah'[9] never to be alone with this woman again."

When we turn to Babylonian sources, we find relatively little which can cast light on our subject. Indirect mention of the use of a sacred object in the taking of an oath is to be found in the time of the third-generation Amora Rav Naḥman, and the first direct mention of such a generation later in the time of Rava. It is Rav Naḥman who relates to a discussion in the Babylonian Talmud *Ned.* 11a with reference to the Tosefta we have already mentioned in part: "'One who takes an oath' by the Torah has said nothing. 'By what is written in it,' 'In it and what is written in it,' his words are binding." In answer to the apparent redundancy of the last two phrases, which the Babylonian Talmud points out, Rav Naḥman offers this explanation: One phrase is that used when the Torah is lying before him, the other when he holds the Torah in his

---

Hageonim is a source for many Palestinian traditions, including responsa of the Palestinian Geonim. See B. M. Levin, "Ma'asim Livnei Eretz-Israel," *Tarbiz*, vol. 1, 82, and, lately A. Grossman, "Bnei Machir and Their Work 'Ma'aseh Hamachiri'," *Tarbiz* (1947), 46, 127, and n. 74. The Book *Vehizhir* itself, which is the source of this story, is a Palestinian work. See S. Asaf, *Miṣifrut Hageonim* (Jerusalem, 1933), 163, and Aptowitzer, *Meḥkarim*, 92. The source of our story is *Sefer Hama'asim Livnei Eretz-Israel*. See Levin, ibid., 87 and Aptowitzer, "Sefer Hefetz and Sefer Metivot," *Tarbiz*, 4, 143. See also S. Lieberman (*Ginzei Kedem* [DL 5, 1939], 184), who is of the opinion that the style is Palestinian. With reference to the oath itself, he writes: "The taking of an oath in this situation is not unusual. The woman would not be considered betrothed even without the oath. Yet to remove suspicion and punishment, the woman was given the oath, as well as to force her to confess. This was why she was not given permission to marry without taking an oath."

A similar story is found in the fragment from *Decisions Regarding Meat upon Coals*, published by Sulzbach in *Jahrbuch der Judische Literarischen Gesellschaft*, Frankfurt, vol. 5, 62. The nature of this work and its place of composition have not been fully explored. It was known a generation before Rashi. Since the majority of those making references to the work are Ashkenazi authorities and Ashkenazi sources, Aptowitzer (in his introduction to *Ravyah* [Jerusalem, 1938], 274) assumed that the work was of Ashkenazic origin. Yet it is very likely that Palestinian sources found their way into this work, as is common in many Ashkenazi works.

[8] *Tesh. Geon.*, edited by N. Coronel (Vienna, 1871), par. 62. See B. Levin, *Tarbiz*, ibid., 84, who is of the opinion that this responsum, like many others in this collection, was drawn from *Sefer Hama'asim*. This is also the opinion of J. N. Epstein, "Toratah Shel Eretz Yisrael," *Tarbiz* II (1931), 322.

[9] In truth, however, the phrase "swear by the Torah" does mean only "taking the Torah" at the time of swearing. It may imply no more than one's saying that "he swears by the Torah," as is found in *T. Ned.* I, 4. Nevertheless, the first meaning here seems preferable.

hand. Even though Rav Naḥman's explanation may not be the true interpretation of the baraita (see Professor Lieberman's remarks in *Tosefta Ki-Fshuṭa*, 402), and even though one may argue that Rav Naḥman's remarks relate only to a resolution of a literary difficulty, it seems very likely that his explanation reflects the custom already current in his time of the use of a Scroll of the Law in the administration of a judicial oath. The two different uses of the Torah referred to by Rav Naḥman— one where the Torah is before the one taking the oath, and the other where he holds it—were current in the Gaonic period.[10]

We find the custom of holding a sacred object during the taking of an oath well-recorded in the time of Rava, pupil of Rav Naḥman, in the well-known story of *kanya de-Rava* ("cane of Rava"). Both Rava and Rav Naḥman were active in determining the way an oath should be taken as well as in extending the area of dispute where an oath would be required—a topic we cannot go into in our present discussion. In the Talmudic story of *kanya de-Rava*[11] the defendant asks the plaintiff to hold his cane, which he had previously hollowed out and into which he had put the *denarim*, while he takes the Torah to swear that he had returned to the plaintiff his money.[12] In the post-Talmudic literature, this story underwent transformation and there is no mention of a Scroll of the Torah. Nevertheless, the way this story is told in the Babylonian Talmud, where the taking of the Torah is only an incidental part of the

---

[10] Where one is required to take an oath according to Torah law or an oath mentioned in the Mishnah (called *gezerta*), then the one taking the oath would hold the Scroll of the Torah in his hands. When, however, a consuetudinal oath only is required, the Scroll of the Torah would be placed on a couch before the one taking the oath.

[11] *Ned.* 25a. On the sources and parallels of this story, see J. N. Epstein, "*Ma'ase Deshushilta Devei Dina*," *Ha'olam*, 25 (1908), 307; *Otsar Hageonim, Nedarim*, Teshuvot, par. 71, n. 1; E. E. Urbach, *Ba'ale Hatosafot*, 3d ed. (Jerusalem, 1968), 200 and n. 38.

[12] This is the universal reading. Such is the version in all readings of the Talmud. In post-Talmudic sources the story underwent great transformation. (See *Otsar Hageonim, Nedarim, ibid.*). No mention is made of a Scroll of the Torah being held at the time of swearing. This variation is not of special significance, since the manner in which the oath was taken is not integral to the story. In *Otsar Hageonim, Ned., ibid.*, we read: "In *Basar al Gabei Gehalim* the version is: The story of the cane of the chain in connection with Raba, concerns a chain upon which was inscribed the Divine Name, and no one who swore falsely could reach it. When this man took the oath, he said to his fellow litigant: 'Come and see that I have sworn the truth.' He went and placed his hand at the top of the chain. His fellow-litigant in anger then broke the cane and what was in it fell out."

In *Teshuvot Hageonim* the stories of the "the cane of Raba" and the "the chain of the court" are mentioned side by side. See *Hemda Genuza* 39 (Jerusalem, 1963), par. 22, the responsa of Rav Natronai, and *Sha'arei Tsedek*, (Saloniki, 1792), 76a, par. 22, the responsa of Rav Hai. These responsa apparently consider these to be separate stories. The chain story is not found at all in Talmudic literature, although there is in *Gitt.* 68a a reference to a chain upon which was inscribed the Divine Name. There, however, there is no connection at all to an oath. The story then of a chain having the power to differentiate between a true and false oath seems to be late.

story, seems to indicate that the custom of holding a Sefer Torah in all manner of oaths, even that of *shevuʿat hesset* ("consuetudinal oath"), as was the case of this particular story, was current already in that part of the Talmudic period. The Geonim, however, did not authorize the use of a sacred object in the taking of a consuetudinal oath, and the early authorities were hard put to explain the Talmudic story in the light of Gaonic practice. The early authorities did not have an appreciation of the historical development, where the distinction between different types of judicial oaths is itself a Gaonic innovation.[13]

There is another important passage in the Babylonian Talmud, also connected with the name of Rava, where the use of a sacred object in general and that of a Sefer Torah in particular in the taking of a judicial oath is mentioned. In fact, this is the only clear and direct mention of such in the entire Babylonian Talmud. The passage is in *Shebu.* 38b. The first-generation Amora Rav quotes the Tosefta *Sot.* 7:4 to explain how a judicial oath is to be administered:[14] "The oath administered is that spoken of in the Torah, as it is written 'And I shall make thee swear by the Lord G-d of heaven' (*Gen.* 24:3)." In the ensuing discussion of this Tosefta passage, the question is raised whether "oath spoken of in the Torah" means that the Divine Name is to be used in the taking of an oath and not an Attribute Name oath. The conclusion of the *sugya* is that the phrase does not come to disallow the Attribute Name oath, but is to be interpreted to require the holding of a sacred object while taking the oath. The Tosefta, then, is taken to refer to the oath-taking ceremony rather than to the intrinsic nature of the oath. The Talmud then quotes the decision of Rava: "Any judge who administers a Divine Name oath is to be considered as one who has erred in what is taught in the Mishnah and is liable."[15] Rashi explains this to mean: "Who has administered a

---

[13] The early authorities, who knew of the Gaonic tradition not to have one hold a Scroll of the Torah in taking a consuetudinal oath, tried to explain the contradiction implied by this story by claiming to see in this oath one required by the Torah. See responsa of *Rabbi Shlomo Ben Adret (RaSHBA)*, vol. 4, par. 272. Asked to explain the contradiction in the story, he explained: It could be said that the story in *Nedarim* is one where the defendant had confessed to part of the debt, or that there was one witness who testified against him. This would require a Torah-oath. The RI Migash, RITBA, and the Meiri give another explanation.

The other way the story is reconciled is that the situation of the story required the taking of a Scroll of the Torah. In truth, there was no legal requirement for such, but the one taking the oath had to use this as a ruse in order to be able to ask the plaintiff to hold the cane for him while he takes the Scroll.

[14] The reading in the printed editions is: "R. Judah said in the name of Rav." München and Florence manuscripts as well as early authorities read: "Said R. Judah." See *Dikduke Soferim*, 43, n. 20.

[15] Rava, who uses the language of Tosefta, explains it in accordance with its simple meaning, as does Ravina. Rava, however, unlike the Tosefta, seeks to teach that only an Attribute Name may be used.

Divine Name oath rather than having required the taking of a sacred object."

It is obvious that the Babylonian Talmud attributes a meaning to the Tosefta which is not in accordance with its simple meaning. The basic meaning of the Tosefta is that some Divine Name is to be used in the oath, not excluding an Attribute Name oath.[16] Rava's original teaching may have meant no more than this: An Attribute Name is to be used and not a Divine Name. A later arrangement of the *sugya*, perhaps even Saboraic, placed Rava's statement within the context of the oath-taking ceremony, where a sacred object is to be used. This later arrangement obviously had in mind the *kanya de-Rava* story and changed what Rava had taught as the Tosefta teaching to harmonize with the story.[17]

A later Amora, Rav Papa of the fifth-generation, is mentioned in the continuation of the *sugya* as having taught that the sacred object to be held must be only a Scroll of the Torah. Phylacteries would not suffice. The Talmud concludes, however, that the law is in accordance with Rava and not with Rav Papa: A sacred object must be used, but not necessarily a Scroll of the Torah.[18]

It seems obvious that the final editors of the *sugya* here were interested in giving firm foundation to the custom of holding a sacred object while taking the oath. It is this custom that we find firmly established in the writings of the Geonim.

---

[16] As does the *Rosh* in his explanation of the view of the Sages (*The Complete Toṣefot Harosh*, Shevuoth, 38b).

[17] There are many indications that this is a late editing. The discussion between Ravina and Rav Ashi of necessity makes this a late *sugya*. It appears as well that Ravina himself still understood Rava's words as being meant to teach that only an Attribute Name is to be used in oaths. The phrases "and this is the law" and "the law is not like this" are clear signs of late editing. Similarly, the expression "and like Rava" is a late connecting link to the new interpretation that only where the oath is by an Attribute Name must there be the taking of a sacred object with it.

[18] The phrase "the law is like Rava, since he is not holding a sacred object in his hand, but the law is not R. Papa" is missing in the München MS, but is found in the printed editions and in MS Florence. If indeed we accept this reading, as seems logical, this appears then as a concluding remark of the editors of the *sugya*. The new interpretation given by the late editors to Rava's teaching became so much a part of the *sugya* that we find certain early authorities who include the later interpretation as part of Rava's original statement, as if this came not from the editors but from Rava himself! See, for example, *Alfasi* to *Shevuot, ibid.*, responsa of the *Rashba*, I, 180, 647.

Since the original intent of Rava's teaching was simply to teach that an oath may be taken only with an Attribute Name, we can now understand a further development in the laws concerning oaths in the time of Rava. According to Talmudic law, no oath is taken in matters concerning real estate. Yet Rava changed this, as is indicated in *Ket.* 87b: "Said Rava, rabbinic enactment [requires an oath.]" It would seem then that since the severity of the oath was lessened with limiting it to an Attribute Name, Rava felt it could now be extended to include even those areas where according to Biblical law no oath is to be taken.

All the sources dealing with our topic in the Babylonian Talmud which we have discussed—Rav Naḥman's interpretation of the baraita in *Nedarim*, the story of *kanya de-Rava*, and the sugya in *Shevuot*—stem from the School of Sura in Babylonian. We have nothing regarding the use of a sacred object in the oath-taking ceremony stemming from the Academy of Pumbeditha. One may surmize, therefore, that the Academy of Sura, which usually followed Palestinian practice, may have taken over Palestinian practice in the oath-taking ceremony as well. It seems plausible as well that in Pumbeditha, and in central Babylonia generally, where the influence of the School of Rabbi Ishmael was stronger than anywhere else, the custom of using a Divine Name rather than an Attribute Name was still in force. It was not necessary, therefore, to add to the awesomeness of the Divine Name oath the requirement of holding a sacred object. It is only during the Gaonic period, when courts refrained from using even the Attribute Name oath, that we find the use of a sacred object as part of the oath-taking ceremony in central Babylonia as well.

The use of a sacred object became extremely important during the Gaonic period when the Geonim substituted the use of *alah* ("imprecation") for all manner of Divine Name or Attribute Name oaths.[19] It is for this reason that support was sought in Talmudic sources for the required use of a sacred object. This explains their particular explanations of the early sources.

The firm establishment of the use of a sacred object in an oath-taking ceremony made it possible for the Geonim to distinguish between oaths which have Biblical or Mishnaic mention and those which came into use only in Amoraic times. Thus, they said, only oaths of Biblical or Mishnaic provenance require the use of a sacred object. But *shavu'at hesset*, the "consuetudinal oath," which was introduced only during the third-generation Amoraic period, does not require such use. It should be noted that the Talmud itself makes no such distinction. The *sugya* in *Shebu.* 41a in marking out differences between oaths of Biblical origin and oaths of only rabbinic provenance—under which category *shevu'at hesset* would also have to be included—does not draw any such distinction, leaving the impression that oaths of rabbinic origin also require the holding of a sacred object.[20] Although Gaonic practice did not require

---

[19] See G. Libson, "*Gezerta* in the Gaonic Period and Early Medieval Period" [Heb.], *Annual of the Institute for Jewish Law*, (1978), 82f.

[20] The early authorities understand this *sugya* in three different ways. One interpretation is that there is no differentiation between a biblical ordained oath and a rabbinic one, since the Talmud does not indicate that "holding a sacred object" is one of the differences. This view is found in the Responsa of the Rashba on several occasions in the name of "there are among the early authorities." See, for example, Part II of the Responsa, 302, 205.

the holding of a sacred object during the taking of a consuedutinal oath, it was nevertheless customary to place a Sefer Torah on a sofa at the time of swearing. Occasionally, the Sefer Torah would be held by the beadle while the oath was administered. Both uses of the Sefer Torah—holding it or placing it before the one taking the oath—were already mentioned by Rav Naḥman in his discussion of a passage in *T. Sot.*, although there is no indication that he differentiated between the consuetudinal oath and other oaths in the use of the Sefer Torah.

The expression *shevu'ah be-Sefer Torah* ("an oath taken with a Scroll of the Torah") frequently found in the Gaonic responsa is a synonym for a Divine Name or Attribute Name oath. When they write, therefore, that "an oath with a Sefer Torah" is no longer customary with them, all they mean is that no Divine Name or Attribute Name oaths are to be administered and only the execration formula alone is to be used. But the Sefer Torah itself was still part of the ceremony.

The conclusion we come to from our survey is that Gaonic custom was not just an independent growth, but rather a link in the long chain of development in the use of oaths. Not only did they draw upon early traditions and customs, but they endeavored to show as well how their own customs were rooted in the teachings of the Babylonian Amoraim, all with the purpose of emphasizing the continuity of the Halakhah.

Another interpretation takes the term "a rabbinically ordained oath" in this sugya not to refer to a consuetudinal oath, but to an oath mentioned in the Mishna. The differences then referred to in the *sugya* are those between a Biblical and a Mishnaic oath, and have no connection with a consuetudinal oath. This view is found in *Sha'are Shevuot* attributed to Ri bar Reuven, chap. 17.

The third interpretation, most widely accepted among the early authorities, is that the *sugya* does indeed deal with a consuetudinal oath, but the difference with regard to the holding of a sacred object is not mentioned because the discussion is only the laws of oaths, but not in the formalities of administration. R. Isaac Migash is the first who gives this interpretation (*Novellae to Shevuot* [Jerusalem, 1976], 75).

THE MARITAL STATUS OF JEWS MARRIED UNDER NON-JEWISH AUSPICES

by

DAVID NOVAK*

1. *Halakhah and the Phenomenon of Secularity*

The question of whether or not two bona-fide Jews, who have married under non-Jewish auspices, are considered to have a *Jewish* marriage is one which has especially concerned halakhists during the past two centuries. Now "under non-Jewish auspices" can mean one of two things: (1) two Jews have married according to the law and rites of a non-Jewish religion; (2) two Jews have married according to civil law and rites only, excluding the law and rites of Judaism, or any other religion for that matter. The two cases are apparently different. In the first case, which was discussed already in the Middle Ages, virtually all halakhists have followed the opinion of the fourteenth-century Spanish authority, R. Isaac bar Sheshet Parfat (*Ribash*), who, in an extensive responsum on the subject, concluded that such a marriage does not have the status of a *Jewish* marriage.[1] In the second case, however, namely civil marriages between two Jews, halakhic opinion has been sharply divided. Some have argued that although a civil marriage between two Jews is manifestly different from a non-Jewish religious marriage between them, in essence both are the same, that is, they are unions deliberately initiated outside the range of normative Jewish marriage. As such they have no valid status in *Halakhah*. Others have argued, conversely, that the difference between the two cases is not only manifest but essential, that Judaism recognizes, *ex post facto* to be sure (certainly prohibiting it *ab initio*, however), contracts made between two Jews outside the range of normative Jewish procedures, and that even marriage is such a contract whose binding power is, however reluctantly, recognized.

---

*M.H.L., Ph.D., Rabbi of Congregation Darchay Noam, Far Rockaway, New York, U.S.A.; Presiding Rabbi of the Beth Din Queens Region Rabbinical Assembly; Member of the Faculty (Philosophy), New School for Social Research, New York, NY.

All translations are by the author.

[1] *She'elot Uteshuvot Haribash*, ed. Lemburg (1805), no. 5. See R. Simon ben Tsemah Duran, *She'elot Uteshuvot Hatashbats*, ed. Amsterdam (1739), no. 47. Cf. *Teshuvot Rashi*, ed. Elfenbein (New York, 1943), no. 171, pp. 191–93.

Since the first responsum written on this subject in 1741 by the *ḥakhamim* of the Portuguese *Yeshivah* "Ets Ḥayyim" in Amsterdam, a considerable literature, both normative and descriptive, has developed about it.[2] My purpose in this paper is certainly not to summarize, let alone analyze, all the arguments pro and con. That would require far greater time and space than has been allotted me. Moreover, several excellent studies, upon which I have freely drawn, have already been published which do just that.[3] Rather, I would like to see the question of civil marriage between two Jews as a paradigm for how modern halakhists have confronted the uniquely modern phenomenon of secularity, a phenomenon which appears to be a *novum*, for which the classical sources have no explicit precedents or rules. In such situations the employment of classical sources by modern halakhists must be by analogy rather than by the strict identification with a previous precedent, or the strict subsumption of a case under a specific rule. Such situations are beyond the capacity of ordinary casuistry. Analogies involve the selective judgment of the authority deciding the new case at hand. If his selective judgment is not to be capricious, then it is clear that in the absence of definite halakhic precedents and rules in this area such judgment will stem from philosophical criteria. Now this does not mean that he simply deduces from these criteria what the law is to be. Rather, his judgment will be to *select* from what the sources already present for his analogies. Furthermore, his philosophical criteria will be drawn from both general *and* Jewish experience.[4] Thus he will have formulated a concept of what essentially characterizes marriage *and* what essentially characterizes Jewish marriage. Although recognizing differences between the two, he will certainly not regard them as mutually exclusive. When new ordinances (*gezerot, takanot*) have been enacted, such philosophical criteria alone have sufficed for their formulation.[5] When, as is our case here, innovative halakhic rulings have been made, then both philosophical criteria and specific legal analogies have gone into their formulation. In this paper I shall attempt to show that those halakhic authorities, who have

---

[2] See A. Freimann, *Seder Ḳidushin Venisu'in* (Jerusalem: Reuben Mass, 1945), 362ff.

[3] See B. Schereschewsky, *Dine Mishpaḥah* (Jerusalem: Reuben Mass, 1967), 83ff., and "Civil Marriage" in *The Principles of Jewish Law*, ed. M. Elon (Jerusalem: Keter, 1975), 371-74; A. G. Elinson, *Nisu'in shelo Kedat Mosheh Veyisra'el* (Tel Aviv: Dvir, 1975); M. I. Mazoz, "*Nisu'in Ezraḥiyim Vetotsotayhem*," *Shenaton Hamishpaṭ Ha'ivri*, 3-4 (1976–1977), 233ff. (For these references I thank Prof. Dov I. Frimer of Touro Law School [New York].)

[4] See D. Novak, *Law and Theology in Judaism* I (New York: Ktav, 1974), chap. 1, and II (New York, 1976), intro.; "Is Conservative Halakhah Possible?: Review–Essay of *Responsa and Halakhic Studies* by Isaac Klein," *JUDAISM* 25/4 (Fall, 1976), 496-98; "Review of *Contemporary Halakhic Problems* by J. David Bleich," *ibid.*, 27/4 (Fall, 1978), 496ff.

[5] See, *e.g., Ket.* 50a.

ruled that a civil marriage between two Jews does have the status of a Jewish marriage, have been more self-conscious of the philosophical criteria employed in their halakhic judgment, and have also been more self-conscious of their explicitly analogous use of classical sources.

2. *Rabbinic Sources*

In the rabbinic sources there seem to be only two possible heterosexual unions between Jews: either Jewish marriage (*kidushin*), or fornication (*be'ilat zenut*). There is no precedent whatsoever for the non-Jewish union between a Jewish man and a Jewish woman.[6] In working up from these sources one has basically two options: (1) everything which is not explicitly *kidushin* is, therefore, fornication; (2) everything which is not explicitly fornication is, therefore, *kidushin*. At this level the argument can move, with equal ease, in either direction. On the one hand, one can argue that Jewish marriage requires that one's intention be for Jewish marriage and *all* that it entails. "Whoever marries does so according to rabbinic jurisdiction (*ada'ata derabanan*)."[7] On the other hand, one can argue that a couple, who have taken upon themselves the public responsibility of living together as husband and wife, can hardly be equated with a couple spending some time together in private lust.

It would seem that this latter point, namely, that a Jewishly informal, sustained, public, heterosexual union is not *ipso facto* fornication, is brought out in the following source in the *Mishnah*.[8]

> A man who has divorced his wife and lodges with her in an inn: The School of Shammai say that she does not require a second *get* from him; the School of Hillel say that she does require a second *get* from him. When is this so? When she has been divorced after sexual consummation (*min hanesu'in*); but both agree that when she was divorced only after betrothal (*min ha'erusin*), she does not require from him a second *get* because he has not yet been sexually intimate with her (*she'ayn libo gas bah*).[9]

The *Bavli*[10] argues as follows:

---

[6] Thus an early rabbinic source reads: "Any act of intercourse (*bi'ah*), which was for the sake of marriage (*leshem kidushin*), gives the woman a married status (*mekudeshet*); and what was not for the sake of marriage does not." *T. Kidd.* 1.3, ed. Lieberman, 276. See *Sifra, Kedoshim*, ed. Weiss, 90d re *Lev*, 19:29; *Yeb.* 37b; *Sanh.* 76a; Elinson, *Nisu'in*, *supra* n. 3, at 26.
[7] *Gitt.* 33a and parallels.
[8] *M. Gitt.* 8.9, ed. Albeck, 299.
[9] The assumption is that there is little likelihood that he would initiate sexual relations under such circumstances. See *M. Yeb.* 4.10 and *Rashi, Yeb.* 41a/bot., s.v. *huts; Ket.* 12a.
[10] *Gitt.* 81a–b.

> Rabah bar Bar Hanah, quoting R. Johanan, said that the dispute concerns a case when the intercourse was observed:[11] the School of Shammai opining that one does indeed make his act of intercourse fornication; and the School of Hillel opining that a man does not make his act of intercourse fornication.

Now it would seem, as pointed out by both *Rashi* and the Tosafists, that the School of Shammai regard anything less than the public utterance of a formal Jewish betrothal statement as something which makes the subsequent act(s) of intercourse fornication.[12] The School of Hillel, on the other hand, seem to recognize the validity of such a marriage *ex post facto*. Since the *Halakhah* is always according to the School of Hillel in such disputes,[13] it would seem that the normative Hillelite view recognizes the validity of what I have termed "informal" unions and that they are not reducible to "fornication."[14]

This line of interpretation is based on a broad reading of the principle, "a man does not make his act of intercourse fornication." It assumes that the case mentioned in the *Mishnah* is but one example of where this principle applies, that its application goes beyond this case. This seems to be the way the principle was understood by certain *Geonim* who added the key word *ḥazakah*—"it is assumed that a man does not make his act of intercourse fornication."[15] Such an "assumption" is seen as applying to a far wider range of cases than that of the *Mishnah* alone.

3. Arguments and Counterarguments

Three factors, nevertheless, seem to mitigate against such a broad reading of the *Mishnah*.

---

[11] "Observed" (*beshera'u'ha*) means that the couple was observed in a position where it could be assumed they were engaged in intercourse (*e.g.*, they were together in a bed), not that the actual physical congress had to be seen. See *Makk.* 7a and *Rashi, B.M.* 91a, s.v. *bemena'afim.* Cf. Maim., *Iṣuray Bi'ah*, 14.6 re *Yeb.* 47b top.

[12] *Giṭṭ..* 81a, *Rashi*, s.v. *beshera'u'ha; Toṣ.*, s.v. *Bet Shammai* re *Yeb.* 107a (see *Toṣ.*, s.v. *ṭa'ma* thereon).

[13] *Erub.* 13a. Only Hillelite acquiesence made the law according to the Shammaites. See *M. Shab.* 1.4; *T. Shab.* 1.16ff.; *Y. Shab.* 1.4/3c; *Shab.* 17a.

[14] That such an arrangment is prohibited (*aṣur*) even though binding (*tofṣin*) is clear from the fact that (1) no new *ketubah* was written and "it is prohibited for a man to live even for one hour with his wife without a *ketubah*" (*B.Ḳ.* 89a; see *Ket.* 57a); (2) no new ceremony was conducted and "a bride where the betrothal *berakhah* has not been recited is like a menstruant" (*Masekhet Kalah*, beg.; see *Yeb.* 36b, *Toṣ.*, s.v. *velo*). See also, *Ḳidd.* 12b (and *Y. Yeb.* 5.2/6d) for the aversion to marriage initiated by intercourse.

[15] Quoted in Maimonides, *Gerushin*, 10.19. For the force of *ḥazakah* in marital matters, see *Ḳidd.* 80a; Maimonides, *Iṣuray Bi'ah*, 1.20–21; *Gerushin*, 10.20. For the difference between *ḥazakah*, which suffices to attest to *ḳidushin*, and actual proof, which is necessary to attest to a *geṭ*, see *Yeb.* 31b and *Rashi* and *Toṣ.*, s.v. *lehatṣalah*; Meiri, *Bet Habeḥirah*, ed. Dickman, 132; Scherescewsky, *supra* n. 3, at 87.

First, the development of the *sugya* in the *Bavli* itself suggests that the editors of the text did not accept this principle as even a valid interpretation of the *Mishnah* at hand, much less a broader principle. For the *sugya* concludes by indicating that the case in the *Mishnah* is considered to be when the intercourse was *not* seen, but that there were only witnesses that the couple was secluded (*edey yiḥud*).[16] The Shammaites are seen as holding that such seclusion need not necessarily lead to the assumption that intercourse did in fact take place. As such we may not assume that the marriage was meant to be resumed. The Hillelites are seen, however, as holding that we may indeed make such an assumption (*vehen hen edey bi'ah*) and, therefore, we may assume that the marriage was meant to be resumed.[17] Thus the question of assumption switches from what we assume was the man's intention to what we assume may be inferred from what the witnesses witnessed.

The second mitigating factor is that Maimonides, in the *Mishneh Torah, explicitly t* rejects the Geonic interpretation as follows:

> All of their arguments seem to me to be very far removed from what is correct ruling (*medarkhey hora'ah*) and it is not proper to rely on them. For the sages only (*bilvad*) enunciated this assumption for the case of when a man divorced his own wife . . . only with his own wife is it assumed that he did not make his act of intercourse fornication, unless he explicates (*ad sheyifaresh*) otherwise . . . it is assumed that every prostitute (*kol zonah*) was engaged in fornication unless the man explicates that it was for the sake of marriage (*leshem ḳidushin*).[18]

---

[16] *Giṭṭ.* 81b.

[17] Interestingly enough, the only other example of when a witnessed act of seclusion, without the audible utterance of a betrothal formula, initiates a marriage is in the case of the levirate (*M. Ḳidd.* 1.1; *Ḳidd.* 13b–14a). Even though the rabbis decreed that it be preceded by a formula—*ma'amar*—analogous to the ordinary betrothal formula (*M. Yeb.* 2.1; *Y. Yeb.* 2.1/3c), even with the absence of such an utterance the marriage is still valid *ex post facto*. This is because the relationship of the *yevamah* with the *yavam* is considered "already prepared" (*zeḳuḳah v'omedet*), viz., because of the previous (childless) marriage to the deceased brother (see *Ḳidd.* 4b/bot.). So, also, in the case in this *Mishnah* it would seem, according to the Hillelites, that the previous marriage to the husband enables him to resume the marriage, even after the divorce, with less formality than would be the rule had no previous marriage ever taken place with him. (The fact is that a marriage has residual restrictions even after divorce. See *Ḳidd.* 13b.) This analogy with the Levirate is important in the reasoning of at least one great later halakhist (*aḥaron*), as we shall see later.

[18] Maimonides, *Gerushin*, 10.19. Maimonides may have regarded the rule that the woman's consent (*Ishut*, 4.1) is required to be a rabbinic qualification since it is inferred from the language of the *Mishnah* (*Ḳidd.* 1.1) by the *Bavli* (*Ḳidd.* 2b—see *Toṣ.*, s.v. *iy*), not from the language of Scripture (*Deut.* 24:1) either directly or indirectly. Note the reference by R. Joseph Karo, *Keṣef Mishneh* thereon to *B.B.* 48b (see Meiri, *Bet Habeḥirah, Ḳidd.*, ed. Sofer, 8). Generally he was reluctant to consider anything Scriptural which was not explicitly there or designated as explicitly there by the rabbis (see *Sefer*

Although Maimonides expresses another view in a responsum,[19] it is clearly the *Mishneh Torah* which carries more halakhic weight.[20] And, indeed, it is this text which has been used by those who argue that anything less than full ķidushin is not a Jewish marriage at all.

Finally, there is the view of the sixteenth-century Egyptian authority, R. David ibn Abi Zimra (*Radbaz*), that if the woman was a menstruant, then we must assume that an act of intercourse between the couple was indeed fornication, because it involves an even graver transgression (*iṣur karet*) than the transgression of non-marital intercourse.[21] This point is usually quoted in the name of *Radbaz* although *Ribash* made it much earlier.[22] This argument has been used by several modern authorities greatly to limit the principle that a man's act of intercourse is not fornication.[23] For every woman who has not properly immersed herself in a *kasher miķveh* is considered to be a menstruant (*nidah*) even if not physically menstruating at the time.[24] Thus in our age, when observant Jewish women are alas in the clear minority, and when Jewish women opting for a civil marriage are surely the least observant of all, it would seem that all their acts of intercourse must be assumed to be fornication—based on this criterion. Certainly one may not assume that such women nevertheless observe the laws of family purity (*ṭahorat hamishpaḥah*).[25]

A broader interpretation of the text in the *Gemara* must answer these three objections.

The reading of the *sugya* we analyzed can also suggest a broader interpretation. For, despite the fact that the editors of the *Bavli* did not see the principle that a man does not make his act of intercourse fornication as

---

Hamitsvot, shoresh 2). In the text in *Ishut*, 1.1 he makes the distinction between pre-Toraitic and Toraitic marriage on the basis of the former being in essence private and the latter public. The woman's consent is only mentioned in the case of pre-Toraitic marriage (see Y. Ķidd. 1.1/58c).

[19] *Teshuvot Harambam* II, ed. Blau (Jerusalem: Mekitsay Nirdamim, 1960), no. 356, 633–34.

[20] Thus R. Joseph Karo, *Shulḥan Arukh*, E.H., 26.1 clearly follows the *Mishneh Torah* rather literally. For the great influence of this work on subsequent halakhists, see I. Twersky, *Introduction to the Code of Maimonides (Mishneh Torah)* (New Haven: Yale University Press, 1980), 531ff.

[21] Quoted in R. Judah Rozanis, *Mishneh Lemelekh* on Maimonides, *Gerushin*, 10.18. See *She'elot Uteshuvot Haradbaz* I, no. 351. For the notion that anything less than the purest religious intention makes an act of initiatory intercourse *be'ilat zenut*, see Y. Yeb. 1.1/2b re T. Yeb. 6.9.

[22] *She'elot Uteshuvot Haribash*, no. 5.

[23] Most notably and influentially, R. Mosheh Feinstein of New York, *Igrot Mosheh*, E.H. (New York, 1961), no. 73, p. 173; no. 75, p. 177. See, also, R. Mordecai Jacob Breisch, *She'elot Uteshuvot Helķat Ya'aķov* II (Jerusalem, 1951), E.H., nos. 183–184.

[24] See *Ṣifra, Metsora*, ed. Weiss, 78a–78b; Maimonides, *Iṣurey Bi'ah*, 4.3.

[25] See, however, R. Jehiel J. Weinberg, *Seridey Esh* III (Jerusalem, 1966), no. 28, p. 83.

applying to the *Mishnah* at hand, this actually frees the principle from the narrow confines of that specific case and allows it to be seen as a general principle which can be applied elsewhere.[26] Furthermore, the parallel discussion of this *Mishnah* in the *Yerushalmi* gives, it seems to me, the most plausible explanation for the difference of opinion between the Shammaites and the Hillelites. The *Yerushalmi*[27] notes:

> R. Jose bar Bun said that the School of Shammai follow their general point of view (*keda'aton*) and so do the School of Hillel. The School of Shammai state that 'man may not divorce his wife unless she was unfaithful (*matsa bah ervah*).' Therefore they say that she is sexually repulsive (*mezuhemet*) to him and he would not be suspected (*hashud*) of having had intercourse with her; . . . The school of Hillel state that 'even if she burned his food.' Therefore they say that she is not sexually repulsive to him and he is indeed suspected of having had intercourse with her.

This too frees the principle for application elsewhere.[28]

As for Maimonides' rejection of the interpretation of the Geonim, which we examined earlier, we do have his contradictory opinion in a little noticed responsum written before the *Mishneh Torah*.[29] Moreover, and more importantly Maimonides himself seems to take a broader view of the situation elsewhere in the *Mishneh Torah*. Thus he writes about a case where a man gave his bride less than the stiupulated *kidushin* sum of money (*pahut mishaveh perutah*) the following, "it is assumed (*hazakah*) that no proper Jew would make his act of intercourse fornication, and now it is in his power to make his act of intercourse a *mitsvah*."[30]

This leads us into the essential question of what constitutes "proper Jews" (*yisra'el kesherim*). The opinion of *Radbaz* (and earlier, *Ribash*) is that this status requires full compliance with Jewish ritual law, particularly the laws pertaining to sexual conduct within marriage. Anything less than this constitutes "fornication." However, there seem to be two types of fornication: (1) neglect of moral rules requiring sexually faithful conduct, that is, that sexual conduct not be allowed *outside* of the marital relationship; (2) neglect of the ritual rules requiring periodic abstinence (*nidah*) and

---

[26] As the rabbis said in situations where similar logic was employed in Scriptural exegesis, "if it does not apply to the specific issue at hand (*im eyno inyan legufo*), apply it to the whole Torah" (*Kidd.* 43a).

[27] Y. *Gitt.* 8.11/49c–d re M. *Gitt*, end. As for the criterion of the HIllelites' for divorce, Meiri (*Bet Habehirah*, ed. Schulsinger, 374) explains that it is an example of a woman's refusal to keep house for her husband. See, also, Novak, *supra* n. 4, at I, 6ff.

[28] Thus, *e.g.*, the *Gemara* sees the principle of "the point in common" (*hatsad hashaveh shebahen*), mentioned in M. *B.K.* 1.1, as not being needed to explain the points in that *Mishnah* and interprets it as a principle meant to include (*l'atuyey m'ai*) what is *not* mentioned in that *Mishnah* (*B.K.* 6a–b).

[29] See *supra* n. 19.

[30] *Ishut*, 7.23 re *Ket.* 73a.

purification (*tevilah*) for the woman *inside* the marital relationship. For those who hold that anything short of full *kidushin* is fornication, there is no legal difference between these two transgressions. Yet, one could make a good case that there is indeed such a legal difference recognized by *Halakhah*. If that is so, then the philosophical judgment which differentiates between these two states will find precedents wherewith to construct its case by analogy. As the late R. Isaac Klein (d. 1979), a distinguished Conservative halakhist in America, wrote:

> It is obvious that we cannot adhere to this criticism today not only among those who dispense with religious marriage, but also among those who are very scrupulous that the marriage be performed strictly according to the requirements of Jewish law. Our experience is that the moral standards of those who have become united through civil marriage . . . compare favorably with the standards of those who have had the benefit of a religious ceremony.[31]

A fruitful analogy concerning the morality of the non-religious can be made with the *Halakhah* of witness, where it is essential to determine who is to be believed in a legal proceeding and who is not:

> One who removes himself from religious propriety (*mumar*) to eat non-kosher meat out of pleasure (*neveylot lete'avon*) is in everyone's opinion disqualified (*pasul*) from witness. But, if he does it rebelliously (*lehakh'is*): Abaye says that he is disqualified; Rava says he is qualified (*kasher*). Abaye says he is disqualified because he is an evildoer (*rasha*) . . . Rava says he is qualified because only a violent evildoer (*rasha dehamas*) is disqualified (*Exodus* 23:1) . . . here is one who is wicked to God but is not wicked to other human beings (*y'eyn ra laberiyot*).[32]

Now, although this is one of the seven exceptions to the rule that the law follows Rava against Abaye, it, nevertheless, represents the view of a major figure in Amoraic jurisprudence. Rava's point, as interpreted by Rabbenu Hananel, is that whereas a person ruled by appetite will more than likely be someone easily bribed, a person ruled by principle—even wrong principle—will act with moral integrity in an area which does not conflict with his non-religious or anti-religious principles.[33]

Despite the fact that the *Halakhah* is not according to Rava in this particular case, it seems, nevertheless, to have influenced Maimonides.

---

[31] *Proceedings of the Rabbinical Assembly* 5 (1933–1938), 485. See B. Cohen, *Law and Tradition in Judaism* (New York: Jewish Theological Seminary of America, 1950), 239–43; Novak, *supra* n. 4, at I, 35ff.; Elinson, supra n. 3, at 139; Mazoz, "*Nisu'in, etc.*," 238ff.
[32] *Sanh.* 27a. See S. Atlas, *Netivim Bemishpat Ha'ivri* (New York, 1978), 31, n. 2.
[33] *Cf. Naz.* 23b where it is stated, albeit in an aggadic context, that "a principled sin (*averah lishmah*) is better than an unprincipled *mitsvah*." This statement, as the very discussion on that page of the Talmud shows, caused later sages much consternation.

For, although Maimonides codifies the traditional requirements that witnesses be observant Jews, he adds two important points:

> One who is disqualified (*nifṣal*) because of a transgression . . . such a person is disqualified (*paṣul*) for testimony. How does this specifically apply? When one transgressed by acts that it is evident to the Jewish people (*shepashaṭ beyisra'el*) that they are transgressions.[34]

Thus Maimonides seems to be saying that contemporary standards of public Jewish propriety determine who is reliable and who is not. By the standards of public Jewish propriety today most Jews would not consider violators of ritual laws to be unreliable as, let us say, professional gamblers, whom the *Mishnah* singled out as examples of persons too unreliable and sordid to be accepted as believable witnesses.[35] Furthermore, Maimonides writes:

> One who has neither knowledge of Scripture nor of *Mishnah*, nor who practices common propriety (*derekh erets*) is assumed to be wicked and disqualified for testimony. For whoever has descended to this level, it can be assumed (*ḥazakah*) that he transgresses in the majority of cases he has the opportunity to do so.[36]

Maimonides even goes further and rules that as long as one is engaged in the practice of *mitsvot*, and particularly charity, and whose public behavior is respectable, such a person's testimony is to be accepted.[37]

4. Natural Law Type Arguments

The difference between Jewish marriage and non-Jewish marriage is consistently maintained in the classical sources. For this reason the Scriptural injunction against marriages between Israelites and the seven Canaanite nations was extended by the rabbis to include all non-Jews,[38] and whatever unions were contracted by Jews with non-Jews are not

---

[34] *Edut*, 11.6. See, esp., *Mamrim*, 2.7.

[35] *M. Ṣanh.* 3.3. See *Sanh.* 24b and Maimonides, *Edut* 10.4. For the question of to what extent even morally reliable gentiles may be witnesses, see *She'elot Uteshuvot Hatashbats*, no. 78.

[36] *Edut*, 11.1 re *M. Ḳidd.* 1.10 and *Ḳidd.* 40b.

[37] *Ibid.*, 11.2.

[38] *M. Ḳidd.* 3.12; *Ḳidd.* 68b re *Deut.* 7:4. Cf. *Y. Sot.* 1.8/17a; *Yeb.* 76a–b; Abrabanel, commentary on *I Kings* 3:1ff. In *Iṣurey Bi'ah*, 12.1, Maimonides based the general prohibition on *Neh.* 10:31 rather than on the somewhat forced exegesis of *Deut.* 7:4 on *Ḳidd.* 68b (see *Toṣ.*, s.v. *binkha*), exegesis which he accepted in his commentary on *M. Ḳidd.* 3.12. Historically this is a more accurate dating of this full prohibition of all gentile spouses. Indeed the Talmud (*A. Zar.* 26b) saw the exegesis of *Deut.* 7:4 as only being the view of R. Simon bar Johai and that the rest of the sages hold that it is a *gezerah* from the time of Ezra.

considered valid even *ex post facto*.[39] Nevertheless, this line of legal application could not be extended to non-Jewish marriages between two Jews because the Scriptural base can only apply to Jews and non-Jews. In Talmudic interpretation there is an important destinction made between the rules based on Scripture or the exegesis of Scripture (*ḳra*), or tradition (*gemara*), and rules based on general reason (*sevara*).[40] Rules based on general reason are acceptable as long as they are not preempted by the former. Clearly the question of a non-Jewish marriage between two Jews is within the proper range of general reason because Scripture and Scriptural exegesis neither eliminate it from having validity, nor do they preempt the judgment that it does have validity.

One can see this type of interpretation at work in the treatment of this question by one of the most fascinating and unique modern halakhists, R. Joseph Rosin of Dvinsk (d. 1936), better known as the "Rogochover Gaon." As in all his writing, R. Rosin's style is extremely terse and cryptic. Nevertheless, when we unpack his statement on the subject of civil marriage, we can see a very significant rational justification—within Jewish tradition—for the validity of such a marriage. Writing in 1929 in answer to a particular question of whether two Jews married in a Russian civil court require a *geṭ* upon the dissolution of their marriage, he writes:[41]

> By definition (*vehageder*) there are two kinds of acquisition of a woman: (1) that she becomes his; (2) that she is forbidden to others by virtue of being a woman who is married and someone's else's *ḳidushin* would not be valid . . . Thus it means that whenever a man specified (*deyihad*) marriage, she is not in the category of a concubine. There is, then, the negative commandment that 'the wife [of the deceased] shall not [marry outside of the family to a strange person],' etc. (*Deut.* 25:5); and there is the positive commandment 'And he shall cleave [to his wife and they shall become one flesh]' (*Gen.* 2:24) . . . Also concerning the gentile warbride (*yefat to'ar*—*Deut.* 21:1) . . . there is marriage (*deyesh bah liḳuhin*) *and Rashi* indicates that this was even before conversion . . . and so the *Sifre* explains that she requires a *geṭ* either before or after her conversion.

R. Rosin concludes that a woman married in such a civil ceremony does require a *geṭ*; however, because of the ambiguity of her situation he suggests that her *geṭ* would require a special formula (*nuṣaḥ aḥer*).[42] Unfortunately, for practical purposes, I know of nowhere where he actually spelled out what such a formula would precisely state.

---

[39] Extending this rule to cover civil marriage would violate the rabbinic principle that "Scripture may not be interpreted totally apart from its ostensive meaning (*dyn miḳra yotse midey peshuto*)" (*Yeb.* 24a and parallels).
[40] See, *e.g.*, *Ḳidd.* 13b and *Giṭṭ.* 6b.
[41] *She'elot Uteshuvot Tsafnaḥ P'neaḥ* (New York, 1952), no. 26, 19.
[42] *Ibid.*, 20.

Despite the fact that R. Rosin himself indicated that there was much more to be said on this subject, his theoretical reasoning, which has bewildered many, must be examined on the conceptual level. The important thing to be noticed is that all of his arguments are taken from either pre-Toraitic or extra-Toraitic rulings.

His first argument is taken from levirate marriage. There the Torah indicates that because of a woman's sexual relationship with her first husband she is considered bound to his family, even if there were no children from this union. (Obviously, if there were children, she is also bound to his family in that her children carry on the family identity and are their father's heirs.) This is pre-Toraitic because we know from the story of Judah and Tamar in *Gen.* 38 that levirate marriage was the norm before the Sinaitic revelation. In fact, the only innovation that the Torah makes in *Deut.* 25 is the institution of ḥalitsah whereby the levirate union can be nullified in advance. R. Rosin's point in citing this seems to be that the sexual relationship between two Jews, publicly acknowledged, has binding consequences. For, as he points out, it is this factor alone, which Scripturally grounds the relationship and gives it legal consequences.

His second argument is taken from the first marriage mentioned in Scripture, that of Adam and Eve. Here we have a statement that the cleaving of a man with his wife (*b'ishto*) makes their relationship a marriage under any circumstances (except a Jew and a non-Jew as we have already seen). Even though such a marriage may not have all the same consequences of a Jewish marriage, as pointed out by the Tosafists R. Rosin cites,[43] it is still considered to be something more than fornication.

His third and most novel argument is taken from the case of the gentile warbride, whom the Torah permits a Jewish soldier to take for a wife, provided that she is thereafter converted to Judaism. Following *Rashi*,[44] as opposed to the Tosafists, R. Rosin indicates that in this case the Torah considers this to be a marriage even before the conversion of the theretofore gentile woman. Moreover, in the background of all this is the rather embarrassing admission by the Talmud that this exceptional dispensation is made as a concession to human nature (*lo dibrah Torah ela keneged yetser hara*), namely, human nature under the stress of a wartime situation with all its anxieties.[45] In other words, the marital norms of the Torah did not invent marriage but took over marriage and its consequences, offering its

---

[43] *Ḳidd.* 21b, s.v. *eshet* re *Ṣanh.* 52b. See *Yeb.* 68b.
[44] *Ibid.*, 22a, s.v. *liḳuhin*. See *Ṣifre, Devarim*, no. 214. Maimonides' view (*Melakhim*, i. 6–7) seems to be the same as that of the Tosafists. See *Radbaz* thereon. This was considered to be a special dispensation (*Sanh.* 59a/bot.) in an offensive war (*milḥemet reshut*—*Ṣifre, Devarim*. no. 211; Maimonides, *Melakhim*, 8.1).
[45] *Ibid.*, 21b/bot.

own subsequent refinements and redirections.[46] Furthermore, R. Rosin compares the warbride with the levirate in that in both cases it is the act of intercourse alone which initiates the marital union. Thus, even in the case of the warbride, which so closely resembles rape, the act of the Jewish soldier, aware of the consequences of his act, is not considered fornication.

R. Rosin's choice of sources, and the line of his reasoning, surely reveal his philosophical judgment of the character of marriage and Jewish marriage. He has come to the sources with a definite concept of human nature and human sexuality. In this type of reasoning he was followed by an influential American authority, the late R. Joseph E. Henkin of New York. Concerning the sexual initiation of marriage, R. Henkin wrote:

> And experience indicates that this is the natural form of acquisition (*kinyan ṭivʻi*).... For when one has brought a woman in and had sexual intercourse with her, she is already bound by virtue of it. And she also demands from him the obligations of marriage. It is also the law of the Noahide from natural norms (*mehanimuṣim haṭiviʻim*) planted in the soul . . . Thus it follows according to what I have written that even without formal sanctification (*beli ḳidesh kelal*) but only that he brought a woman into his house for the purpose of marriage (*leshem ishut venisuʻin*), this act of intercourse which he did with her afterwards is as if there were witnesses.[47]

This line of reasoning, which we have seen developed by R. Rosin and R. Henkin, is based on two related strains in Jewish thought. (1) The institutions which prevailed before the giving of the Torah (*ḳodem matan Torah*), – although transformed by Sinaitic revelation, still retain some of their validity for Jews even after that revelation.[48] (2) The Noahide law and institutions, which were normative even for Jews before the Sinaitic revelation, are "natural law" in the sense that they reflect basic human inclinations and reason.[49] Now it is true that both of these points have been disputed in the history of Jewish thought. However, they do have important adherents.[50] R. Rosin and R. Henkin, ultimately

---

[46] See *Bereshit Rabbah*, 44.1.

[47] *Kitvey R. Yoṣef Eliyahu Henkin* I (New York, 1980), "*Perushey Ivra*", 2.1 See *ibid.*, "*Lev Ivra*," 12ff. See, also, *Mordecai, Kidushin*, no. 533, and R. Jonah Landsofer, *Sheʻelot Meʻil Tsedaḳah* (Sdelkov, 1835), no. 1, 8.

[48] See, *e.g.*, R. Tsvi Hirsch Chajes, *Torat Neviʻim*, chap. 11 in *Kol Ṣifrey Maharatz Chajes* I (Jerusalem, 1958), 63ff.; *Encyclopedia Talmudit* I, 296b–297a; *Otsar Haposḳim* 10 (Jerusalem, 1967), 12 (the view of R. Silberstein); Mazoz, "*Nisuʻin, etc.*," 243.

[49] See Saadyah Gaon, *Emunot Vedeʻot*, 9.2; Maimonides, *Melakhim*, 8.11, and D. Novak, "Law and Ethics in Maimonides' Theology," *The Solomon Goldman Lectures* III (Chicago: Spertus College of Judaica, 1982), 11ff.

[50] This whole topic is the subject of my recent book, *The Image of the non-Jew in Judaism: An Historical and Constructive Study of the Noahide Laws* (New York: The Edwin Mellen Press, 1983).

basing themselves on their own reasoning, have selected a venerable opinion in the history of Jewish thought. That opinion has in turn enabled them to select that halakhic option which sees civil marriage as *kidushin*, albeit *ex post facto* and with displeasure.

This line of reasoning, especially in its purely legal aspects, is buttressed, it seems to me, when we examine some of the discussions at the beginning of the tractate *Kidushin* in the *Bavli*, where the theoretical foundations of the institutions of Jewish marriage are discussed.

At the beginning of this tractate the *Gemara* notes that the *Mishnah* refers to "acquisition" (*ha'ishah niknit*), whereas the *Mishnah* at the beginning of the second chapter refers to "sanctification" (*ha'ish mekadesh*).[51] The former term is considered Scriptural, whereas the latter term is considered rabbinic. Even though "sanctified" (*mekudeshet*) can simply mean "exclusively mine," the Tosafists point out that with no other chattel does such an exclusive relationship exist. Therefore, the later use of the term *mekudeshet* seems to indicate that the uniquely religious character of the Jewish marital relationship is something subsequent rather than prior in the development of Judaism. It is seen as analogous to the relation of objects dedicated to the Temple (*hekdesh*).[52] Moreover, along the lines stressed by R. Rosin and R. Henkin, at least the *Bavli* emphasized that the whole institution of marital acquisition (*kinyan*) is essentially connected to Abraham's acquisition of the field of Ephron the Hittite, a precedent preceding the Sinaitic revelation.[53] According to many scholars this section of the *Gemara* is a product of the Geonic period (*Seborayim*), after the official editing of the *Bavli* text.[54] Thus it can be seen as a summary of the whole development of rabbinic thought on the institution of Jewish marriage.

Furthermore, the rabbis note what is considered binding in betrothal formulas:

> How is acquisition effected through money? He gave her money or its equivalent and said to her: 'behold you are sanctified (*mekudeshet*) to me; betrothed (*me'ureset*) to me; behold you are my wife (*at li l'into*)'—she is sanctified.[55]

---

[51] *Kidd.* 2b.
[52] S.v. "*d'asar.*" See *Me'ilah* 18a–b and *Tos.*, s.v. *eyn*. Nevertheless, *kidushin* is considered even more exclusive than *hekdesh*. See Y. *Kidd.* 3.1/63c.
[53] *Kidd.* 2a–b. See *Tos.*, s.v. *ukhetiv*, and *ibid.*, 13a, *Tos.*, s.v. *leshem*.
[54] See *Igeret Rav Sherira Gaon*, ed. Lewin, 71, and D. Halivni, *Mekorot Umesorot, Nashim* (Tel Aviv: Mosad Bialik, 1968), 628, n. 6.
[55] *Kidd.* 5b. This may reflect the notion that even Jewish marriage can be seen as a civil contract as well as a religious covenant, although, unlike Roman law, it can only be initiated (and) terminated by the man. See Y. *Kidd.* 1.1/58c and B. Cohen, *Jewish and Roman Law* I (New York: Jewish Theological Seminary of America, 1966), 383–84.

It is clear from the majority of the acceptable terms of betrothal that they have no religious connotation and simply indicate a public act of betrothal consciously agreed upon by both parties. In fact, based on the situation where the sole criterion seems to be whether or not both parties are aware of the marital consequences of their words and deeds, the *Bavli* mentions the statement of R. Judah in the name of Samuel that "whoever is unfamiliar with the procedure (*ṭiv*) of Jewish divorce and marriage should not become involved in any situation where they are the subject of discussion (*lo yehe lo eṣek imahen*)"[56]—with a member of the opposite sex. Of course, valid betrothal ultimately does have religious consequences in that it is an institution structured by *Halakhah*; however, the phenomenology of the situations discussed by the *Gemara* clearly indicates that a permanent heterosexual relationship between two Jews is the essence of what is being presented—nothing more.

5. *The Scope of the Halakhah*

The basic philosophical question at issue in this whole dispute, it seems to me, is not only about the character of Jewish marriage *per se* but, also, about the *Tendenz* of the entire halakhic process. The question can be formulated as follows: Is the halakhic process, in confronting new phenomena, to be centripetal or centrifugal? Is it to restrict or expand its scope?[57] Those who advocate the Jewish invalidity of civil marriage are in fact restricting the scope of the *Halakhah* by constituting civil marriage as an extra-halakhic reality. Conversely, those who advocate its Jewish validity are expanding the scope of the *Halakhah*.

We can see the centripetal approach in the arguments presented by two modern halakhists, the late R. Jehiel J. Weinberg of Montreux, Switzerland (d. 1966), the former rector of the Orthodox Rabbinical Seminary in Berlin, and the late R. Jacob M. Toledano, the former Sephardi Chief Rabbi of Tel Aviv. Interestingly enough, their reasoning drew upon the same pre-Toraitic and extra-Toraitic institutions that were used by R. Rosin and R. Henkin, who, nevertheless, came to opposite conclusions than they.

R. Weinberg, albeit as a suggestion rather than as a practical halakhic ruling (*lemaʿaseh*), reasons that a civil marriage should be regarded

---

[56] *Ibid.*, 6a. This is the view of R. Azriel in *Tos.*, s.v. *lo*. However, *Rashi*, *Ri* the Elder and *Riṭba* interpret the passage to refer to an incompetent professional (*dayan*) who is supervising marriage, not to the couple themselves marrying. In the context of 5b–6a, which is the halakhic origin of this statement, R. Azriel's view seems to be more correct. The statement is repeated on 13a–b in an aggadic context. There, in the transposition, the views of *Rashi et al.* seem properly to belong. For in the context of 6a the Gemara is discussing when a man and a woman are engaged in a dialogue with marital consequences (*gufa: haya medaber im ha'ishah*). On 13a–b the context is a gathering of rabbis.
[57] See Novak, *supra* n. 4, at II, 129–31.

as we would regard a Noahide marriage between two gentiles. Just as in Noahide marriage publicly known cohabitation is sufficient to initiate marriage, so permanent public separation is sufficient to terminate the marriage.[58] R. Weinberg bases himself on Maimonides and, then, attempts to see civil marriage analogously.[59] I have argued elsewhere that Maimonides' views cannot be used for any such precedent, even by analogy, because such an analogy presupposes the validity of concubinage as a sort of second-class Jewish marriage. Maimonides was clearly (and controversially) opposed to concubinage and equated it with fornication.[60] R. Weinberg's purpose in even making such a novel suggestion was to alleviate somewhat the *agunah* problem, that is, to remove as many women as possible from the category of being fully married (*eshet ish*) and, therefore, making them no longer at the mercy of oft-times uncooperative husbands who will not give them *giṭṭin*, even when they clearly should do so. It seems as though he believed that some small measure of victory in this especially vexing contemporary dilemma could be won for Traditional Judaism in what is in fact a retreat.

R. Toledano suggested that concubinage be revived, following those medieval authorities (*rishonim*) who refused to accept Maimonides' condemnation of it.[61] Following the view that a concubine (*pilegesh*) does not require a *geṭ* to be divorced, he advocated that Jewish couples actually be given the choice whether they want full Jewish marriage (*ḳidushin*), with all its consequences, or partial Jewish marriage (*pligshut*), with all its

---

[58] *Seridey Esh* III, no. 22, 46–47. The most radical suggestion of all was given by the Reform leader, R. Samuel Holdheim, who advocated, using some of the same sources we have presented here, that all matters of marriage (and divorce) be considered civil contracts only, *ab initio*. No one committed to the halakhic system could possible advocate such willful abrogation of basic Jewish institutions. See *Ueber der Autonomie der Rabbinen und das Prinzip der juedischen Ehe* (Schwerin: Kurschner, 1847), 198ff. (I thank Prof. Ismar Schorsch of the Jewish Theological Seminary of America for this reference.)

[59] *Melakhim*, 9.8.

[60] See *Ishut*, 1.4, and *ibid.*, 4.4 (and *She'elot Uteshuvot Haradbaz* IV, no. 1296). For those who opposed Maimonides on this point, at least theoretically, see R. Abraham ben David of Posquières (*Rabad*) on *Ishut*, 1.4, and on *Na'arah Betulah*, 2.17; Nahmanides, *Teshuvot Haramban*, ed. Chavel (Jerusalem: Mosad Harav Kook, 1975), no. 105; R. Solomon ibn Adret, *She'elot Uteshuvot Harashba* IV, no. 314; *She'elot Uteshuvot Haribash*, nos. 398, 425. See Novak, *supra* n. 4, at I, 159, n. 26. For open endorsement of concubinage, see R. Jacob Emden, *She'elot Uteshuvot Yabets* II, no. 15.

[61] *Otsar Ḥayim* 6 (1930), 209. See Z. Falk, "Al Hanesu'in shel Kohen Ugershah," *De'ot* 27 (1965), 35; Elinson, *supra* n. 3, at 91. Cf. R. David Tsvi Hoffmann, *Melamed Leho'il* III (Frankfurt-am-Main, 1932), no. 8, 16–17. R. Toledano's view is based on the Talmudic opinion that a concubine is not married (*uvelo ḳidushin*—Ṣanh. 21a). See Y.Ket. 5.2/29d and L. M. Epstein, "The Institution of Concubinage Among the Jews," *Proceedings of the American Academy for Jewish Research* 6 (1934–1935), 183–84. Cf. *She'elot Uteshuvot Harashba* V, no. 242.

different consequences.[62] This too would help alleviate the plight of many *agunot*, the assumption being that *gittin* are often difficult to obtain from the type of secularists who would opt for this *de facto* civil marriage, albeit under Jewish auspices.

At the risk of sounding irreverent about the opinions of these two great halakhists—which I am not—I cannot help but react to their suggestions, designed as they were to alleviate a very real contemporary problem in Jewish life,[63] with the American jest, "the operation was a success, but the patient died!" In other words, their solution to the *agunah* problem was too good in that, if the Jewish public, especially the Jewish female public, found out about it, Jewish marriage with its greater contemporary liabilities and fewer contemporary assets, would become an option only fit for fools.[64] After all, the children of a Jewish woman civilly married are unquestionably Jewish,[65] the monetary benefits of the *ketubah* are today purely symbolic in that all now defer to the law of the secular state in monetary matters; and those civilly married are hardly ostracized in the contemporary Jewish world, which openly tolerates far greater infractions of Jewish tradition. Clearly the *Tendenz* of the halakhic process has been to make Jewish marriage more not less attractive to Jews.[66]

Surely the halakhic process in the past, although at times employing the institutions of the non-Jewish world to deal with specific problems, did so reluctantly and preferred devising its own internal solutions. Many examples could be cited.[67] Elsewhere I have argued that the only

---

[62] A number of modern authorities make the need for a *get* contingent on the intention of the couple civilly marrying, viz., if they civilly married because they lived in a society (*e.g.*, Communist) where religious marriage cannot be obtained, but they intended to live as much of a Jewish life as possible, then a *get* is required; if, on the other hand, they intended not to have a Jewish religious marriage, then a *get* is not required. See R. Ben Zion Uziel, *Mishpatey Uziel* 1.2, *E.H.*, no. 59; Schereschewsky, *supra* n. 3, at 90–91; Mazoz, "*Nesu'in, etc.*," 268–70.

[63] As for the status of children born of a second marriage, after the dissolution of the first civil marriage, most authorities hold that they are not *mamzerim*. See Mazoz, *op. cit.*, 246. A number of authorities, however, still require a *get*, not because they believe a civil marriage to be binding, but because they are concerned that the public might think that a Jewish marriage was dissolved without a *get* (see Yeb. 88b/bot). See Hoffmann, *Melamed Leho'il* III, no. 20, and *Otsar Haposkim* 10, 11.

[64] Indeed, R. Menahem Meiri noted that if Jewish women knew of the lowly status of women according to Scriptural law, they might have left Judaism! See *Bet Habehirah*, Kidushin, 8.

[65] See *Gitt.* 79b and *Rashi*, s.v. *gita*.

[66] See, *e.g.*, Yeb. 38b and *Rashi*, s.v. *v'Abaye*; *Ket.* 84a and *Rashi*, s.v. *mishum* (cf. Tos., s.v. *leketubat*).

[67] See, *e.g.*, M. Gitt. 9.8; Gitt. 88b, and Tos., s.v. *uba'akum*. Also, see, *e.g.*, *She'elot Uteshuvot Harashba* VI, no. 254, who agonized that the principle "the law of the state is the law" (*dina demalkhuta dina*—B.B. 54b and parallels) takes too much away from Jewish legal autonomy.

real solution to the *agunah* problem in our day is the revival of the rabbinic power to annul marriages (*afkaʻat ḳidushin*), to be used cautiously and sparingly, of course.[68]

In conclusion we can see that like all "landmark" cases with which halakhists have had to deal in the past, the question of the Jewish status of a civil marriage between two Jews, and the judgment of modern secularity it entails, involves (1) a philosophical view of the character of marriage and Jewish marriage; (2) a selective drawing from a very wide range of sources; and (3) a philosophical view of the historical *Tendenz* of the whole halakhic process itself.

[68] "Annulment in Lieu of Divorce in Jewish Law," *Jewish Law Annual* IV (1981), 188ff.

THE USE OF EXCESSIVE FORCE BY A PEACE OFFICER: ONE HALAKHIC OPINION*

by

S. M. PASSAMANECK**

Since 1976 I have served as an auxiliary chaplain with the Los Angeles County Sheriff's Department. During these past six years, I have observed hundreds of deputies performing the incredible variety of tasks that are the ordinary routine of a modern police officer. My experiences with law enforcement personnel led me eventually to look into what the *halakhah* might have to say on the subjects of police and law enforcement: hence this paper.

The halakhic bibliography on police and police work is not large; as a matter of fact it is quite small. But material exists. A few broad strokes will suffice to demonstrate that the Jewish legal system has recognized the importance and the duties of some sort of police agency.

To begin with, there is the Bible. *Deut.* 16:18 commands the establishment of judges and officers. The term used for officers, *shotrim*, is the term presently used to indicate police. Maimonides in *Hilkhot Sanhedrin* 1:1 enlarges upon the ancient commandment, which had been reiterated in *B. Sanh.* 16b, and specifies that the officers have the power to bring persons suspected of "crookedness" (Maimonides' term, not mine) before the court for trial. That is to say, they have the power to arrest. Curiously, the principal duties of the officers are to patrol the streets and marketplaces to maintain lawful practices in the various shops. They are, in effect, market inspectors. But Maimonides does go on to assert that anyone in whom the officers shall see "crookedness" is to be brought to the court. While the emphasis is clearly placed on the policing of commercial activity, this last clause can easily be expanded to cover all manner of criminal behavior. Moreover, the officers are to be armed, and that, too, suggests that these enforcement personnel do not necessarily limit their patrols to inspection of weights and measures.

---

*This paper was prepared for oral presentation, in which sources were cited during the delivery of the text itself. The sources, which are relatively few, are found in the text thus obviating the need for extensive footnotes.

**Professor of Talmud and Rabbinics, Hebrew Union College, Los Angeles.

Maimonides even prescribes the establishment of a sort of vice squad, with only the thinnest of Talmudic basis for it. In *Hilkhot Yom Tov* 6:21, the rabbinical court is charged to appoint officers at the times of religious festivals. These officers are to patrol riverbanks and orchards in order to prevent men and women from gathering at such places to drink, to dine, and possibly to commit unlawful acts. Such patrolmen are also charged to warn all Jews against mixed gatherings on private property, lest they drink too deeply and fall into sin.

These two references to Maimonides' codex provide a sufficient point of reference for the place and role of police in traditional legal thought. David Nativ's recent Hebrew article[1] gives us plenty of both halakhic and aggadic detail on police, and police work, and their role in Jewish society.

While traditional sources do not provide abundant material on police work, the same cannot be said for the modern press and electronic media. Modern media, which reflect the tastes and interests of modern society—including the Jewish members of that society—present us with an inexhaustible flow of information of all kinds on police and police work. Clearly someone, or some ones, believe that we are all more or less interested in the police. They send us data of all kinds, sober or sensational, for or against, and the data pour forth without pause. Those someones in the media are probably correct. There is a massive general interest in police and police work, and especially in the matter of police powers.

The phrase "law and order" has become a critical part of modern conversational idiom. It connotes, among other things, a sense of police power, and an image of the police officer, whether menacing or benign. On a less popular, or perhaps more technical, level, lawyers and judges, not to mention legislators, wrestle daily with problems and situations stemming from police authority in the areas of search and seizure, evidence, and the exercise of arrest powers. Not the least of the vexing questions, guaranteed to make headlines in the press and on the air, is the use of force by police officers, particularly when such force appears to be excessive or brutal. A charge of police brutality immediately becomes a topic of public and private debate and harrangue.

The subject of excessive force brings me to my specific topic. A full exploration of the matter in the light of traditional Jewish sources will take us far beyond the time period allotted to my presentation. The examination of one text, however, can be accomplished.

There is a most illuminating text on the matter of excessive force. To the extent allowed by the content of that text, and reasonable inferences

---

[1] D. Nativ, "Police Service in the Light of Judaic Sources" (Heb.), *Techumin* I (5740), 372–84.

which can be drawn from it, I shall try to examine this one traditional opinion on a police matter that continues to exercise reasonable, and unreasonable, people concerned with the frayed fabric of modern society.

The text is responsum No. 180 from part one of Rabbi Jacob Reischer's *Shevut Ya'akov*. The volume first appeared in Halle in 1710. Reischer was born in Prague, about 1670. He was a brilliant scholar and enjoyed a widespread reputation as a first-class legal authority. Reischer had already served as a rabbinic judge in Prague and elsewhere before he was called to serve as Av Bet Din in Ansbach, the capital of Bavaria, in 1709. The first volume of his responsa followed shortly after.

There is no internal evidence on the precise origin of the case we are about to consider, but a south German or Czech provenance is at least reasonable. The date of the case is similarly obscure, but a date sometime after 1695 and before 1709 is probable.

I shall begin with the question and a brief analysis of it. Reischer's reply is given in three parts, corresponding to the three questions raised. Only the first two parts, however, speak to the point under notice. I shall go through those parts of the answer in some detail, but the third part will receive only brief treatment. The author prefaces his entire response with a most interesting sentence of introduction. I shall also comment on that sentence in due course. Finally, I shall make an observation or two which I hope will not be out of place as conclusion.

Here then is the question put to Reischer:

> "Reuben acted disrespectfully toward a deputy of the court; he struck the deputy in the presence of the court. The deputy turned and struck Reuben merciless blows with his club (inflicting) severe wounds. In truth, according to medical opinion, it would be thought impossible to administer a beating like that with a club like that.
>
> "Is the deputy of the court to be held liable since it had been possible to save himself (*i.e.* protect himself) without giving this severe beating?
>
> "Further: is there ground for liability since the injury caused was not appropriate to the weapon used?
>
> "Further: the deputy of the court does not wish to have this case heard before this court (*i.e.* the one in whose presence the incident occurred), but rather before the higher court in this city."
>
> The questioner then respectfully asks for guidance in the matter.

Much detail that would be of interest to us is omitted from the brief question. First, what was the deputy's official status and capacity? What was he doing in court and what was he entitled to do? The deputy, we must assume, enjoyed some official status. He was a duly appointed officer of the court; whether his commission was permanent or temporary is not important. He was not an ordinary citizen at that time and place; he was armed and presumably exercising the duties of a bailiff or a marshall, or perhaps a deputy sheriff. Then who was the person who acted disrespectfully towards the court's deputy? We do not know that either. One might jump to the conclusion that the deputy had brought the person before the court under arrest, and the person, Reuben, was none too delighted to be up on charges. There is nothing in the text, however, to support such a conclusion. Reuben might have come to court of his own volition to answer some charge, and begun, for some unknown reason, to act disrespectfully. Reuben might have been a criminal defendant, or he might have come on some civil matter, or he might have come to prefer charges against someone else and for reasons unknown, or for no reason at all, acted disrespectfully. Or perhaps Reuben was there in court with someone else, some other plaintiff or defendant, and again for reasons unknown or no reason at all, he acted disrespectfully and struck the deputy. I should like to point out that very reasonable and decent appearing ladies and gentlemen can and do become enraged at police officers engaged in the lawful exercise of their duties. They become disagreeable and offensive in the extreme, and for no good reason. The officers may be entirely civil and polite, but there are indeed citizens who simply explode when stopped regarding some traffic offense or when they see a noisy drunk removed from a public restaurant. Most people are suitably respectful when respectfully approached, but some are not. I have seen enough of both types during my years of patrol observation.

But Reuben was more than disrespectful. He hit the deputy. I have seen that too, more than once. The fact that Reuben struck the deputy would of course have a bearing on the modern analysis of the case. Reuben would be arrested in the State of California for an alleged violation of Chapter 243b PC,[2] battery on a peace officer engaged in the performance of his or her duties. If convicted, Reuben would face a fine of $1,000, and up to a year in the county jail.

In any event, Reuben hit the deputy and the deputy responded with vigor, with so much vigor in fact that the enquirer makes a point to say that one would not even imagine such wounds could be the result of a clubbing. The deputy beat a mighty tatoo on the hapless Reuben. What is surprising here is that no one in the court seems to have stepped in to stop the thrashing. Apparently the deputy stopped when he was satisfied that Reuben's disrespect had been properly punished. It is inconceivable that any officer, marshall, or bailiff could continue to strike anyone in a courtroom today without causing a riot. If this incident occurred today

---

[2] The initials "PC" refer to the California penal code. Similar provisions appear in other state and federal penal codes in the United States.

in California and, assuming that Reuben was under arrest, the officer would be arrested under Ch. 147 PC, which covers inhumane and oppressive treatment of prisoners. If convicted, the officer wouuld be dismissed and face a fine of up to $2,000. No doubt the officer would face federal charges for violation of civil rights. If Reuben were not a prisoner or under arrest, the officer would be charged with violation of Ch. 149 PC, assaulting or beating a person under the color of authority, without lawful necessity, in other words, unlawful excessive force. The officer could expect punishment by a fine not exceeding $5,000, or a year in jail, or state prison, or both. And no doubt there would be civil rights violations to answer for here as well. But in that rabbinic court, almost 300 years ago, the officer was not pulled off Reuben as far as we were informed. Perhaps no one wanted to take on the deputy at that point, perhaps many things. But we do not know.

The two questions raised are simply these: First, there was excessive force and violence; is there any liability on that ground of the excessive nature of the beating alone? Second, given the severity of the wounds, is there any liability for them?

The second possible ground for liability appears to be a logical extension of the first. If excessive force is impermissible in this case, then there should be liability for the injuries so caused. If excessive force is not, however, a ground for liability, then the severity of injury should not be a ground for liability, either, since why allow the beating itself and then make the deputy pay compensation for the severity of the injuries. The questioner does not draw attention to the relation between these two questions, but they would seem to be logically sequential.

The request for a change of venue does not apparently bear on the matter of excessive force.

Reischer begins his response with the assertion that he will take up the questions in order; but not, he says, for the benefit of the enquirer alone. Presumably he is going to give a definitive statement on the case. He goes on to explain why the answer is not only for the enquirer—he says: . . . "later authorities have already warned us concerning the *akh* and *rak*, as a debate on the *halakhah* of whether or not there should be liability for excessive force. . . ." Reischer refuses to enter into a debate; he eschews the "buts" and the "excepts" of legal discourse. It would seem that he feels the necessity of stating a clear judgment one way or the other. The delicacy of legal debate would presumably leave too many loopholes, too many exceptions. One senses that it is too important a matter to be left half settled. There is no indication that Reischer is settling a debate which has already polarized opinion; he simply wants no equivocation at all in his own answer.

We now turn to the answer and we shall see how successfully the respondent avoided equivocation.

Reischer begins his response by declaring that the law in this matter is, apparently, simply put in the Talmud, *B. Baba Kamma* 28a. The author cites the provision that whereas, according to scripture (*Deut.* 25:11, 12), the woman who rescues her husband from an attacker by seizing the assailant's genitals, is to lose her hand,[3] the rabbis commute the biblical punishment to a money payment. The transcription of this text in the responsum is unfortunately somewhat garbled and contradictory. A large and important element of the talmudic text is omitted. The omission of course does not reflect on Reisher's understanding of the argument; he certainly knew it very well indeed. There are, however, many occasions for inadvertent error in manuscript transcription and typesetting, careful proofreading notwithstanding.

I shall give the author's version first and then review the fuller text from *Baba Kamma*.

The author transcribes as follows: does the pecuniary liability not apply when she has no other less drastic means of saving her husband? The answer is no. When she has a less drastic option available, she is exempt. The latter portion of the rule provides, on the basis of *Deut.* 25:11: "she stretches out her hand," an exemption from liability for a deputy of the court who employs excessive force. We understand, therefore, that even where the woman has a less drastic option available to her—and she uses the more drastic means of rescue—he (presumably the deputy in a similar case) is exempt from liability.

According to the version, the woman would never be liable; certainly not when she must use extreme force, and even when a lower level of force would be sufficient but she proceeds to a higher level immediately. Thus the talmudic penalty cannot be applied in any case.

The last portion of the citation states that the deputy is *also* exempt from liability for excessive force *even* in a case where the woman used excessive force when she need not have done so. It seems therefore that we have an element of confusion in the logic of the interpretation of 25:11—the exemption rule for the deputy is extended to cover the woman, yet the phrasing implies that the deputy's exemption is somehow based on the woman's exemption: the deputy is *also exempt*, even in the case where the woman, who is exempt, could have used a less drastic level of force but did not do so.

The point Reischer is driving at is ultimately clear: the officer is not

---

[3] During the question and answer period, it was pointed out that the verb "thou shalt cut off" (her hand) *vekatsotah*, is an unusual form, which in rabbinic parlance is occasionally used to indicate, or can indicate, the act of determining or fixing a sum of money. Therefore, the rabbis who commuted the corporal penalty to a money payment were not departing from nor distorting the meaning of the biblical text. The paper here mentions only that the amputation was eschewed in favor of a money payment; clearly, in terms of the text, this was an entirely proper reading of the text by the rabbis.

liable for use of excessive force. But the *Baba Kamma* citation is not at all well put; there is room for some confusion, which one need not ascribe to any fault on the respondent's part. The confusion concerns the woman, not the officer, and his exemption is the essential part of the argument.

The section of *Baba Kamma* in question provides as follows: the pecuniary liability applies when the woman has a less drastic option but does not use it. When she has no option except extreme force, she is not liable. The text eventually states that where the woman has no other option except extreme violence, her hand becomes like "a deputy of the court" and she is exempt. Again the point is clear; the officer is not liable even in a case of excessive force. The talmudic version does however suggest the circumstances in which the woman, taking the law unto herself, would be liable for extreme violence.

Reischer underscores the rule of exemption for the deputy by reference to Rabbenu Yeruḥam's *Toledot Adam V'hava*, Ch. 31, Sec. 2, as quoted in the *Bet Yoṣef* to *Ṭur Ḥoshen Misphaṭ*, Ch. 8, end. Rabbenu Yeruḥam declares that a deputy of the court has the right to use force against a reluctant arrestee and is not liable for any injury to the arrestee's person or property even if the deputy employs an excessive level of force.

Three brief observations on my part should round out this part of the responsum. First, excessive force simply means a level of force beyond what is minimally required to subdue a a person. One does not use an elephant gun to get a mosquito. Second, the matter of life-threatening or deadly force is not mentioned. As a rule, police agencies permit officers to use deadly force only when the life of the officer, or of others in the vicinity, appears to be in immediate danger. Police shootings are routinely subjected to the most detailed and scrupulous investigations—by professional investigators, the press, and citizens at large. And that is as it should be. Third, the liability in point in *Baba Kamma* appears to refer to a pecuniary penalty for *boshet*, the price put on the victim's public embarrassment consequent upon an injury caused by an assailant. At this point, Reischer's argument does not distinguish between liability for injury and liability for embarrassment. One assumes that he has, at least, both in mind and that for his present purpose the distinction is not relevant. It will however become relevant as the discussion proceeds. The matter of penalty will come up again shortly.

The *Shulḥan Arukh*, *Ḥoshen Mishpaṭ* 8:5, gloss restates the right of the deputy to use force, without fear of liability, against the person or property of a person reluctant to obey, but the text does not go into the matter of excessive force without liability. That point is made by the *Ṣefer Meirat Eynayim* commentary thereto: a deputy of the court may exercise excessive force against a person reluctant to obey the law and incur no liability by using such violence. No distinction between embarrassment and injury *per se* is drawn in the commentary or the text.

At this point, Reischer introduces another argument based on the commentary *Nimuke Yosef* to Alfasi on *Baba Kamma* 27b. Despite Reischer's reluctance to debate, he now does indeed show that the deputy's exemption from liability for excessive force does not escape some challenge. The commentary discusses the talmudic rule that, where a person is faced with irreparable harm (as were presumably the woman and her husband in the previous argument), the person may lawfully act on his or her own behalf to protect his or her property (and person). The person may use force even to the extent of striking the adversary 100 times with the blade of a hoe. The commentator restricts this violence asserting that the 100 blows were lawful only where some less drastic option is simply not available and extreme force is the only recourse. Obviously, says the commentator, the position of the deputy vis-à-vis a person who does not obey the law is similar. The implication of this, says Reischer, is that the deputy has the right to use excessive force only when less drastic approaches are not available. If excessive force is used when lesser force would suffice, the deputy would be liable for the damage caused.

When we consider the facts of our case, the deputy is clearly liable under this argument, but of course Reischer has not come to the end of his opinion.

Two comments here: first, the right of self help is the logical foundation for the police authority to use force. Reischer does not cite the next few lines of commentary which pose the rhetorical question: should the right to use violence granted a private person for his protection be greater than the similar power granted to a deputy of the court? Second, the reference to 100 blows with the blade of a hoe is, I believe, a hyperbole, pure and simple, representing an extreme level of violence. Anyone who has ever been in a hand-to-hand fight knows that 100 punches, not to mention blows with a club, will very likely inflict mortal injury—long before the hundredth blow has been struck.

The author now reconciles the two arguments: the latter one for some degree of liability and the former one against it. He simply restates the talmudic provisions of *Baba Kamma* 28a, in the light of the *Nimuke Yosef* commentary to Alfasi on *Baba Kamma* 27b; and he goes on to suggest a distinction between injury and degradation as a significant consideration in the assessment of liability. In any case, this reconciliation seriously qualifies the deputy's apparent exemption given in *Baba Kamma* 28a. This former discussion concluded that if the woman who is protecting her husband has no recourse other than to seize the genitals of his assailant, her hand becomes like "a deputy of the court," who is certainly exempt from liability if he has no recourse except extreme violence since he acts under the authority of the court. If, however, the deputy need not have resorted to extreme force it would, one gathers, appear logical to the *Nimuke Yoṣef* that even a deputy of the court would be liable for injury caused by unnecessarily exercising such force. Then Reischer asserts that one may possibly reconcile the two views by saying that in the case of the woman, any exemptions mentioned apply only in the matter of payment for degradation, which we noticed may be presumed to be the liability involved there, while in the matter of injury *per se*, it is logical that there be liability.

On this basis, then, the deputy of the court could be held liable for injury of the victim, but not for his degradation, in a case of excessive force.

We recall that Reischer did not want to enter into legal debate in this case. In a sense he does not. He does not weigh the validity of one argument against the other. He appears at least simply to state each argument, one for liability and one against, so that the enquirer can make his own choice. This is not debate, but it is equivocation. The answer is not at all as clear as it might be were he to favor one argument or the other. But the next element may at least offer a hint about which argument Reischer himself prefers.

The author now turns to the matter of whether or not the deputy was liable for the severity of Reuben's injuries since the weapon used was not appropriate for causing the wounds inflicted. Reischer cites *B. Baba Kamma* 91a, *Ṭur Ḥoshen Mishpaṭ* 420, and *Shulḥan Arukh Ḥoshen Mishpaṭ* 420:28. There we have the rule that a weapon used in an assault and wounding is to be examined by the court to determine whether or not it could have caused the injury sustained. If the court determines that the weapon could not have caused the injuries sustained, the attacker is not liable for injury, but he is liable for degradation consequent upon the injury. Reischer does not refer to the liability for degradation or embarrassment. Indeed he argues for the deputy's exemption from any culpability without reference to the special categories under which a fine is calculated. The author's silence on the matter of embarrassment rather suggests that he dismisses it, otherwise a word or two on it would certainly be in order.

Reischer then argues with the opinion of Solomon Luria expressed in Luria's commentary to *Baba Kamma*, Ch. 8. Luria wrote regarding excessive force that it seems to him that the attacker is liable—for injury no doubt—under the laws of Heaven. Apparently the human rabbinical court cannot impose liability, but the heavenly court can. Luria reasons that liability before the heavenly court is appropriate because a case of excessive force is not of lesser import than the case of A who frightens B and owing to the fright B suffers injury. A is in this case not to be held liable for B's injury in a human court, but the heavenly court can hold him liable as an indirect cause of injury.

Reischer takes immediate exception to this and declares that excessive injury is not at all like the matter of fright. It is rather a normal and reasonable assumption that B would react to fright in such fashion that he could sustain injuries. But with excessive injury, it is not a normal and reasonable assumption that one could inflict injury with a given weapon over and above what might be expected from the use of that particular weapon. So much for Luria.

Reischer next strengthens his argument against any liability, human or divine, for excessive injury. He quotes *B. Baba Kamma* 55bf., where we are informed that there are four acts for which one is liable before the heavenly law, but not the human law. Although indeed there are many more than four such acts, the Gemara explains that these four needed specification in order to preclude the possiblity of arguing that the perpetrators of these four acts were guiltless even at heavenly law. One of the four acts is the bending of a farmer's standing grain in such a way that an unusually strong gust of wind can carry a spark into it; one might argue that there should be no liability even at heavenly law. The Talmud thus informs us that such an argument is not admitted.

Reischer proceeds that if in the matter of excessive injury one contends there should be liability under the law of heaven on the analogy of the spark and grain case, then one would be propounding a most remarkable law. He writes that, on any view, fire is a mobile cause of damage. That is to say, the wind carries sparks; the relation among the bent grain, the spark, and the wind is clear. This is, however, simply not the case regarding the weapon. Certainly it would not occur to anyone that a person could inflict more than a reasonably estimable degree of injury with a particular weapon. This is quite reasonable unless of course Satan had taken a hand in the incident, brought his own accusations against the victim, and the attacker was constrained by satanic power to inflict brutal injuries. Luria himself mentions this possibility. Even in this situation, Luria would hold the attacker liable under the laws of heaven. Reischer clearly implies that there should be no liability at all if the deputy acted under satanic constraint; after all, he could not help himself and constraint is valid plea for the defense.

But surely, our author contends, there is no liability whatsoever for excessive injury in this case. This is supported by the unqualified language of both the Talmud and the post-talmudic legal authorities who declare exemption from liability for excessive injury, with no word at all about any liability under the laws of heaven. This argument concludes Reischer's analysis of excessive injury: apparently no liability, human or divine, obtains in the affair.

The author next declares that the deputy's case is to be heard before the court in which the incident occurred. He cites supporting authority to deny any change of venue. But this last matter is not to the point of this paper. I include it only to provide the answer to the third question just in case anyone was wondering about it.

Let us return to the matter of excessive injury. Reischer's answer on this matter would seem to reflect an attitude on the problem of excessive force. On that point our author did not debate, he simply put two strong arguments: one for liability and one against it, without apparently favoring one or the other.

I have already suggested that there seems to be a logical relation between liability for excessive force and liability for excessive injury. If the excessive force is unlawful, then some liability for injury naturally would follow. If the excessive force is lawful, then why should there be liability for the injuries? Since there is no liability for the injuries, it seems that our author implies, in a veiled manner to be sure, that non-liability for excessive force is to be preferred. After all, what is the point in saying that the act itself is illegal and then denying the victim compensation for the results of that act? Further, it would be bizarre to allow compensation for a reasonable degree of injury but not the excessive part of it: the injury is one indivisible agony. Our author quite properly did not even flirt with such a notion. On the basis of the answer to the second question, then, Reischer very indirectly appears to come down on the side of non-liability for excessive force.

The obvious question is why he was so obscure, if he was really in favor of one argument over the other. An answer to this question is not obvious. We can only make a suggestion. Perhaps for him the arguments were evenly balanced. Either one was acceptable. He did not care to take sides among the learned masters of the past on this point of law. Indirection and subtlety were the only choice therefore to resolve the matter; but for those who would care to impose liability for excessive force, surely the way is open, the supportive argument is there. Then, again, for reasons quite unknown and unknowable, he chose not to choose.

We have concluded the story of Reuben who disported himself badly and hit a deputy who grievously thrashed him for such folly. It is time for a few observations. In a modern legal opinion on such an incident, one would expect to find, embedded in the necessary review of the relevant law of course, some indication of moral attitude, express or implied, towards the principals in the drama. Somehow, we would be given to understand what the jurist senses to be ethically right or wrong. Clearly there is no such underlying tone present in this responsum unless we assume that the indirect exoneration that I have suggested is also taken to be an expression of the author's moral position. That aside, the author avoids any moral judgment or censure, blame or praise, when he easily could have inserted such remarks. Indeed many responsa from many periods reflect a measure of express moral opinion along with the required explication of the law. Its absence in this case, where one might expect it, is a minor mystery. I suppose that one could infer something from this apparent silence, but I prefer not to infer anything.

The absence of a clear moral position leads us, however, to a further consideration. The *halakhah*, not to mention the non-legal portions of Jewish tradition, discloses a highly refined sense of fairness and ethical perspective. This requires no supportive detail here; examples abound. But fairness and ethics are not mutually exclusive of tough-mindedness, and it seems that this responsum is a case in point. The law strives to protect many interests. The values of public order, maintenance of the peace, and respect for the officers of the community are also to be prized and defended. *Shulḥan Arukh Ḥoshen Mishpaṭ* 8:4, 5, among other texts, emphasize this. The degree of protection these values receive can, so it seems, take an extreme form. The right to protect one's person and property goes so far as to allow 100 blows with the blade of a hoe under certain circumstances, and certainly the officers charged with the duty of maintaining public order enjoy the same rights, if not greater ones, to resort to force if necessary. Thus we may infer that the Jewish legal tradition has a rather high tolerance for violence in the protection of peace and order.[4] Violence, when necessary, is not to be avoided. It is as

---

[4] One of the participants suggested to me privately that the inference that "the Jewish legal tradition has a rather high tolerance for violence in the protection of peace and order" is questionable if it is based upon this one responsum, which, admittedly, appears to be unique. Indeed, it was suggested that a responsum by its nature represents, by and large, the unusual, and therefore a single text is not too solid a basis for inference, particularly in regard to a matter as delicate as what Jewish tradition would or could say today about violence under color of authority and police use of excessive force. The remark is a thoughtful one and merits consideration.

First, the apparent uniqueness of this responsum really tells us nothing about the frequency of violence in the Jewish communities of Europe or elsewhere prior to the projected date of the responsum. Since the text mentions no other responsa on the matter, one gathers that such material was scarce at best. Yet medieval society did have a violent side and there are enough responsa extant that clearly show Jews involved in fights and homicide. Perhaps the matter was settled in the streets or did not require a learned rabbinic disquisition to settle outstanding matters. Further, we should not expect, nor do we find, that Jewish communities had a regular police force in any modern sense.

The London metropolitan police are generally held to be the first such force, and they were organized in 1829. Thus it follows that Jewish legal literature discloses no significant corpus of rule on police and police procedures. Yet the *halakhah* does refer to the matter of "disrespect to the officer of the court." The mere presence of such a punishable offence puts us on notice that acts of disrespect could, and no doubt did, occur.

What is clear from this one text, even if we take it as record of a unique instance, is that, to a greater or lesser extent, violence in defense of public order was approved. There was no ground in the legal tradition to reject it out of hand as inherently repugnant. The tradition, in fine, showed a rather high tolerance for it. At least, there is a place for it; it is not to be avoided, as improper or un-Jewish. This inference is not, however, a last word on what other attitudes the Jewish legal tradition, interpreted today, might reveal towards

legitimate a part of the system as any other means of protecting life and property. This tolerance is not of course to be taken as a license for all manner of untrammeled force in any situation. I shall not specify what this tolerance for violence implies in our own society. You can do that for yourselves if you wish. We should, however, be aware that Jewish law neither requires nor constrains us to take a single uncomplicated view of self-protection or of police power. The community also has rights, and these are enforced by, among others, the police agencies.

Finally, we may observe that when and if a community feels it must sanction excessive violence by its peace officers, we may raise legitimate questions concerning the stability, the morality and the future of that community. But those proper questions should be raised about specific communities and particular societies in which the excesses occur. The right to resort to force, when necessary, for the preservation of order, and the suppression of crime, remains a crucial part of society's mechanism for self-preservation and survival. If that force becomes excessive, it can be dealt with either as our author did, or by other means.

The use of excessive force, especially by the police, who are customarily trained and instructed to use minimal force, is always a serious and potentially explosive matter. Our legal tradition appears to offer us one sober and reasoned view of the problem that does not succumb to transient emotions.

---

this matter. It is only an indication of the very openness of the *halakhah* in this particularly delicate area of modern law.

GEṬ AND *GEṬ SHIḤRUR*

by

DANIELA PIATTELLI*

This paper is concerned with the history of the introduction of written documents in Jewish law, with particular reference to the document of enfranchisement of the slave (*geṭ shiḥrur*) and to its relationship with the *geṭ* of a woman. The sociological and legal relations that form the background to this development prove to be of considerable interest.

The provisions of biblical law which refer to the enslavement of a member of the Covenant community show that the relationship between the slave and his master was far closer to that between a hired labourer and his employer—where a free man voluntarily undertook the obligation to provide labour—than to that between a master and a slave whom he had bought, and who was therefore considered as property. These sources show that the status of the enslaved man did not involve any change of his position in the legal system; at the latest, he was to be restored to his family group when the year of the Jubilee came round, and his rights to his ancestral property would then be restored to him.

No legal formality was required in order to prove that the end of the period of labour had come, and that the man was therefore freed from all the bonds which had attached to the former relationship.

That is the position in the "legislative" sources.[1] The prophetic literature, however, does provide evidence that a public declaration in solemn verbal form seems to have been introduced about the period of the Exile. The Book of *Nehemia* (5:1–13) tells us that under the Persians the Jews were reduced to such a state of poverty that they were compelled to hand over their children as guarantee for the payment of debts, since they had exhausted all other forms of security. Sensitive to this problem, Nehemia convened an assembly of the people and persuaded the creditors to bind themselves before the priests, and thus in solemn form, to execute an act of remission of the debts. The act of remission was by solemn declaration; no thought seems to have been given at that time to the addition of a written document which would provide evidence of the

---

*Professore Associato di Istituzioni di Diritto Romano, Professore Incaricato di Diritti dell' antico Oriente Mediterraneo, Università di Roma (Scuolo di Perfezionamento).

[1] *Ex.* 21: 2–3, *Lev.* 35: 39–43, *Deut.* 15: 12–15.

renunciation of the creditor's rights over the debtor, let alone the restoration to the bondsman of his full legal capacity.

Another passage of prophetic literature provides further indirect evidence that thought was not yet given to the institution of a written document, even for its probative function. Invoking an image popular with the prophetic literature, the Book of *Isaiah* (50:1, 52:3) compares the relationship between God and Israel to a marriage tie. The prophet sees Israel as an unfaithful wife who has been dismissed, but not divorced; he remarks that there has been no delivery of a bill of divorce. To stress further the fact that the bond between God and His people still persists, the prophet points out that God never sold the people as slaves, since no money was paid. Nor can God be said to have intended to give up His rights over Israel, since no money had been paid to the creditors by way of ransom.

The use made by the prophet of these legal concepts in order to illustrate the character of the bond which unites God to his people shows clearly that at that period—probably towards the end of the Exile—while a written document was already constitutive of divorce, it was not yet even required evidence for the remission of a debt. The repayment of the money was the only method recognized for terminating both the debt and the form of enslavement to secure it.

The use of a solemn declaration before the priests must have constituted the earliest mechanism of giving freedom, used in order to avoid cases analogous to that described in *Jer.* 34. There, we are told that in the reign of Zedekiah the people had bound themselves to the King by means of a covenant to release all their brothers and sisters who were serving as bondsmen, at the end of the sixth year (as required in *Ex.* 21). But this covenant was only partially performed. After freeing the bondsmen, many creditors suddenly had second thoughts, and retook possession, despite the original enfranchisement. According to the sources it seems, therefore, that Jeremiah considered it could be appropriate to *require* a solemn, public declaration, in the presence of the priests, in order to ensure that freedom would not again be denied.

Social change must have brought about further consideration not only of this situation regarding enslaved members of the Covenant community, but also a wide range of other cases, such as that of slaves of foreign origin. In their case, as in that of prisoners of war, the early sources tend to stress their separation from their original ethnic groups, and to favour their incorporation as members of the Covenant community. *Gen.* 17:12-13 provides for the circumcision of a male foreign slave, and the legislation of Exodus has the circumcised slave take part in the Passover rites (*Ex.* 12:44-45), from which however the foreign slave and the foreign labourer were excluded. *Deut.* 21:10ff. deal with the woman prisoner of war whom her master wishes to keep for himself.

The provisions regarding shaving of her head, shearing of her fingernails, and stripping her of the dress she wore when captured, all constitute actions which testify to the final removal of the woman from the bonds of her original group. Here too it is a ceremonial act, and not yet a written document, which testifies to the significant change of status.

It was only to foreigners, according to the law of *Leviticus* (25:44ff.) that the term "slave" could legally be applied. Such foreign slaves alone could be the subject of a contract of sale, and once they became the property of the man who had bought them, they could remain perpetually in that condition, forming also part of his estate. The slave of foreign origin who agreed to enter the Covenant (by conversion) was in a very peculiar situation; by virtue of this act his position theoretically became equal to that of a person born into the Covenant community, but his servitude could remain permanent, unlike that of the (native) Jew who entered bondage. This situation must have prompted reflection on the part of the interpreters of the Law.

The *Damascus Document* (14:2) now tells us of a norm which forbade the sale of male or female slaves who had agreed to enter the Covenant community. Are we entitled to infer from this that they sought to overcome this difficult legal situation by treating the slave of foreign origin as if he were a free man who had placed at the disposal of another not his person but his services?

Unfortunately, the data at our disposal are too fragmentary to enable us to risk an answer. What the new discoveries do appear to show is the existence of a real interest, at least in some circles, in all those situations which could result in uncertainty as to legal status.

Apart from the passage from the Damascus document just mentioned (a passage known already from the manuscript found in the Cairo genizah), the version found in Qumran Cave IV (which contains some previously unknown sections of the Damascus Document), includes rules regarding the status of proselytes. These rules regulate the limitations on admission to the future Temple of proselytes and bastards, but may well also carry implications for the legal status of these groups in more mundane matters.

Further noteworthy evidence is provided by *Targum Onkelos* to *Leviticus* 19:20. The biblical text states that the death penalty for adultery shall not be applied when this crime is committed by a man having marital relations with a married woman slave (*shifḥah*) who had not been ransomed or freed in some other way (*vehafdeh lo nifdatah o ḥufshah lo nitan lah*). Instead, the man must merely bring a guilt offering (*asham*), since—as the text states—the woman was not freed. In Onkelos, the fact that the woman has not been ransomed or freed in any other way is interpreted as meaning that her freedom had not been granted either by money or by a document of liberation (*bekhaspa . . . bishṭar*):

uqvar arei yishkov im itta shikhvat zar'a vehi amta ahiyda liqvar ve'itpraka la itpriykat bekhaspa o heruta la ityehiyvat lah bishtar bikurta tehei la yumtun arei la ithararat

These sources cast light upon some of the discussions preserved in the rabbinical sources. For the sake of brevity, I shall mention only the Gemara to *Gittin* 4:4 (39b). There, the question is raised whether payment of money effects the liberation of a slave in the same way as does delivery of a document. On this, the opinion of the School of Rabbi Akiva is said to prevail: it is not money, but the document of liberation, which effects the manumission, according to these interpreters of the Law.

It is well known that Targum Onkelos was compiled on the basis of material coming from the School of Rabbi Akiva. Thus, by combining the talmudic evidence with that found in parallel sources, we may conclude that at least some of the controversies regarding problems of status were solved in the time of Rabbi Akiva by accepting the principle that a written document could provide the most reliable evidence of the granting of freedom, and that it therefore became in that period a necessary and sufficient condition for the attribution of the status of freedom.

Some of the most interesting evidence on this matter comes, not surprisingly, from the interpretation of the sources regarding the status of the married woman—a theme of constant concern in the legislative sources, as well as to their interpreters.

The compiler of the Book of *Deuteronomy* already considered that the safest way to eliminate any uncertainty regarding the status of a lawful wife—as to whether she was now free or remained still married—consisted in the handing to her of a bill of divorce. This act alone entitled her to seek the repayment of the *mohar* and restored to her the capacity to contract a new marriage in the future.

Later on, under the Hasmonaeans, and thus in the period of the greatest creativity of rabbinic law, fostered by the strengthening of an independent Jewish state, that concern was expressed in a well-known legal provision introduced by Shimon ben Shetah. In order to protect the legal wife against unjustified divorce by the husband, his obligation to repay the *mohar* was equated to any other obligation arising from debt, in that it was to be guaranteed through the insertion in the document attesting to the existence of the debt of a clause which provided a legal mortgage over all the property of the divorcing spouse.

In the period of Rabbi Akiva, the document of liberation must equally have been considered the safest means to determine the status— free or slave—of a woman who was guilty of forbidden relations; when the woman had previously been enslaved, the document of liberation was thus the only means by which the judge could decide whether the offenders had committed the crime of adultery.

Given that the *get* and the *get shiḥrur* were responsive to conceptually analogous objectives, it is natural that they were built up according to a substantially identical pattern.

The documents from the Judaean Desert tell us that by the time of the last Jewish revolt against Rome, the pattern of the divorce (*get*) had already been completely elaborated. Although thus far we have no comparable new discoveries of documents of liberation, it may perhaps not be too risky to suppose that the pattern of the *get shiḥrur* was also at least well on the way towards complete elaboration.

It seems possible that external factors may have hastened this process of elaboration. The problem of exact ascertainment of the status of a free man or slave must have been felt all the more urgently once the Jewish communities lost not only sovereignty, but also autonomy. For then, certainty of status became a necessity not only within the Jewish legal system, but also for its external effects, in ascertaining whether an individual belonged to a recognized religious community or not.

We should not underestimate the importance of the fact that the earliest traces of a document of liberation of a slave are found only in biblical commentaries, such as Targum Onkelos; or of the fact that the rabbinic sources seem to agree in pointing to Rabbi Akiva (active under Hadrian) as the interpreter of the Law whose opinion was unanimously accepted, and to whom we owe the earliest systematisation of the subject.

This same problem probably affected not only the Jewish communities which had by then lost all autonomy, but also the newly-formed Christian communities. With regard to the latter, the Church Fathers provide information which, properly evaluated, may throw light on the period before the first Constitutions of the Christian emperors on the subject.

In Epistle 185, *de correctione Donatistarum* (*P.L.* 33, c.799), Augustine writes a few words which are full of meaning from the historical and legal points of view:

> Timore fustium et incendiorum mortisque praesentis, pessimorum servorum, ut liberi abscederent, tabulae frangebantur. debitoribus chirographa reddebantur.

In moments of danger, says Augustine, slaves could be freed by breaking the tablets of their enslavement, and debts could be cancelled by returning the (creditor's part[2] of the) chirograph. History tells us that such events really took place. Josephus (*Bell. Jud.* 2:427) recounts that in 66 C.E., as the Roman siege became intensified, the archives of Jerusalem were put to flame in order to eliminate all traces of debt.

---

[2] See *Tobit* 5:1–3, Pseudo-Asconius, in *Verr.* 2, 1, 9; and further D. Piattelli, *Concezioni Giuridiche e Metodi Costruttivi dei Giuristi Orientali* (Milan: Giuffrè, 1981), 159, 177.

Returning to the more strictly legal aspect of the matter, we must integrate Augustine's formulation with the more detailed description of the rules governing manumission of a slave in Church, which Augustine himself provides in another work:

> Servum tuum manumittendum manu ducis in Ecclesiam. Fit silentium, libellus tuus recitatur, aut fit desiderii tui prosecutio. Dicis te servum manumittere, quod tibi in omnibus servaverit fidem ... Ut manumittas servum tuum, frangis tabulas eius (*Serm.* 21, 6, *P.L.* 38, c. 145).

So the servant was presented *in Ecclesia*. Before the onlookers the master read the document and, to show his will that the servant be freed, broke the tablets attesting the status of slavery.

This is not the occasion on which to discuss the problems inherent in *manumissio in Ecclesia*, and the analogy between it and liberation in the Synagogue which seems to have been widespread amongst Jewish communities living in the diaspora right up to the second century C.E., according to papyrological and epigraphic sources. It is impossible to deal with these problems without a preliminary study of the ultimate ties of these institutions with liberation in the Temple, which had been widespread in the East since the most ancient times. What matters for present purposes is the fact that we may infer the existence amongst the Christian communities of a practice of drawing up written documents. Given this practice, it became possible to require the reading of this document in the course of *manumissio in Ecclesia*.

We may rightly conclude that the practice of drawing up such written documents reflected provincial customs. It was unknown to the Romans themselves, who adopted it in their legal transactions only at a later period, under the influence of peoples for whom the written form constituted the very essence of the contract. In particular, the written document (or chirograph) to which Augustine alludes was widely used in the provinces to provide evidence of the existence of a debt. Roman soldiers living in the provinces also made use of it. We have only to recall *P. Mur.* 18, of 171 C.E., which is precisely this—a chirograph attesting the existence of a money loan contracted by a Roman soldier, who probably belonged to the 10th legion Fretensis, stationed perhaps in the toparchy of Herodium or in that of Ein-Gedi.

The peculiar character of the chirograph lies in the fact that it is a private written document. Its probative value is therefore far inferior to that of deeds drawn up before a public official in a public registry, as is the case for example with the documents coming from Dura Europos. One can readily understand that the value of the chirograph was limited strictly to its recognition in church, and that it was certainly not possible to obtain through it the Roman citizenship which normally came with the granting of freedom. Imperial sanction was needed in order to confer upon the chirograph this latter function. Such imperial sanction was perhaps conferred by the constitution of Constantine in 316, which is incorporated in the Justinianic Code under the rubric *de his qui in ecclesiis manumittuntur* (C.1,13,1). Here, the emperor declares legal the fact that:

> propter memoriam facti vice actorum interponantur, qualiscumque scriptura, in qua ipsi vice testium signent.

To provide evidence of an event it was sufficient, instead of witnesses, to have writing, the signatures on which will themselves serve as witnesses.

COERCION IN CONJUGAL RELATIONS

by

NAHUM RAKOVER*

A. Introduction

The right of a man to have sexual relations with his wife against her will has come under legislative discussion in recent years in Israel.

According to section 152(1)(a) of the Criminal Law Ordinance of 1936, "Any person who (a) has unlawful sexual intercourse with a female against her will by the use of force or threats of death or severe bodily harm, or when she is in a state of unconsciousness or otherwise incapable of resisting . . . is guilty of a felony and is liable to imprisonment for fourteen years. If such felony is committed under paragraph (a) hereof it is termed rape."

This section was replaced by section 345 (marginally headed "Rape") of the Penal Law, 1977. (This Law is a consolidated version of existing statutory criminal law, prepared by the Constitution, Law and Justice Committee of the Knesset under its general power but without authority to change the substance.[1]) Section 345 originally read as follows: "A person who has sexual intercourse with a female, not being his wife, against her will by the use of force or threats of death or severe bodily harm . . . is liable to imprisonment for fourteen years."

The original term "unlawful" was thus construed in the 1977 version so as to exclude from the offence of rape involuntary intercourse during marriage, on the view that "rape" of a wife is not "unlawful." When objection was raised to this assumption of the role of interpreter, there were second thoughts by the Knesset and "unlawful" was restored and "not being his wife" deleted from the final text of the 1977 law.[2]

That, however, still left open the question whether to force intercourse upon one's wife was an offence under the Penal Law or, indeed, rape at all.[3] Later in 1978 a Knesset committee, dealing with possible

---

*Deputy Attorney-General, State of Israel; Professor, Bar-Ilan University.

[1] Sec. 16(e) of the Law and Administration Ordinance, 1948.

[2] See sec. 16(h) *ibid.*

[3] See *Abu-el Kia'an v. Attorney General* (1954) 18 *PD* (IV) 200 and *Khatib v. Attorney General* (1960) 20 *PD* (II) 136.

changes in the law of rape, was divided over retaining "unlawful" in section 345 of the Penal Law.[4]

This aspect of the matter was subsequently considered by the Ministry of Justice in connection with a Bill for a sexual offences enactment, in the relevant section of which "unlawful" does not appear. The introduction to this Bill now before the Knesset emphasises that marriage is no defence to a charge of rape.

The present study is concerned with the position taken by the Jewish law, the *Halakhah*, in this regard. The subject, almost inevitably, falls into two parts. First, does a wife owe her husband any duty to have sexual relations and, if so, the extent of the duty? Secondly, is the duty, if it exists, enforceable? The effect this study has had upon Israeli case law and the recent legislative proposal is set out in an appendix.

B. *The Duty to have Sexual Relations—Source and Nature*

1. *The Duty of the Husband*

The duty which a husband bears towards his wife in respect of sexual relations is derived from Scripture (contrary, as we shall see, to the wife's corresponding duty). According to *Exodus* xxi, 10, "*she'erah kesutah ve'onatah lo yigra*," usually translated as "her food, her raiment and her conjugal rights he shall not diminish." Some of the authorities seek to base the husband's duty on the term *onatah*, others on the term *she'erah*, and still others derive it by logical inference.[5]

There is also the view of R. Eliezer b. Yaakov in the Talmud which, as understood by a Gaonic authority, obviates the need for any scriptural proof text.[6] This view has been explained by a leading rabbi of the last century, the Netziv of Volozhin, in the following manner: "Reason tells us that (the man) is so bound. It is, as we well know, for this purpose that a bride enters into marriage, and she is forbidden to find her pleasure elsewhere because of her husband. Hence, if he denies her sexual relations, she is deprived of her right. Even for denying her the pleasure of bearing children, he may be compelled to divorce her and pay her

---

[4] The committee's conclusions (Part 2) were submitted to the Ninth Knesset on 14 June 1978.

[5] *Mekhilta de R. Yishmael, Mishpaṭim* 3 (Horowitz-Rabin ed.), 258–59, "*ve'onatah* means sexual relations according to R. Yoshiah. R. Jonathan said: How do we know sexual relations? By inference—since the matters for which *ab initio* she was not married may not be diminished, all the more so regarding that for which she was married. Rav said: *she'erah* means sexual relations." Ketubot 47a–48b.

[6] *Ketubot* 48a: *She'iltot de R. Ahai Gaon*, 60. Commentary of R. Solomon b. Shabtai Anav in *She'iltot* III, (Mirsky ed.), 187; for an identical view *cf.* Y. *Ketubot* V, 7 for the parallel passage to the *Mekhilta*, n. 5 above. According to *Sefer Yere'im* 191, the duty to have sexual relations is not biblical but rabbinical. *Semag*, Negative Precepts 81, is to the same effect.

ketubah . . . since she is not his captive to be deprived of her pleasures."[7] Here the right of the woman to sexual relations is stressed and from that follows the correlative duty of the husband.

Although the source of the husband's duty lies in the religious precept (*mitsvah*) of conjugal relations, R. Solomon b. Adrat (Spain, 1235–1310) points out that in addition spouses are mutually bound in conjugal obligations as a necessarily implied incident of marriage.[8] And he goes on to say further that the religious precept is dependent upon the obligation. In the absence of the obligation, the religious precept will not come into effect. "The religious precept arises only because of her and not him, since he is bound to her," with the result that if a husband solemnly vows to abstain from intercourse with his wife, thus putting an end to his obligation towards her, the religious precept will no longer apply to him.[9]

Discussion of the different sources to which the husband's duty is attributed is not merely an academic exercise but involves significant practical consequences. If the source is Scripture, he may be debarred from "contracting out" and any condition he may seek to introduce is a nullity.[10] If his duty rests on his presumptive obligation, the spouses may validly agree to a condition releasing the husband from maintaining conjugal relations.

Moreover, there is some authority for saying that even if the source is Scripture, release from the duty may be obtained by the woman agreeing on her part to waive its observance[11] or by stipulation prior to marriage.[12] In this view, therefore, because the duty of conjugal relations

---

[7] *Birkat HaNetziv* to the *Mekhilta ad locum*; cf. *Ha'Emek She'elah*, ibid.

[8] *Novellae* of *Rashba* to *Nedarim* 15b. Cf. *Shitah Mekubetset* to *Ketubot* 63a that sexual relations are fundamental to marriage. See also *ibid.*, 71a, and *Bah* to *Sh.Ar.E.H.* 67. Likewise, Nahmanides to *Baba Batra* 126b. Cf. also Maimonides, *Hilkhot Ishut* XIV, 6; id. *Hilkhot Nedarim* XII, 9; the apparently contrary view expressed by Maimonides in the passage preceding the last citation can be explained.

[9] See further, on the obligation of conjugal relations, B. Schereschewsky, *Family Law in Israel* (Jerusalem: Rubin Mass, 1967, 2nd ed.), 180 (in Hebrew).

[10] *Ketubot* 56a and *Rashi ad locum*. Cf. Maimonides, *Hilkhot Ishut* VI, 10, who distinguishes between sexual relations, which may not be made conditional, and the other incidents, such as matters of property, which may. Y. *Baba Metzia* VII, 7 seems to take the view that sexual relations may also be made conditional (S. Lieberman, *Tosefta Kifshuta, Kiddushin*, New York: Jewish Theological Seminary of America, 1973, III, 7 n. 29).

[11] *Resp. Tashbetz* I, 94, in dealing with conditions, observes that although the rule is that if the man stipulates that he is under no obligation, the stipulation has no effect; it is otherwise, where the condition is that the woman will forego intercourse. See the *Novellae* of *Nahmanides* to *Baba Batra* 126b; K. Kahana, *Birkat Kohen*, 79.

[12] *Havat Yair* to *Rif*, *Baba Metzia* VII (54a, 5) relying on *Rashi* to infer a new rule— where a man stipulates before marriage that his wife should not be entitled to food, raiment and conjugal rights from him, the stipulation (even as regards conjugal rights) will be valid.

is *jus dispositivum and not o jus cogens*, it depends on the husband.[13]

It should be noted that the *mitsvah* of conjugal relations differs in important respects from the *mitsvah* of bearing children. The former will subsist even when the latter has already been fulfilled or when for some reason the woman cannot conceive.[14] Again, whilst the husband can be released by his wife's waiver from conjugal relations, he cannot be so released from the precept to have children.[15] "The precept of conjugal relations and the precept to have children are obviously separate matters and independent of each other."[16]

2. *The Duty of the Wife*

There is no Biblical or Talmudic source which directly imposes upon a wife the duty of conjugal relations. It may, however, be inferred from the Talmudic discussion of the case of a woman taking a vow debarring her husband from having intercourse with her, where the view is taken that he need not formally annul the vow to dispose of it (as in other instances he might), since she is bound (subject) to him in this respect.

> If she vows 'The pleasure of cohabitation with me is forbidden to you,' why do we need an annulment; she is in any event bound to accord it to him? If, however, she says 'The pleasure of cohabitation with you is forbidden to me,' it is as R. Kahana stated: Where the vow is 'the pleasure of cohabitation with me is forbidden to you,' she may be compelled to cohabit; but if it is that 'The pleasure of cohabitation with you is forbidden to me,' he can annul the vow.[17]

As we observed above, Rashba explains that to be bound to have sexual relations follows from the mutual obligation of spouses to cohabit. His argument is that although the woman is not commanded to have conjugal relations, any vow by her denying them to her husband will be of no effect and for that reason will obviously not require annulment since she is bound to him.

---

[13] See *Gilyone HaShas* to *Nedarim* 15b: "it appears that the entire obligation derives from what he himself has undertaken, and if he wishes not to bind himself in this manner he is entirely free to do so. Hence it is not divinely ordained." *Cf. Rashba* as in text to n. 9 above.

[14] *Resp. Igrot Moshe, E.H.* 102: "conjugal relations do not depend on the possibility of conception but are part of a husband's obligation towards his wife, to give her pleasure and not cause her pain, just as is the case with food and raiment, as explained by *Tosafot* to *Ketubot* 47b."

[15] Maimonides, *Hilkhot Ishut* XV,1: "A woman may permit her husband after marriage to abstain from conjugal relations provided that he has fulfilled the command of 'be fruitful and multiply' by having children. Otherwise he remains bound by the obligation until children are born to him, for that is a positive commandment of the Torah."

[16] *Maggid Mishneh ad locum.*

[17] *Nedarim* 81b; see also 15b and *Ketubot* 71b and text to n. 42 below.

R. Abraham MinHahar (Carpentras, fourteenth century) regarded this "servitude" as a concomitant of the kinyan of sexual relations based on the term "take" in the verse "if any man take a wife" (*Deut.* xxii, 13).[18]

A similar approach is taken by the Netziv of Volozhin in explaining that kinyan in the context of marriage involves being bound only as regards sexual relations.[19] Beyond that, no kinyan occurs. Accordingly, if a wife takes a vow prohibiting her husband from having sexual relations with her, formal annulment of the vow by the husband is unnecessary and she will be compelled to yield to him, since it is for this purpose that she was "taken." When Scripture speaks of "the purchase of his money" (*Lev.* xxii, 11)[20] in connection with the acquisition of servants, that goes only to the fruits of their labour. Similarly, a wife is only subject to her husband with regard to conjugal relations,[21] because although a wife is generally compared to her husband's servants, it was clear to the Sages that whatever she earned by her own labours belonged to her and therefore the only matter in which she was subject to him (like his servants) was in regard to conjugal relations.

As regards such conjugal relations, whilst the man cannot forbid himself intercourse in contravention of the explicit precept "her conjugal rights he shall not diminish," no similar prohibition affects the woman. Her duty in this regard is implied from the verse "if any man take a wife and go in unto her" (*Deut.* xxii, 13). Hence for this purpose alone is she "taken" by him.[22]

3. *Conjugal Relations when the Husband is Repulsive to his Wife*

It would appear from Maimonides that the wife's obligation to permit conjugal relations is limited. "A woman who denies her husband sexual relations is called a *moredet* (a rebellious wife). If, upon being asked why she has rebelled, she replies that her husband has become repulsive to her and she cannot willingly cohabit with him, the husband

---

[18] Commentary to *Nedarim* 15b, *cf. RaN* to *Nedarim* 20b and *Shitah Mekubetset, ibid.*, to the effect that a man may do as he pleases with his wife since the Torah places her in his possession (kinyan).

[19] In this regard, see *Novellae* of *Rashba* to *Gittin* 75a; Resp. *Mahane Hayyim* II, E.H. 44; Resp. *Sho'el u-Meshiv* III, iii, 9 (*ad finem*).

[20] See *Yevamot* 66a.

[21] *Torah Temimah* to *Lev.* xxii, 11: "the term kinyan applies to all things that come to a person by right and not merely those he acquires by money purchase (as in *Ruth* iv, 5, 10) but this does not mean that a wife is in reality something purchased like a slave, since a slave becomes the absolute property of his master whereas only the income of the wife's possessions are acquired by her husband and that not according to Biblical law but by rabbinical takanah."

[22] Resp. *Meshiv Davar* IV, 35.

will be compelled duly to release her since she is unlike a captive woman with whom he may cohabit despite her aversion."[23]

Whilst many of the early authorities are not in agreement with Maimonides, that the man must give his wife a divorce in these circumstances,[24] they uphold the underlying principle that the woman's obligation ceases when she finds him repulsive.[25,26]

Moreover, the implication of Maimonides' formulation of the rule is that a woman will only become a *moredet* if she denies her husband conjugal relations in order to aggrieve him. This aspect is repeated a number of times by Maimonides in regard to a woman being declared a *moredet* and to her duty to permit conjugal relations. "If she has rebelled against her husband in order to aggrieve him, saying that she has done so because he acted in some way or other. . . ."[27] "She is treated in this manner if she has rebelled in order to cause him anguish."[28] And in speaking of her obligation, "The Sages also commanded the wife to be chaste in the

---

[23] Maimonides, *Hilkhot Ishut* XIV, 8.

[24] On the various views relating to compulsory divorce on the grounds of "repulsiveness," see M. Shapira, "Divorce for Reason of Repulsiveness," *Diné Israel* 2 (1971), 117–53; Z. Warhaftig, "Compulsory Divorce in Practice," *Shenaton HaMishpat HaIvri* 3–4 (1976–77), 153–216, at 183; A. Halevi-Hurwitz, *Kuntres HaBerurim* (1975).

[25] It could be advanced that in Maimonides' view the wife's plea that her husband is repulsive to her does not release her from conjugal relations and these remain in full effect, but because he is hateful to her and she is therefore unable willingly to have sexual relations with him she is entitled to a divorce to release her from her duties. (Divorce, however, is not merely to protect the woman against involuntary relations since, were it so, in the event of there being no suggestion of that, he could not be compelled to give her a *get* and the wife would be entitled to conjugal relations, but because she does not obtain satisfaction by reason of his repulsiveness she becomes entitled to a divorce.) To this argument, it may be said that even assuming that it is correct, *Rema* in fact decides that where a woman has good grounds for the plea of repulsiveness, she may be allowed separation from her husband (Sh.Ar.E.H. 77, 3) and therefore she is under no obligation to maintain conjugal relations. (This form of separation must be distinguished from that where it is a woman's right, approved by the court, to live apart from her husband in another place until the matrimonial residence is changed, or where the husband applies to court. In these cases separation does not arise in order to negate the husband's right to conjugal relations: see M. Corinaldi, "The Relief of Temporary Separation . . . and its development in the Rabbinical Courts," *Shenaton HaMishpat HaIvri* (1974), 184–218; Warhaftig, *supra* n. 24, at 169–72.)

[26] See Rabbinical Courts Judgments I ,327, citing *Bene Ahuvah* to Maimonides, *Hilkhot Ishut* XIV, 15, who maintains that according to Maimonides a wife is not in the same category as a captured woman, nor equally when the husband claims she is distasteful to him will he be held captive to her. The court reasoned that in such a case the husband has no need to force himself upon her if she is so distasteful, whereas in the reverse situation the wife suffers greatly and needs protection. The court, however, did not deal with the question whether the husband may lawfully compel his wife to submit to his advances.

[27] Maimonides, *Hilkhot Ishut* XIV, 9. See text to n. 36 below.

[28] *Ibid.*, XIV, 11–12 ("a betrothed woman who refuses to marry in order to hurt the man is truly a *moredet*").

home . . . and not refuse her husband in order to pain him . . . but at all times attend to his wishes."[29,30]

The view that a wife is not subject in any way to her husband in their conjugal relations is apparently taken by R. Moses b. Joseph of Trani, *Mabit* (Safad, 1500–1580). In his *Kiryat Sefer* on Maimonides, he writes: "The *moredet* who says her husband is repulsive or that she wishes to pain him for some reason or another is not compelled to cohabit with him since she is unlike a captive woman who can be compelled to submit to sexual relations with a man she does not desire. Just as she is not to be compelled to accept food and raiment if she does not wish to be maintained (by her husband), so also with regard to conjugal rights. Alternatively, Scripture speaks of 'her conjugal rights' and not simply of 'conjugal rights,' with the result that these depend on her own free will; the rights are hers and not the husband's."[31]

That the wife cannot be compelled to have sexual relations and the right is hers exclusively must not, however, be taken literally, since a woman who refuses sexual relations to her husband may well be declared a *moredet*, with all that involves.[32] *Mabit* must therefore be taken to have in mind only the matter of compulsion but no further; the right is equally that of the husband and sanctions will attend impairment of that right.

---

[29] *Ibid.*, XV, 18. *Cf.* the difficulties raised by *Hagahot Maimoniyot* from *Shabbat* 140b and by *Leḥem Mishneh, ad locum*, and the solution suggested by *Birke Yosef* to *Sh.Ar.E.H.* 15, 3 and *Ma'aseh Roke'ah* to Maimonides, *ad locum*. According to *Eliyahu Rabba* to *Sh.Ar.O.H.* 240, 17, it is a serious transgression for a woman to ask, even jokingly, for some material consideration before allowing intimacy.

[30] Equally regarding the husband's duty to his wife, Maimonides lays down that the husband will transgress the negative precept in *Ex.* xxi, 10, if he denies her in order to cause her distress; *Hilkhot Ishut* XIV, 7. See also his *Sefer HaMitzvot*, Negative Commandment 262. *Sh.Ar.E.H.* 76, 11, is to the same effect. According to *Resp. Alshekh*, 50, a transgression will also occur when the husband has no intention of aggrieving his wife. See in addition *Be'er Hetev* to *Sh.Ar.E.H.* 100, 16, and *Ma'ase Roke'ah* to Maimonides, *Hilkhot Ishut* XIV, 7. According to *Ritba*, cited in *Shitah Mekubetset* to *Ketubot* 48b, a husband's refusal to have intercourse when unclothed for reasons of modesty will make a *get* exigible from him; in the same circumstances, the wife will be treated as a *moredet*, "for this is not the way of love." See also a response of HaRav Kook printed in *Tehumin* I, 9–10, and Kanievski, n. 68 below.

Resp. Maḥane Ḥayyim (R. Ḥayyim Sofer) *E.H.* II, 41, distinguishes between permanent and temporary rebelliousness: the latter occurs when the intention is to cause pain, the former when there is no such intention. (According to *Maḥane Ḥayyim*, *Onah* consists of the act of intimacy. See *Resp. Ketav Sofer E.H.* 102 and Rabbinical Courts Judgments I, 344.)

[31] *Kiryat Sefer* to Maimonides, *Hilkhot Ishut* XIV. See text to n. 37 below.

[32] Further on the law relating to the *moredet*, see Scherescheswky, *supra* n. 9, at 185 *et seq.*

C. Compulsion of the Wife

1. General—the Absence of Consent

We have seen that in some circumstances (as when the husband is repulsive to her) a woman is not under obligation to be intimate with her husband. Where, however, the obligation is fully effective the question arises whether the husband may, so to speak, take the law into his own hands and enforce the obligation by forcing himself upon her and ravishing her. Apart from the whole problem of "self-help" in Jewish law, it is enough to say that forcible sexual relations differ so substantially from voluntary relations that they do not constitute "self-help" and effectuation of the right to voluntary cohabitation.

The answer to the question posed above is to be found in the source of the obligation generally. As we said earlier, the source lies in the obligations undertaken by a woman on entering into marriage and its scope must be delimited accordingly. Any agreement by the woman on that occasion to her husband having his desire against her wish forcibly will clearly be of no effect.[33] We need not discuss the validity of an express condition between spouses regarding involuntary sexual relations or the effect of such a condition should the woman subsequently retract.[34] Assuming even that the condition takes effect and that the woman may not go back on it, is it to be implied from the very existence of marriage? The answer is that although the woman's duty is a necessary concomitant of marriage, there is no condition implied that he may ravish her.[35]

---

[33] Even were it contended that in earlier times a woman would consent to forcible intercourse, it is the existing situation as it is today that concerns us.

[34] On the application of the negative commandment, "thou shalt not add thereto" (*Deut.* iv, 2; xiii, 1), see the observations of Luria, n. 35 below. The view of Luria given by the Talmudic Encyclopedia, title "*Ḥovel*" (XII, 681, n. 23, and 683–84), that waiver is effective, is not acceptable. Even in the absence of such a negative commandment, a person cannot stipulate irrevocably to suffer in his or her person, mentally or physically, and may therefore always resile from the stipulation. See the distinction made by Abulafia, *Yad Ramah* to *Baba Batra* II, 80, between the acquisition by submission of a right that affects property adversely (*ḥazakah*) and a similar right affecting a person as such (or to create a serious nuisance like malodour or to invade a person's privacy). The distinction and the "victim's" right to abrogate any conditions that might have been made voluntarily are explained more fully and succinctly by Nahmanides, *Novellae* to *Baba Batra* 59a.

[35] *Cf.* Luria, *Yam shel Shlomo* to *Baba Kamma* III, 21, who demonstrates that the Talmudic rule that a husband is liable to damages for hurting his wife physically during intercourse applies with equal force to other circumstances, even under provocation, on the presumed ground that by virtue of marriage she is under the implied obligation to hearken to his wishes. Even if a condition in this regard were to be implied by entering marriage, it would have no effect since it would be in contravention of "Thou shalt not add thereto." The rule, Luria adds, applies to intercourse which is clearly basic to marriage; a man must control and moderate his desires and not hurt his wife; *a fortiori* in any other situation.

What then, it may be asked, is the value of the woman's obligation if it depends on her own free will to have intercourse? What is there to prevent her from "blackmailing" her husband and obtaining benefits in consideration of their cohabiting? Although the woman must agree and in this sense is "bound" to do so, and non-compliance may entail sanctions, the conjugal relations may not occur through physical force; they may only be "coerced" through the legal measures prescribed in the case of a *moredet*, the loss of the value of her *ketubah* and of her other rights, and delivery of a *get*. As Maimonides put it, "If she has rebelled against her husband in order to aggrieve him, saying that she has done so because he acted in some way or another or because he reviled her or because he provoked quarrels with her and the like, she is to be warned by the *bet din* that if she persists in her rebellion, she might well incur the loss of her *ketubah*."[36]

2. Refusal of the Woman to Cohabit

(a) Where a refusal to cohabit is not such as to distress her husband grievously and is indeed justified, a wife will not necessarily lose any of her rights since she is not bound to cohabit in circumstances such as these.

Thus, with regard to the frequency of cohabitation, R. Joseph of Trani, *Maharit* (Turkey, 1568–1639) took the view that the wife's duty is proportionate to the husband's duty to maintain conjugal relations (in accordance with his calling and status as explained in *Mishnah Ketubot* V,6), and no more, since she is not captive to him to have intercourse at all times. "Certainly she is not subject to him incessantly when she does not wish it, and she will not become a *moredet* unless she contends that he is repulsive to her or distresses her but if she claims that she need only submit to conjugal relations on the occasions prescribed by the Torah she may not, it seems, be compelled."[37]

R. Rafael Aaron b. Shimon in his *Bat Na'avat HaMardut* reports a case that came before his *bet din* in Egypt, in which on a complaint that the husband came to her incessantly during the night, leaving her intolerably sleepless and exhausted, the wife was not declared a *moredet* and was exonerated from refusing intercourse; she was also permitted to claim divorce without loss of any of her rights, although the husband insisted that as the woman was his lawful wife his desires had to be met in accordance with Scripture.[38] The circumstances showed that the woman was suffering real torment and that the husband was behaving like an animal.

---

[36] Maimonides, *Hilkhot Ishut* XIV, 9. See text to n. 27 above.
[37] *Resp. Maharit* I, 5, cited in *Kenesset HaGedolah E.H.* 77; *Tur*, n. 7, *ibid.*, and *Be'er Hetev*, *ibid*. See also *Bat Na'avat HaMardut* (1977) II, 1.
[38] *Ibid.*, II, 2.

This judgment and the observations of *Maharit* cited above were adopted by R. Avadyah Hadayah in the Jerusalem Supreme Rabbinical Court: "A woman is not to be declared a *moredet* on the complaint of her husband when she is justified in her refusal"[39] to have excessive intercourse.

(b) We have already noted that in dealing with a *moredet* whose husband was repulsive to her Maimonides held that a wife is not the captive of her husband in matters of intercourse "to her aversion." What is the situation where aversion is not an element? According to *Mabit*, the rule is not confined to "repulsiveness" but extends to a refusal in order to cause him grievous pain. Thus a woman is released from any duty to cohabit unwillingly.[40]

R. Solomon Luria (Poland, 1510–1573), a contemporary, it may be observed, of *Mabit* of Safed, took the same view. Dealing with the case of a woman being compelled to work, he shows that Maimonides' rule that she may be chastised into obedience must give way to the remarks of *Rabad* that he had never heard of a woman being so chastised. Luria goes on to say that although according to one Talmudic authority a refusal to work may also make a wife a *moredet*, the question is why she should be penalised by being declared a *moredet* and losing her *ketubah*, if chastisement is available. The idea of a person not living in a "hornet's nest" will not apply because the husband controls his wife and may punish her. Granted that a *moredet* with regard to cohabitation cannot, we say, be chastised since she may not be forced into sexual intercourse that is obnoxious to her, but in the case of work that argument is not available.[41] From all this it follows that Luria held quite simply that a wife is not to be chastised regardless of whether she is a *moredet* because of "repulsiveness" or because she wishes to aggrieve her husband.

3. *Coerced Cohabitation*

We may now return to our Talmudic sources. It is possible perhaps to infer a right in the husband to compel his wife to fulfil her duty towards him in accordance with R. Kahana's dictum in the Talmud that where a woman forbids her husband under vow cohabitation with her, she may be compelled to cohabit.[42] The term "compelled," however, in the context of marital relations, is sometimes construed as imposing a

---

[39] *Resp. Yaskil Avdi* V, 69.
[40] Clearly this "liberty" may entail loss of her rights as a *moredet*.
[41] *Yam shel Shlomo*, Baba Kamma III, 21. *Cf.* the observations of *Resp. Divre Ḥayyim* II E.H. 41, that the rules regarding a *moredet* do not arise in the case of a woman who, though in love with her husband, "rebels" because her father finds him distasteful.
[42] *Nedarim* 81b. See text to n. 17 above.

duty contrary to the wishes of the person concerned and in the event of a refusal enforcing observance of the duty by denying that person certain of his or her rights but not by physical means. Hence R. Kahana's dictum as such cannot be understood as empowering the husband to use physical compulsion.[43]

Thus, for example, regarding the duty to live in Israel, we read:

> Where (the husband) wishes to go up (to the Land of Israel) and (the wife) does not, she may be compelled to do so; otherwise she may be divorced without her *ketubah*. If she wishes to go up and he does not, he may be compelled to do so; otherwise he must divorce her and give her her *ketubah*.[44]

On this passage, R. Shimon b. Zemah Duran (Algiers, 1361–1444) commented: "This compulsion is only financial, the loss of the *ketubah*, physical chastisement not being mentioned but divorce. Wherever compulsion is mentioned without divorce it is financial."[45]

The exclusion of physical chastisement is not restricted to those cases where the express sanction is loss of the *ketubah* or divorce with the *ketubah*, but it applies generally; where compulsion is mentioned without divorce, it is of a financial nature.[46]

The term "compelled" also occurs in connection with the work which a woman is bound to perform, and opinion is divided over its precise meaning. According to the *Mishnah*:

> R. Eliezer said that even if she brought (her husband) a hundred bondswomen, he may compel her to work in wool since idleness leads to unchastity.[47]

Maimonides holds that "they compel any woman who refuses to work at anything she is under obligation to perform, even by physical chastisement."[48] To this *Rabad* objected, "I have never heard of women

---

[43] A. Wasserman, *Kovetz Shi'urim* to *Ketubot* (Lithuania, 20th cent.), 231, finds the term "compel" difficult, since her children would be the issue of ravishment, included in the nine groups referred to in *Nedarim* 20b (see text to n. 60 below). This difficulty is, however, dispelled by the view taken in the text.

[44] *Ketubot* 110b, the source of which is *Tosefta Ketubot* XII, 5, where the reference to divorce and the *ketubah* does not, however, appear.

[45] *Resp. Tashbetz* III, 86.

[46] See *Resp. Mabit* I, 139, and Rabbinical Courts Judgments I, 98. According to *Resp. Rashba* I, 1192, where a woman urges that she wants to bear a son who will support her in old age, her husband will not be actually compelled to divorce her in spite of the reference in *Yevamot* 65 to compulsion where it is taken to be financial, her *ketubah* being supplemented. See also *Resp. Rosh* 53, 6.

[47] M. *Ketubot* V, 5 (*Ketubot* 59b). At 61b as well it is stated: "For it was taught: (the husband) may not compel her to wait upon his father . . . but he may compel her to feed straw to his cattle. R. Judah said: Nor may he compel her to work flax."

[48] Maimonides, *Hilkhot Ishut* XXI, 10.

being physically chastised; instead their requirments and maintenance are reduced until they give way."[49] Maimonides, however, does not permit the husband to do the compelling himself but assigns the process to the court;[50] as he says, "they compel, etc." As we observed above, Maimonides rules that a woman who pleads her husband's repulsiveness as the reason for not having intercourse is released from her obligation in this regard since she is not his captive.

4. "*A man may do whatever he wishes with his wife*"

There is another source that requires examination:

> R. Johanan said the Sages held that the law does not follow the view of Johanan b. Dahabai, but a man may do whatever he wishes with his wife.[51]

That "a man may do whatever he wishes with his wife" would suggest that he has no need to obtain the wife's consent to intercourse. This, however, is not the case, as emerges from the development of the argument in the *Gemara*. The argument begins with a statement by Johanan b. Dahabai:

> The Ministering Angels told me four things: people are born lame because (their parents) overturned their table (practiced unnatural intercourse), dumb because they kiss "that place," deaf because they converse during cohabitation and blind because they look at "that place."

This means a person may not follow these practices and if he does the issue he may have will be maimed in one way or another. To this, R. Johanan asserts as above, implying that these practices are not morally reprehensible and no dire results need be feared. It is in this sense that his remark is to be understood since there is nothing in the *Gemara* to indicate that a wife may be forced to submit to the practices mentioned.

---

[49] Cf. Rabad,' *HaSagot* to Maimonides, *loc. cit.*, and his remarks cited in *Ritba*, *Novellae* and *Shitah Mekubetset* to *Ketubot* 63a, that in the view of R. Huna a woman who refuses to work is not treated as a *moredet*. "But if her *ketubah* cannot be reduced, how is she to be compelled? Mere words will be of no avail. To use the rod and the scourge is not something one does to a woman. Compulsion is therefore only exercisable through the *ketubah*." See *Migdal Oz* on this passage.

[50] Me'iri, *Bet HaBeḥirah* to *Ketubot* 63a, notes in the name of Maimonides that he may himself compel her by beating and imprecation. *Yam shel Shlomo* to *Baba Kamma* III, 21, also notes that Maimonides permits the husband himself to use physical force, if his wife refuses to work, just as a master may compel his servant. See *Ma'ase Roke'aḥ* to Maimonides, *ad locum*.

[51] *Nedarim* 20b. See *Rosh ad locum* on the meaning of "overturning the table."

5. Unnatural Cohabitation

The view that a woman cannot be forced into having sexual relations is not inconsistent with the foregoing. The *Gemara* immediately goes on to tell of

> A woman (who) appeared before Rabbi and complained, 'I set a table before my husband but he overturned it,' to which Rabbi replied, 'My daughter! The Torah has permitted you (to him) and what can I do for you?' A woman appeared before Rav and complained 'Rabbi, I set a table before my husband but he overturned it,' and Rav replied 'How does it differ from a *binita* (a small fish which may be cooked any way one wishes)?'

Here again there is no mention of intercourse being carried out by force. The fact that the women complained can be explained by their apprehension that their respective husbands were not allowed to act in the manner indicated, but not that they were in fact opposed to such cohabitation. The only inference to be drawn is that a woman must agree, but not that the man may thus force himself upon her against her wishes.[52]

This is what *Rabad* has to say in the matter. The unnatural practices which the sages permitted may only occur when a wife has been persuaded to indulge in them. If, however, they are forced upon her, he is certainly a sinner of whom it is said, "the soul that is without knowledge is also not good" (*Prov.* xix, 2). The second part of this verse, "And he that hasteth with his feet sinneth," the Sages observed, refers to a man who insists on repeated intercourse. It is he who is called a sinner even when he wishes thereby to ensure that he has male children, *a fortiori* when he engages in unnatural practices without his wife's consent. Some authorities hold that a man may have unnatural intercourse when his wife desires intercourse but not in the particular form he wants it, thus differing from the case where he wants repeated intercourse against her wishes, since then her refusal goes not to the form of the act but to the act itself, witness the case of the woman who appeared before Rav in the account above. According to these authorities, this was a case where the woman was unwilling. *Rabad*, however, argues that that is not sufficient since it is possible that the woman was persuaded to act as she did and that all she came to ask was whether any religious prohibition was involved.[53]

---

[52] It is not to be necessarily inferred from Rabbi N. H. Z. Berlin (president of the Bet Din in Altona, Hamburg and Wandsback), *Atze Arazim* to *Sh.Ar.E.H.* 25, 1, that the husband is empowered to use force but that it depends upon the wife's wishes because she must consent, for otherwise she becomes a *moredet*. So also Netziv of Volozhin in his *Resp. Meshiv Davar* IV, 35, may be held to take the view that compulsion consists of the woman being declared a *moredet*, as explained in the text to n. 42 above.

[53] *Ba'ale HaNefesh, Sha'ar HaKedushah* (Ka'apah ed.), 122–23. See the comment of *RaN* mentioned in n. 18 above. Apparently he does not permit this to be done forcefully. See also *Resp. Igrot Moshe E.H.* 63, 3.

Rabad's view that a woman may not be compelled to have abnormal intercourse is cited as the law in *Ṭur*.[54]

A stringent decision is reported by R. Elazar Azkari. "Here in Zefat in the year 5308 (1548) a woman appeared before R. Joseph Karo, R. Isaac Masud, R. Abraham Shalom, R. Joseph Shagis and a number of other rabbis and complained that her husband had unnatural intercourse with her, and they excommunicated and publicly disgraced him, saying that he ought to be burnt at the stake. Finally they expelled him from Eretz Yisrael."[55]

In a later case, a woman who "rebelled" against her husband because he indulged in unnatural intercourse with her was held not to be a *moredet* and the husband was ordered to divorce her. "Where the man is evil in his deeds and always has unnatural intercourse, as in sodomy, God forbid, and it is known that the woman suffered very much physically, and this had been going on for so long a time that she could no longer bear it and rebelled against him because he was repulsive,[56] in these circumstances, R. Abraham di Boton (the author of the commentary *Leḥem Mishneh* on Maimonides) decided that the woman was not a *moredet* at all and must be given a divorce without loss of her *ketubah* and her interim maintenance, since the situation was irremediable and the intimacies of marital life could not be supervised."[57]

R. Avadyah Hadayah held similarly in a case involving an appeal of a woman who complained of unnatural cohabitation. After citing the view of *Rabad*, that the woman's consent is essential for the practice to be permissible, he went on to say that "even those who would permit it do so only when the woman is willing, but if a husband forces it upon the woman he is called a sinner. . . . All the more so when a man indulges excessively in unnatural intercourse against the wife's wishes."[58]

6. *The Prohibition of Intercourse Against the Wife's Wish*

Not only is there no source to be found entitling a man to ravish his wife, but there is Talmudic authority for positively prohibiting marital

---

[54] *Tur E.H.* 25. See *Be'er Hagolah* to *Sh.Ar.E.H.* 25, 6, referring to *Shne Luḥot HaBrit* 100, which seems to rely on *Sefer Haredim* (see next note). See also *Eliyahu Rabba* to *Sh.Ar.O.H.* 240, 2.
[55] *Sefer Haredim, Mitsvat HaTeshuvah* II (*ad finem*).
[56] *Bat Na'avat HaMardut* II, 3.
[57] Resp. *Edut BeYa'akov* (R. Abraham di Boton), 36. See Resp. *Yabia Omer* V, 14, regarding exemption from providing maintenance.
[58] Resp. *Yaskil Avdi* VI, 25. See *Ben Ami* v. *A.G.* (1964) 18 *P.D.* (III) 225, 231–32, where Cohn J. points out that in contrast to the situation in England, Jewish law does not treat unnatural intercourse with a woman as an offence since it is explicitly permitted in the Talmud, citing the sources referred to in the text to nn. 51 and 52 above. But as has been explained in the text, "overturning the table" is only permissible with the woman's consent; otherwise it is forbidden by the Torah.

relations against the woman's desire:

> Rami b. Hama said in the name of R. Assi: A man is forbidden to force his wife to abide by the precept (of marital relations) since it is written "And he that hasteth with his feet sinneth" (*Prov.* xix,2). R. Joshua b. Levi stated: Whoever forces his wife to abide by the precept will have unworthy children. . . . So again was it taught: "Also without the consent the soul is not good" (*ibid.*) refers to the man who forces his wife to abide by the precept.[59]

And again, R. Levi commenting on the verse, "And I will purge out from among you the rebels and them that transgress against me" (*Ezek.* xx, 38) observed:

> This refers to children of the (following) nine categories—children of fear, children of ravishment. . . .[60]

According to *RaN ad locum*, the "rebels" and the "transgressors" are the children conceived in the course of a transgression. *Rabad*, on the other hand, interprets the verse as referring to the male participant in intercourse when either the wife was raped or the intercourse took the form of one of the above categories, both the child and the male himself being affected and the latter called a rebel and transgressor.[61]

Further, the extra-canonical tractate *Kallah* states that children born of sexual relations by ravishment suffer from defects—lameness, blindness, muteness, deafness—from their very conception, because, as R. Eliezer says, intercourse occurred without the woman wanting it, or as R. Joshua said, because during intercourse she cried out that she was being raped.[62]

Explaining the difference between these two opinions, *Rabad* remarks that it turns upon whether the woman was ultimately persuaded to have intercourse, as the passage from *Eruvin* indicates.[63]

The prohibition of intercourse by force is given as the *Halakhah* by Maimonides: "And the Sages forbade . . . a man to come upon his wife by force when she is in fear of him,"[64] or alternatively, "a man may not

---

[59] *Eruvin* 100b. According to Emden, *ad locum*, this is so although done in performance of the commandments regarding conjugal relations and the bearing of children. To the same effect Y. Kalez, *Sefer HaMusar* (Jerusalem, 1973), VI.
[60] *Nedarim* 20b.
[61] *Ab'ale HaNefesh Sha'ar HaKedushah* (Ka'apah ed.), 122. See *Bet Yoṣef* to *Sh.Ar.O.H.* 240, who so understands from *Rabad*.
[62] *Kallah* 8, cited in *Menorat HaMe'or* (Alnaqua) X and Kalez, *supra* n. 59. See also *Kallah Rabbati* I, 11.
[63] *Ba'ale HaNefesh*, *loc. cit.* See *Pri Megadim* to *Sh.Ar.O.H.* 240 and I. Seligman, *Ma'ayan Ganim* (Vilna, 1914), 6a, commentary on *Kallah*. *Rabad* is cited in *Tur O.H.* 240 and *Tur E.H.* 25.
[64] Maimonides, *Hilkhot Issure Bi'ah* XXI, 12.

ravish his wife and have intercourse by force but only when she consents and in joyful circumstances."[65] Likewise, the *Shulḥan Arukh* rules: "A man may only have intercourse when his wife is willing; if she does not desire it, he must persuade her,"[66] or again, "if he is wrathful with her, intercourse is forbidden until she is persuaded."[67]

In recent years R. Jacob Kanievski has written that "according to *din Torah* it is forbidden to have intercourse when the wife is not induced by physical contact, embrace and kisses and desires to have connection. Otherwise, as explained in *Pesahim* 49b ("just as a lion tears it prey and devours it and has no shame, so an *am ha'arets* strikes and cohabits and has no shame") it is a heinous offence to act in a manner that causes one's wife anguish even if with the best and most pious of intentions, since a man may not treat his wife as a captured slave."[68]

D. *Conclusions*

Unlike the marital duty of the husband which derives from Scripture, the corresponding duty of the wife emerges from talmudic inference as part of the obligations she undertakes on entering marriage.

This difference is of importance when defining the extent of the wife's duty. Her duty is not to be extended by implication to include submitting to ravishment since to that she certainly did not agree or undertake to tolerate when she married. Accordingly, a husband is not entitled to force sexual relations upon his wife.

On the other hand, it cannot be denied that the wife's refusal will entail sanctions, but these are remedial in the area of family law: the woman may be declared a *moredet*, she may be divorced, lose her *ketubah*, and so on.

There is nothing to confute this view in the Talmudic sources, which indeed condemn sexual compulsion itself as being sinful, although several other sexual practices are regarded as permissible. Further, cases are at hand in which the courts have actually treated with the utmost severity husbands who have forced themselves upon their wives against their wishes.

The Sages regarded unseemly relations as disrespectful of the woman and contrary to the precept that a man should honour his wife

---

[65] *Hilkhot Ishut* XV, 17. In *Hilkhot De'ot* V, 4, this rule figures among those especially recommended to the *talmid ḥaham* for conducting himself in a pure and holy manner.
[66] *E.H.* 25, 2.
[67] *O.H.* 240, 3. That the children of a hated wife may become rebels and transgressors (*Nedarim* 20) is probably the reason for not compelling a *moredet*. See *Ritba Novellae* to *Ketubot* 63b. See also *Ra'ah, Novellae, ad locum,* and *Resp. Yabia Omer* V, *E.H.* 14.
[68] *Igeret Kodesh* (Jerusalem, 1978), 7, published anonymously.

more than himself.[69] For the Sages marriage was a source not of pain and anguish but of life.[70]

APPENDIX

Originally this study took the form of an opinion written by the author at the request of counsel in the first case heard in Israel that directly raised the question of whether a man can be guilty of the rape of his wife: *Cohen v. State* of Israel (1981) 35 P.D. (III) 281. This opinion was put in before the District Court at first instance, by consent of the parties (*State of Israel v. Cohen* [1980] P.M. [1] 245).

In two earlier cases before the Supreme Court the matter had been discussed but not decided since in neither was the woman held to be the lawful spouse of the accused.

The facts in Cohen were fairly simple. The defendant was charged with having on two occasions attacked his wife with violence in order to have intercourse with her against her wish and having caused her injury; on the first occasion he had his way with her but on the second her brother came to her assistance. The parties were subsequently divorced.

In the District Court the indictment was (as well as for assault causing actual bodily harm under section 380 of the Penal Law, 1977) for rape under section 345. During arguments the facts were admitted on behalf of the accused and the claim made that these facts could not sustain a charge of rape since that was an offence that could not be committed between spouses in view of the meaning of "unlawful" in the relevant section of the local Criminal Code Ordinance and the state of the law in England and in most jurisdictions in the U.S.A. where the Common law rule generally prevailed, although some departure from it had occurred in recent times.

After considering in some detail the opinion of the present writer, the court adopted in full the conclusions at which he had arrived, more particularly the view that even if the wife's duty regarding intercourse was an implied condition of marriage, the husband had no right to compel its fulfilment by the use of force which in fact was forbidden; that of course did not preclude the remedies available to the husband in a proper case of a "rebellious wife." In the result, the defendant was convicted and sentenced to three years' imprisonment.

---

[69] *Yevamot* 62b, and Maimonides' *Hilkhot Ishut* XV, 19: "the Sages pointed out that a man should respect his wife more than himself and love her as he loves himself."
[70] *Ketubot* 61b. See *Resp. Maharam b. Baruch* (Prague ed.) 81, who condemns any man who transgresses the precept to excommunication and dire punishment. See also *Yam shel Shlomo* to *Baba Kamma* III, 21, who cites the above and expands on it; *Sh.Ar.E.H.* 154, 3 and the notes of *Rema* and *Be'er Hagolah ad locum*; *Resp. Tashbetz* III, 8; H. Palagi, *Kaf HaḤayyim* I, 11.

The defendant appealed against the conviction and the sentence. After an exhaustive analysis by Bekhor J. (who delivered the main judgment of the Court) of the relevant statutory provisions of the Penal Law, 1977, and such previous Israeli cases that were in point, the Supreme Court dismissed the appeal. The lower court was upheld in its finding that "unlawful" was a constituent element of rape. This term was to be construed by reference not merely to the enactment in which it appeared but the law generally which in this instance clearly comprehended Jewish law. "Unlawful sexual intercourse" would occur where the man had no right under law to have intercourse with the woman in question. That law included the personal law of the parties, as defined by the Palestine Order in Council of 1922; in the present case that was indisputably Jewish law. The term was not to be taken as referring merely to a woman who was not the wife of the defendant, as was evident from the amendment of section 345 of the Penal Law, 1977, passed after doubts had been voiced as to its exact import.

The Supreme Court then contrasted the position in Anglo-American law and other legal systems and referred to some of the literature on the subject. The judgment went on to cite with approval views voiced in the earlier cases highly critical of the Common law rule as being inconsistent with human rights and the institution of marriage.

Since the applicable personal law here was Jewish law, the Court carefully reviewed the present writer's opinion, its arguments and the authorities cited and found that modern enlightened views on the question accorded with the Talmudic rule that a man may not force intercourse upon his wife.

The Court also adverted to a parallel opinion by another expert, Dr. B. Lipshitz, put in by the defendant. This opinion concurred in express terms with the conclusion of the present writer but maintained that the wife's refusal did not abrogate the husband's right but merely limited it by excluding the use of coercion without attaching any legal consequences. The Court refused to adopt this understanding of the law. It accepted fully the distinction made by the present writer between the wife's refusal to fulfil her marital obligations other than that relating to intercourse and her obligation regarding intercourse. In the latter case, the use of force is expressly forbidden. The argument that, although debarred from forcing himself upon his wife, the husband is nevertheless not rendered criminally liable if in fact he does so (especially as in Jewish law no express penalty is prescribed for the act), was rejected by the Court. Intercourse will be unlawful and constitutes an offence within the meaning of secton 345 of the Penal Law, 1977, if it occurs against the wishes of the wife, is effected by the use of force, and is prohibited by the parties' personal law. A wife is a free human being, not given over to her husband's caprice.

Whilst the above appeal was pending, the Bill of the seminal *Ḥok Yeṣodot Hamishpaṭ* (Law of the Fundamentals of Law) (which in general terms replaces reference to English law under the previous rule by reference to the Jewish heritage, in the event of no solution to a problem being found in enacted law or by analogy) was debated in the Knesset. In the course of the debate and in reply to hostile criticism from certain quarters about the regressive nature of Jewish law, the then Minister of Justice, Mr. Sh. Tamir cited, *inter alia*, as a concrete example of the progressiveness of Jewish law, the District Court judgment in *Cohen* and the findings of the present opinion that the wife is not in any absolute sense bound to submit to intercourse and that if she refuses, physical coercion may not be resorted to, the only "remedy" available to the husband being to have her declared a *moredet*, by proper process of law.

DINA DEMALKHUTA DINA

by

SYLVAN JAY SCHAFFER*

One area of *halakhah*, the Jewish law, which has received relatively little attention is the principle of "*Dina demalkhuta dina*," loosely translated: "the law of the kingdom is the law." This principle has two primary applications: first, under *dina demalkhuta* certain aspects and holdings of civil law are accepted as part of the halakhic system; second, the legitimacy of certain civil legislation and requirements is recognized by *halakhah*. It should be mentioned at the outset that *dina demalkhuta* does not mean that the civil law is accepted in toto as a substitute for Jewish law. Rather, it means that certain parts of the civil law are accepted under certain circumstances to supplement the *halakhah*.

The source of *dina demalkhuta* is found in the tractate of *Gittin* (10b). The Mishnah there validated most documents executed in non-Jewish courts and attested to by non-Jews. The exceptions were documents related to emancipation and divorce. The Talmud differentiated between deeds of sale and deeds of gift. The deeds of sale attested to by non-Jews were more obviously acceptable since they were merely evidence of a transfer which was accomplished by other means, *i.e.*, money. Therefore, the validity of the deed itself was only of secondary importance. However, in a gift situation, the deed itself must be valid in order to serve as an instrument of transfer. Therefore, Samuel explained that the deed was acceptable under the principle of *dina demalkhuta*, since it was acceptable in civil courts. The *halakhah* thus utilized the civilly determined legal status of the deed to find a halakhically valid transfer.

The *Talmud*[1] mentions three other specific areas where *halakhah* accepts civil law to some degree. The first concerns the Parthian law that one cannot claim title to land until after 40 years of unchallenged ownership. Rabbi Samuel b. Meir[2] in his commentary on that rule explains that although Jewish law requires only three years of such ownership, the Parthian regulation supersedes the Jewish under *dina demalkhuta*.

---

*J.D., Ph.D., Attorney and Clinical Psychologist; Visiting Scholar at the Hastings Institute for Bioethics in Psychiatry and Law; Faculty, City University of New York; Private Practice.

[1] *B.B.* 55a.
[2] *Ibid.*

The two other areas discussed in that portion of the Talmud involve the effect of not paying taxes. In the first of these situations, the *halakhah* recognized that if one failed to pay his real property taxes he would forfeit ownership of the land to the person who did pay the taxes based on the principle of *dina demalkhuta*. In the second situation, however, the Talmud qualified this rule in a situation in which the land was to be forfeited for failure of the owner to pay the head tax. The Talmud said that in such a situation *dina demalkhuta* would not apply, since the confiscation of the land for failure to pay the head tax was arbitrary. Thus, there are some limitations on the application of this principle.

A second, related application of *dina demalkhuta* concerns the recognition by the *halakhah* of the legitimacy of legislation and actions of the civil government such as the levying and collection of taxes. Should the Jewish law require a Jew to cooperate with the collection of taxes by the civil government? The *Talmud*[3] cited Samuel's principle of *dina damalkhuta in* questioning a statement by the *Mishnah*[4] that under certain circumstances it might be permitted to evade taxes. The Talmud was concerned that this would violate *dina demalkhuta*. The answer given was that it was permitted to refuse to pay certain unjust taxes, *i.e.*, when the tax is unlimited or when the tax collector is acting without proper authority from the king.

The last point, that it is proper to ignore civil law under certain circumstances, raises an important moral and philosophical issue related to *dina demalkhuta*: if the law of the land is unjust, does *dina demalkhuta* nevertheless apply? The answer is that it would not,[5] since such unjust rules would be classified as "*gazlenuta demalkhuta*," the "robbery of the kingdom" and not its law.

There is some discussion in the Talmud and commentaries clarifying the legitimacy of the power of the civil authorities. The *Meiri*[6] and the *Vilna Gaon*[7] derive the source of the civil authority from "*Parashat Hamelekh*," the "*Chapter of the king*" in the Second Book of *Samuel* (chap. 8). They explain that although one intention of Samuel was to warn the Israelites about the dangers of having a king, and what the king would impose on them, Samuel was also delineating the legitimate powers of a king (among them taxation).

Although the Meiri and the Vilna Gaon apply this authority to all kings, Jewish and non-Jewish, in Israel and in the Diaspora, *Toṣefot*[8]

---

[3] *Ned.* 28a.
[4] *Ibid.*
[5] Maimonides, *Hilkhot Gezelah Va'avedah*, chap. 5, sections 14 and 18; *Ḥoshen Mishpaṭ* 369, section 8 in *Ramo*.
[6] Commentary, *Nidd.*
[7] Commentary, *Ḥoshen mishpaṭ* 369, subsection 34.
[8] *Sanh.* 20b.

regard this authority as restricted to Jewish kings ruling over all of Israel. Generally, however, the *halakhah* accepts the position of the Meiri and the Vilna Gaon that *dina demalkhuta dina* covers all kings in all places.

In the *Talmud*,[9] Rava develops *dina demalkhuta* by explaining that since the king has the authority to confiscate trees to build a bridge, his agents have the authority to act on his behalf and determine the method by which these trees will be collected. Thus, even if the responsibility for providing trees falls on the entire community, the agents may collect the entire quota from one person who must comply under *dina demalkhuta*.

There is a second, relatively new approach to the source of *dina damalkhuta, that of the last s* Rabbi of Kovno, Rabbi Avraham Shapiro, described in his work the *Dvar Avraham*.[10] He derives *dina demalkhuta* from the principle "*hefker bet din, hefker*," the authority of the *bet din* to confiscate property and give it to another. The *bet din* may do this even in a situation in which there was no "*kinyan*," formal acquisition. Thus, the authority of the *bet din* is not derived from the Torah since there was no *kinyan*, but rather from the governmental power of the *bet din*. Rabbi Shapiro applies this approach to non-Jewish civil courts as well, which serves as the source of *dina demalkhuta*.[11]

It is crucial to note that *dina demalkhuta* applies only to economic and civil matters and not to religious laws, *i.e.*, a civil law stating that pork is considered kosher would not be recognized by *halakhah*.[12]

Another possible limitation on *dina demalkhuta* arises according to the Tosafist *Rabenu Yona*[13] even in monetary situations when both parties are Jewish. He limits *dina demalkhuta* to situations arising between a Jew and a non-Jew. However, when both parties are Jewish, they are subject to Jewish law exclusively. The *Hazon Ish*[14] seems to agree with this position. It is possible, however, that even when both parties are Jewish, *dina demalkhuta may apply when there is no* applicable Jewish law which would be contradicted by such an application,[15] or when such laws are for the general good and are subsumed under the government's power to keep law and order (rent control, price controls, and traffic laws).[16]

---

[9] B.K. 113b.
[10] Jerusalem, 1969, vol. I, 12a; and H. Schacter, "Dina Dimalchuta Dina," *Journal of Contemporary Halacha* I/1 (1981), 103–32.
[11] Gitt. 36b.
[12] L. Landman, *Jewish Law in the Diaspora: Confrontation and Accommodation* (Philadelphia: Dropsie College, 1968), 124.
[13] Quoted in the *Rashba Gitt.* 10b.
[14] End of volume *Hoshen Mishpat*, essay 16, section 1.
[15] Schachter, *supra* n. 10, at 123.
[16] B.B. 89a; Schmuel Shilo, *Dina Demalkhuta Dina* (Jerusalem: Jerusalem Academic Press, 1974), 175.

Finally, one major area of concern involves *dina demalkhuta* and criminal activity. There is a halakhic prohibition against "*meṣirah*," turning over a Jew to a non-Jewish government for imprisonment. This is not, however, a blanket shield for Jewish wrongdoers. For example, the *Talmud*[17] relates that several prominent rabbis were policemen for the Roman government. Although they were not lauded for serving in these positions, neither were they prohibited from doing so.

A Jew may turn over a Jewish criminal to legitimate non-Jewish authorities when the crime also violates Jewish law, *i.e.*, murder or theft.[18] In addition, as with most *dina demalkhuta* issues, there is also the concern that violation of the civil law would constitute "*ḥillul hashem*," disgracing the name of the Almighty.[19]

Generally, most civil monetary laws are quite similar to those of Jewish law so that there is little conflict between the systems. However, there are some areas, such as inheritance, which provide the potential for conflict and thus require careful planning and Rabbinic consultation. Certainly, even if *dina demalkhuta* were not applicable, the principle of "*kiddush hashem*," sanctifying the name of the Almighty before non-Jews, would require compliance with civil law where halakhically permissible.

[17] *B.M.* 83b–84a.
[18] Schachter, *supra* n. 10, at 118.
[19] *Ḥoshen Mishpaṭ*, chap. 28, section 3.

EXTENSIVE AND RESTRICTIVE INTERPRETATION OF TERMS IN RABBINIC HERMENEUTIC

by

*NORMAN SOLOMON**

Any attempt to describe rabbinic legal reasoning must somehow account for the *middot*. The lists of *middot* which occur in early rabbinic writing are the first attempt we know of to enumerate and characterize the modes of inference from Scripture.

Daube[1] and Lieberman[2] both saw clearly that the *middot* are not principles of logic, and that Schwarz[3] and others erred in contending that they derived, perhaps through Shemaiah and Avtalyon, from the Aristotelian syllogism; such links with Greek thought as may exist were rather with the Alexandrian commentators and rhetoricians. Aristotle himself[4] distinguished clearly and emphatically between logic and rhetoric, syllogism and enthymeme; a further distinction between rhetoric and hermeneutics is important, and it is to the latter category that the *middot* belong.

Little attempt has been made to describe the development in the use of *middot* beyond the tannaitic period; there has, indeed, been a tendency to regard the system, or at least its specific versions, as arising fully-fledged from the brain of select individual *tannaim* such as Rabbi Ishmael. The dating of talmudic texts and the establishment of the correctness of their received attributions being so problematic, this failure to perceive the growth outline of the system is not surprising. Michael L. Chernick's[5]

---

*Lecturer in Jewish Studies, Selly Oak Colleges, Birmingham, U.K.

[1] D. Daube, "Rabbinic Methods of Interpretation and Hellenistic Rhetoric," *Hebrew Union College Annual* 22 (1949), 239–64; idem, "Alexandrian Methods of Interpretation and the Rabbis," in *Festschrift Hans Lewald* (Basel: Helbing & Lichtenhahn, 1953), 27–44; idem, "Texts and Interpretation in Roman and Jewish Law," *Jewish Journal of Sociology* 3 (1961), 3–28.

[2] S. Lieberman, *Hellenism in Jewish Palestine* (New York: Jewish Theological Seminary of America, 1962), 47–82.

[3] A. Schwarz, *Der Hermeneutische Syllogismus in der Talmudischen Literatur* (Karlsruhe, 1901).

[4] Aristotle, cf. *Analytica Priora* 70a and *Rhetorica*, passim.

[5] Michael L. Chernick, "The Development of Kelal U'ferat U'khelal and Ribbui U'mi'ut We-ribbui in the Talmudim and Midrashim"—a Ph.D. thesis (unpublished) at Yeshivah University (1978).

recent study, based on form criticism, of the use of *kelal uferat* and *ribbui umi'ut* is thus warmly to be welcomed, though regrettably it was not available in time to be taken into consideration fully in the present study. The work is important not only within rabbinic studies themselves, but also in assessing the historical links, if any, between rabbinic and Hellenistic or Roman thought; both Lieberman and Daube commit errors which arise from the failure to establish correctly just when and where which particular Hellenistic rhetor, Roman jurist, or rabbi, actually formulated the idea or principle under discussion.

I propose to make here some observations about a particular group of *middot*, *viz.* those relating to the interpretation of general and specific terms; they are sometimes expressed in a terminology revolving around the words *kelal* and *perat*, sometimes in that built around the words *ribbui* and *mi'ut*. Similar stages of development could certainly be shown in the use of other *middot*.[6]

Origin of the Terminology

A well-known passage,[7] of which we possess several versions, attributes seven *middot* to Hillel, amongst them *kelal uferat* and perhaps also *perat ukhelal*. *Sifra*,[8] in a section which has found its way into the daily liturgy, lists no less than nine *kelal uferat*-related *middot* amongst the nominally thirteen, but in reality sixteen, it attributes to Rabbi Ishmael. Can we take it, then, that the basic *middah* of *kelal uferat* was first formulated by Hillel at the beginning of the first century, and then more than a hundred years later was elaborated by Rabbi Ishmael to include some more exotic forms of inference? An examination of the extant materials relating to Hillel and Rabbi Ishmael fails to support this view. In the admittedly scant sources we have for Hillel's teachings there is not a single instance of his use of *kelal uferat*, whether in those terms or otherwise, though the reports[9] of his debate with the Bnei Bathyra do carry recognizable instances of his use of other *middot*. The materials relating to Rabbi Ishmael have recently been comprehensively studied by Gary L. Porton, who finds that seven of the nine *kelal uferat*-related *middot* attributed to Rabbi Ishmael are nowhere instantiated in the sources attributed to him.[10] *Kelal uferat* itself is attributed to him once

---

[6] Compare, for instance, the Third Stage development in the systematization of *hekesh* and *gezerah shavah* as reflected in a *sugya* such as *Gittin* 41b.

[7] *T. Sanh.* 7 (end); *ADRN* 37.

[8] *Sifra*, Introduction. It may be significant that in *Sanh.* 86a the 'thirteen *middot*' are cited without reference to Rabbi Ishmael.

[9] *T. Pes.* 4: 1, 2, *Pes.* 66a, etc.

[10] Gary L. Porton, *The Traditions of Rabbi Ishmael* (Leiden: E. J. Brill, 1976–1982), 4 vols., at IV, 201f.

in *Sifra* on Numbers, three times in the *Talmud Yerushalmi and once in the Bavli*; *kelal uferat ukhelal* is found in his name once in *Tosefta* and three times in the *Yerushalmi*. One might add to Porton's findings that nowhere in the *Mishnah* does either word, *kelal* or *perat*, occur in the technical sense in which it is used in these *middot*; one can hardly put this down to Akiban provenance of the Mishnah, especially as Porton has shown[11] that the alleged difference in exegetical method between the schools of Ishmael and Akiba is largely illusory.

A close examination of those texts in which Rabbi Ishmael is represented as using *kelal* and *perat* reveals by and large that they do not purport to be authentic statements of Rabbi Ishmael, but rather legitimate uses of an exegetical principle he is said to have propounded. Typical is the *sugya* in Y. *Terumot* 11:2. The Mishnah deals with the liability of a non-Cohen to payment of the value plus a fifth of *terumah* liquids he drank in ignorance of their status. In justifying the view of Rabbi (E)liezer, who holds him liable, the Yerushalmi suggests that his view coincides with that of Rabbi Ishmael, who interpreted by means of *kelal uferat*, for such an interpretation of *Lev.* 11:34 would support the view that one would be liable for value plus a fifth after consuming *any* liquids produced from *terumah*. Note that there is no claim here that R. Ishmael himself used the *middah* of *kelal uferat* in this context, or even that he ever spoke about the problem at all. There are other *sugyot*—for instance, that in *Erubin* which we shall discuss at length later— in which the *kelal uferat* inference is important, but which were nevertheless presented in their earliest form without the name of R. Ishmael; the *Erubin sugya* occurs in *Sifre* and *Bavli* without Ishmael's name, but in the *Yerushalmi* with it.

It seems, therefore, that despite the attribution of *kelal uferat* to Rabbi Ishmael and his teacher, Neḥunyah ben Hakaneh, and notwithstanding the tradition tracing it back to Hillel, the actual terminology was not commonly used, perhaps not even coined, until the late second or third century. Evidently it became popular swiftly. As it was attached to the name of Rabbi Ishmael, perhaps being developed by his disciples, an attempt was made in third-century Palestine to attach his name to arguments couched in the characteristic terminology. It is likely that this attempt was made in the Palestinian schools, for scarcely any such arguments are attributed to him in the Bavli; even the well-known statement that he used the *kelal uferat* hermeneutic is attributed in the Bavli[12] to the Palestinian R. Yoḥanan.

The *ribbui umi'ut* terminology is considerably older, at least in the form of verbs rather than abstract nouns, being found in the *Mishnah*

---

[11] *Infra*, n. 17.
[12] *Shebu.* 26a.

and in indisputably early tannaitic materials. It is worth noting, so often is it glossed over, that the traditional view[13] is that R. Ishmael used not only *kelal uferat* but also *ribbui umi'ut*; conversely, we have examples[14] of the attribution to R. Akiva of the use of *kelal uferat* hermeneutics, though these are far fewer than the examples of the attribution to R. Ishmael of the use of *ribbui umi'ut*. Close examination, moreover, shows that those traditions—at least one of them a Mishnah—in which Rabbi Ishmael is said to use *ribbui umi'ut* are not only older than the *kelal uferat* ones, but present the *ribbui* argument as an integral part of the tradition, not in a form in which it looks, as with the *kelal uferat* pieces, that the name of Rabbi Ishmael has been grafted in at some stage, or that the author is presenting an argument which he puts into the mouth of Rabbi Ishmael but which is not a genuine tradition of the master.

Kelal Uferat, Ribbui Umi'ut — The First Stage

We are now in a position to describe the First Stage in the development of the *kelal uferat* and *ribbui umi'ut* hermeneutics.

In the years up to approximately 200 rabbinic hermeneutics had progressed on the whole on non-formal lines, that is, the modes of inference were not themselves formalized. It is unlikely that the terms *kelal* and *perat* were used other than rarely and then only towards the end of the period, though that is not to deny that specific inferences, later formulated in *kelal uferat* terminology, were in fact made earlier. The nouns *ribbui* and *mi'ut* were probably not in common use either; though the verbs from which they are derived were certainly part of the rabbinic vocabulary of inference at a much earlier stage, they are 'natural' Hebrew in which to express the ideas of inclusion and exclusion. But whilst one can easily say "*marbe ani et . . .*" or "*mema'et ani et . . .* ," the verbs *kalal* and *parat* are not so used in second-century Hebrew—"*poret ani . . .* ," indeed, would mean "I itemize" rather than "I exclude." Moreover, all four abstract nouns—*kelal, perat, ribbui* and *mi'ut*—tend to disjoint the syntax when they are actually used in the inferential process. Their natural place is not in the process of inference itself, but in *talking about* the process of inference; they are "*meta-inferential*," a "*second-order language*" about inference. Hence we need not be surprised to discover that their use becomes common only after 200. This is the period of the late tannaitic schools, of which we still lack a comprehensive picture. The Ushan period, from about 140, has been well and oft[15] portrayed by the indefatigable J. Neusner as

---

[13] See the references in Meir Ish Shalom's (M. Friedmann) commentary, *Meir Ayin*, on "*Sifra*" (Breslau, 1915), 20.

[14] *E.g.*, Y. *Erub.*, 3:1.

[15] *E.g.*, in J. Neusner, *History of the Mishnaic Law of Purities*, vol. 22 (Leiden: E. J. Brill, 1977), 294.

that in which the conceptual basis of the laws received its characteristic mould, and he has recognized the immediate post-Ushan period as one of systematization. In the first half of the third century we have the evolution of the schools who bridge the gap between the *tannaim* and *amoraim*, and I am suggesting that this is the period in which talk *about* inference from Scripture, rather than the actual *making of* inferences, becomes important.

Why should such a change take place just at this time? Whereas the period from 70 had seen much genuine legislative activity, with scriptural justification mainly in a supporting role, and even at Usha legislation continued while the system was being ordered and articulated, legislative activity was severely circumscribed by the publication of the Mishnah itself. The legislators had become interpreters, and there could be no movement other than through accepted, agreed modes of interpretation; hence, the need to talk *about* ways of interpretation, to name and categorize them, and to form them into an effective tool in their own right for progress in Torah. It is a serious error of historical perspective to view the rabbis of the first and second centuries as guided and restrained in either legislative activity or biblical interpretation generally by norms, such as the *middot* ascribed to Rabbi Ishmael, which belong to the third and later centuries.

There is ample evidence of the formulation of different vocabularies for expressing modes of inference from Scripture. Albeck[16] has pointed out how consistently the terminology of each of the halakhic midrashim is shaped. He writes: "It should also be noted that the individual terminologies of sections of the *midreshey halakhah* derive not only from their sources, but have been formulated and fixed by the compilers." As a simple example he instances the use of *"lehotsi"* for "exclude" (as a mode of inference) in *Mekhilta*, and in *Sifre* on Numbers, whereas *Sifra*, and *Sifre* on Deuteronomy, use *"perat l . . . ."* He notes how when citations from the *midreshey halakha* appear in the Talmuds they often lack their distinctive "home" terminology. It would appear, therefore, that the early third century bore witness to the emergence of a number of competing terminologies in which to formulate and describe the processes of scriptural inference. *Kelal uferat, ribbui umiʻut*, were the two basic languages which emerged for expressing extensive or restrictive interpretation of biblical terms; though the *ribbui umiʻut* language had stronger roots in conventional Hebrew usage, the new tendency to the utilization of abstract nouns put the two languages on a par.

It is important to understand that at this stage the two 'languages' do not necessarily indicate two different inferential procedures, though in the Second Stage (see below) the attempt is made to distinguish between them as modes of inference. In this First Stage, though, it is simply the

---

[16] H. Albeck, *Mavo Latalmudim*, 2d ed. (Tel Aviv: Dvir, 1975), 99 (transl. N.S.).

case that some schools—tradition instances that of R. Ishmael—use *kelal uferat* language, while others—some instance that of Rabbi Akiva—use *ribbui umi'ut language.*

In view of all this it comes as no surprise that, as Gary L. Porton has shown,[17] there is little in fact to choose between the extant exegetical traditions of R. Ishmael and those of R. Akiva. Nor, indeed, need we puzzle over the confusion which exists as to the allegiance of others, for instance Rabbi,[18] to one school or another, or raise our eyebrows when the Jerusalem Talmud[19] names Rabbi Akiva as the originator of *"kelalot uferatot"*! Nor is it by any means necessary to appeal to the distinction between aggadic and halakhic methods of inference in order to explain how it is possible for the thirty-two *middot* attributed to Rabbi Eliezer, son of R. Jose of Galilee, to include *middot* expressed in each of the languages; at this early stage, the languages were not yet seen as contradictory.

Bearing in mind that at Stage One the languages are understood simply as forms of expression to clarify and systematize earlier inferential procedures we can also see how easily lists could have been compiled of the *middot* of Hillel or other rabbis. The third-century teachers were neither reminiscing nor romancing; they were trying to describe, largely in their own language, what sort of inferences their predecessors had made. The increasing complexity of the hermeneutic process was perceptively expressed by them in the attribution of increasing numbers of *middot* to succeeding generations; seven to Hillel, thirteen to Rabbi Ishmael, thirty-two to the Ushan Rabbi Eliezer son of Jose. The listing is a characteristic activity of this period, perhaps alluded to almost contemporaneously by R. Abbahu[20] in his amiable application of *1 Chronicles* 2:55 to those who "turn the Torah into numbers . . . fifteen women exempt their sisters-in-law from levirate marriage, thirty-six offences in the Torah carry the penalty of excision, there are thirteen rules about the remains of a clean bird . . ." Though Rabbi Abbahu's examples are all to be found in our Mishnah there are independent grounds on which to consider several of them late incorporations; but exactly who the *"sofre sefurot"* were who "turned the Torah into numbers" we do not yet know.

In sum, in Stage One we see a far-reaching innovation in rabbinic Judaism. No longer are we simply making inferences from Scripture, we are considering and discovering *how* we make those inferences, and we are forced to create new languages to make such discourse possible. We indicated above that the decline in the legislative freedom and authority

---

[17] *Supra* n. 10, at IV, 205f.
[18] *Men.* 28b.
[19] *Y. Shek.* 5:1.
[20] *Ibid.*

of the rabbis was a factor in this move to enhance the power of interpretation, to demonstrate its certainty. In the ongoing polemic with Christianity in Palestine another factor is to be seen; if only it were possible to demonstrate and establish incontrovertible methods of scriptural interpretation the Christian claim to scriptural fulfilment could be firmly discredited.

Kelal Uferat, Ribbui Umi'ut — The Second Stage

Although we stated above that the use of two 'languages', that of *kelal uferat* and that of *ribbui umi'ut*, did not necessarily presuppose two basically different systems of inference, the momentum arising from the purely linguistic differences would of itself tend to create differences in the range of application of the rules. That such is the case we may readily infer from a *Tosefta*[21] passage—probably the earliest passage to represent Rabbis Ishmael and Akiva as differing in their allegiance to *kelal uferat* and *ribbui umi'ut* respectively, though neither is presented as exclusively using one or other of the formulae. Commenting on *Lev.* 5:2, *Tosefta* maintains that Akiva found *kelal uferat* inapplicable to the verse, whereas Ishmael (but some read Simeon!) did apply it.

Only at a much later stage do we find the two formulae regarded as contradictory principles of interpretation. The *terminum ad quem* for this position would be the first half of the fourth century, for we find Abbaye commenting on it; however, the difficulty of dating the source materials means that one cannot definitively rule out a somewhat earlier date.

Let us now examine what is perhaps the main *sugya*[22] in which an attempt is made to define the precise modes of operation of *kelal uferat* and *ribbui umi'ut*, and hence the difference between them.

Deuteronomy 14 states that the tithe, both of animals and crops, must be taken to Jerusalem and consumed there. The rabbis refer this passage to the Second Tithe, *ma'aser sheni*, brought in the first, second, fourth and fifth years of the sabbatical cycle. The produce itself need not be taken to Jerusalem, but may be commuted to money, and the money spent in Jerusalem:

> "There you shall spend it as you will on cattle or sheep, wine or strong drink, or whatever you desire. . . ." (*Deut.* 14:26, NEB)

There are three terms, or groups of terms, in this sentence. "Spend it as you will" is general; "cattle or sheep, wine or strong drink" is a string of specific terms; "whatever you desire" is again general.

This verse would seem to be irresistible to anyone wanting to test out a hypothesis about the interpretation of general and particular terms.

---

[21] *T. Shebu.* 1:7 (Zuckermandel ed.), 449.
[22] *Erub.* 27b, 28a, and parallels.

Kelal uferat ukhelal, ribbu umi'ut veribbui—how can one miss it? Yet *Sifre did* miss it, for it uses neither terminology in inferring from the verse that one may buy with one's *ma'aser sheni* money only *"peri miperi vegidulo min haarets"*—food, drink or condiments made from "fruit that reproduces" (*i.e.*, food of vegetable origin) or "that which is nourished from the earth" (*i.e.*, animal foodstuffs)—but not salt or water.

We could not hope to find a better illustration of the way in which third-century exponents of the various schools of interpretation worked over the material before them and married it, with or without the bride's consent, to their own system of exposition. For in passages which must surely date from late in the same century both Talmuds cite what can only be rehashed versions of the *Sifre*. The verse is the same idiosyncratic wording—but the terminology of the schools has been subtly woven in. The *ribbui umi'ut* schools—according to the Bavli, Rabbis Judah ben Gadish and Eliezer (Eleazar?)—interpret in their language, Rabbi Eliezer (or whoever puts the words in his mouth) concluding that "brine" is excluded from the list of permitted purchases, Rabbi Judah ben Gadish that salt and water are excluded. The *kelal uferat* lobby— the Bavli gives no names, the Yerushalmi instances both Ishmael *and* Akiva—interpret in *their* language, the resulting exclusions ranging from salt and water to such exotica as truffles and locusts. All of them offer recognizable versions of the *"peri miperi"* summation.

I am here concerned not with the literary development of the *sugya*, but with changes in the use and understanding of the *middot*. We can already see one aspect of the Second Stage of development. No longer are the *middot*, as in the First Stage, merely convenient labels of conventional inferential processes; they have taken on a life of their own, and the unnamed rabbis who use them pseudepigraphically are shaping them into well-defined hermeneutic procedures. The Yerushalmi here is less well-developed than the Bavli, for it still allows a wide range of interpretation to arise from the use of *kelal uferat*, and thus finds it possible to ascribe its use to *both* Rabbi Ishmael *and* Rabbi Akiva. The Bavli has defined its use of *Kelal uferat* in a more circumscribed fashion; it therefore assumes that a slightly different interpretation of the verse, viz. a smaller list of exclusions, could only arise because a different principle of interpretation, to wit *ribbui umi'ut*, was being used.

It is essential, if we are to make sense of the development of talmudic reasoning, to describe the relationship between *kelal uferat* and *ribbui umi'ut as conceived in the Bavli at* this stage.

The basic problem faced by the rabbis confronts any jurist, judge or lawyer who is called upon to interpret a text or a statute or to apply a precedent. How extensive or restrictive should his interpretation be? If the statute or whatever is couched in general terms, which particular instances does it comprehend? If—as in a casuistic system, or one where precedent is to be taken into account—specific instances are given, how does one move from the specific instance to a case which is not identical with it in all respects? Every jurist would dearly like to have some rule of thumb by which to make such inferences; the rabbis, devising the *kelal* and *ribbui* rules, were trying to provide just this. They are suggesting that close investigation of the biblical text reveals general and specific—extensive and restrictive—terms, and that by attending carefully to these terms one can determine just how broad or narrow one's interpretation should be. Imagine three concentric circles. The outermost corresponds to the *kelal* or the *ribbui*; the innermost corresponds to the specific instance or instances, *peratim* or *mi'utim*. The middle circle includes all those instances to which the law should apply; it is of greater radius than the circle which is defined only with reference to the specific instances, but of lesser radius than that defined by the law as based on the general term. How do we fix the radius of the middle circle? Here, in the Second Stage of development, this is still to some extent dependent on the individual interpreter. Nevertheless, one definite indicator emerges; if we interpret with *ribbui umi'ut* language we will define a circle of greater radius than if we use *kelal uferat* language.[23]

The Second Stage is that in which we see the descriptive vocabularies of the First Stage transformed into fairly clearly defined rules for interpretation.

What are the causes of this transformation?

Up to a point, it results from the inner dynamic of the hermeneutic process, that is to say, the tendency of its language habits to consolidate themselves as rules.

The transformation would also seem to satisfy a basic need of later *tannaim* and their successors. Inference from general rules to specific cases[24] is very much less problematic than that from specific to general, or from specific to other specific cases. The former can often be represented in deductive form, that is, with formal logical validity. The latter can never be represented in this way, but always implies the use of some more general rule by which the inference can be justified; jurists have referred[25] to such general rules as 'second order rules,' and they have speculated as to how far such rules can or ought to be incorporated in the law system itself, and how they relate, for instance, to general social or philosophical considerations. Now, in the active phase of rabbinic legislation, which we may take as ending at Usha, we find that the rabbis, whether consciously or not,

---

[23] Compare the treatment of the two systems of interpretation as it appears in *Bekh.* 37a–b.

[24] See D. N. MacCormick, *Legal Reasoning and Legal Theory* (Oxford University Press, 1978). Chaps. 2 and 3 deal with deductive justification, essentially the inference from general to particular.

[25] *Op. cit.*, chap. 5.

tend to be guided in their decision-making by those ethical, social and political considerations which belong to the realm of 'second order rules'; texts are easily interpreted in conformity with such considerations, though this fact is obscured often enough by the weight of hermeneutic devices later inserted in our source materials. After Usha, however, there is a fundamental change, a reluctance to rely on second-order justification, a search for certainty within the received holy text itself. The elevation of the hermeneutic rules to the role of prime justification for textual interpretation fills the vacuum created by the reluctance to argue on the basis of general ethical and moral principle. A rational approach, one which would reach decisions by weighing up circumstances and principles, yields to what is perceived as a safer, rule-based, mechanical one.

Once again one sense overtones of the polemic with Christianity. If Scripture is to be the final court of appeal, the best defence lies in securing the process of interpretation, not in argument on general principles.

Kelal Uferat, Ribbui Umi'ut — The Third Stage

The Third Stage focuses on the attempt to make the utilization of the *middot* an exact technique.

The circle analogy in the previous section points to a defect in the technique as it stood at Stage Two. The middle circle represents the extension of the law when the terms defining the outer and inner circles have been taken into consideration. But how is one to gauge the distance between the inner and middle or middle and outer circles? A man is taller than a mouse but shorter than a carthorse; this enables us to distinguish him from an ant or an elephant, but how do we know how to relate his size to that of a kangaroo?

The rabbis saw the need to *quantify* the *middot*, to determine exactly the radius of the middle circle—if they could not succeed in this, then interpretation, even by means of the *middot*, would retain an element of subjectivity, for one rabbi might interpret more or less extensively than another. They attempted to achieve this aim by grafting into the *middot* their notion of *tsedadim*, 'relevant aspects' of particular cases or categories in law. Each case (category, etc.) has some *tsad* or *tsedadim* in virtue of which it is decided in a particular way; the relationship between this and *ratio decidendi* should be explored. The concept of *tsedadim* is at least as old as the completed Mishnah. For instance, in the first *mishnah* of *Baba Kamma*, where the main categories of tortious liability are set out, we read that *hatsad hashaveh shebahen*, their common *tsad*, or operative factor, is that they are likely causes of damage, that the owner is responsible for them, and that if they cause damage the person responsible must make restitution with the best quality land. As well as the *tsad hashaveh*, the common operative factor, the Mishnah lists the specific operative factors (it does not actually use the word *tsad*) of the individual categories of liability. It is certainly of importance that the development of the rabbinic idea of the *tsedadim* be studied in depth; perhaps it has been neglected as it is not included in any of the formal lists of *middot*. Dr. Jacobs' excellent study[26] of the relationship between *binyan ab* and Mill's "method of agreement" highlights the logical aspects of this form of argumentation, but it needs to be supplemented by (a) a careful historical account of ways in which the technique of investigation of 'relevant aspects' developed and (b) an assessment of the juristic significance of the concept of *tsedadim*, including its relationship with *ratio decidendi*.

At any rate, we find that by late amoraic times *tsedadim* are being used in an attempt to quantify degrees of similarity between cases; the rabbis are asking, with regard to how many *tsedadim* can we compare case A with case B? The *sugya* discussed above illustrates this. The question is raised[27] as to whether *kelala kama davka* or *kelala batra davka*; in a *kelal uferat ukhelal* sequence which *kelal* is definitive, the first or the second? If the second, we read, the *middah* operates as follows: *perat* is followed by *kelal*, and the rule of *perat ukhelal* is that everything similar to the *perat* in even one respect (*tsad*) is included; the first *kelal* restricts the application of the law to cases that resemble the *perat* in two *tsedadim*. If, on the other hand, it is the first *kelal* which is definitive, the *middah* operates as follows: one starts with *kelal uferat*, and the rule of *kelal uferat* is that application of the law is restricted to the instances enumerated in the *perat*; the final *kelal* is instrumental only in extending the application to instances closely similar to the *perat*, that is, to those similar in *three tsedadim*, aspects. Applying the analogy of the circles, we find that they are now conceived as having radii whose lengths are determined as small whole multiples of the length of one standard *tsad*. The innermost circle contains only the case actually enumerated in the *perat*, the next circle cases which share three common factors with the *perat* (if *kalala kama davka*) or two common factors (if *kelala batra davka*), the outermost circle contains those cases which resemble the *perat* even in one respect. Beyond the outermost circle lie all those cases which are not thought to resemble the *perat* in any way.

It is significant that though the *sugya* in *Erubin* applies this analysis only to the *kelal uferat* system, a parallel *sugya* in *Nazir*[28] applies it to *ribbui umi'ut*. This shows conclusively how late a development is this attempt to graft the *tsedadim* idea into the mainstream of *middot*. It is

---

[26] L. Jacobs, *Studies in Talmudic Logic and Methodology* (London: Vallentine, Mitchell, 1961), 9f.
[27] *Erub.* 28a.
[28] *Naz.* 35b. As in the *Erubin sugya* this analysis is absent form the parallel Yerushalmi passage.

not, of course, possible at this stage to assign an exact date to the process. However, it is clear that it was a Babylonian development not earlier than the fifth century. I find no trace of it in the *Yerushalmi* (though commentators have tried to read it in), and in the *Bavli* it occurs in discussion of a ruling attributed to Ravina, and is presented in language which is at least late amoraic and possibly seboraic.

There is a high degree of artificiality in this Third Stage type of argument. Is the quantification of degrees of legal relevance at all a possible enterprise? Can one ever be sure that one has exhaustively enumerated all the operative features in a legal decision, let alone that the maximum allowable number of such features is just four? Surely there should be some system of weighting as between *tsedadim*, for some must be more important than others? As in so many enterprises the search for certainty produces a system which may have inner coherence and consistency but which has forfeited connection with the outer world in which it is to be applied.

We need not be surprised that after the talmudic period rabbinic legal development eschewed use of all hermeneutic *middot* other than the *kal vaḥomer*; even those authorities[29] who held that in principle all *middot* other than *gezerah shavah* could be applied without a supporting tradition refrained in practice from applying them.

A Note on Kohlberg

It might be thought that there is some analogy between the account given here of the development of rabbinic modes of legal reasoning and the account given by Lawrence Kohlberg of what he claims is a universal human pattern in the development of moral thought.

Kohlberg[30] treats of three levels of moral development, subdivided into six stages. The three levels are labelled[31] by him preconventional, conventional and postconventional, the latter being referred to also as autonomous or principled. Important for us are stages 5 and 6, the subdivisions of the postconventional level. At stage 5 there is "an emphasis upon the possibility of changing law in terms of rational considerations of social utility" (rather than freezing it in terms of stage 4 "law and order"). At stage 6 "logical comprehensiveness, universality, and consistency" guide the decisions of conscience. Kohlberg is adamant that stage 6, just because it provides a more adequate basis for moral decision-making, is "more moral"[32] than the earlier stages. However, it is

---

[29] *Cf. Toṣafot Sukk.* 31a, s.v. *veri savar*.
[30] Lawrence Kohlberg, "From Is to Ought," in *Cognitive Development and Epistemology*, ed. Theodore Mischel (New York: Academic Press, 1971), 151-235.
[31] *Op. cit.*, 164, 165.
[32] *E.g.*, on p. 214f. He uses impressive words like *differentiation, integration, prescriptivity*, and *universality* (all on p. 216) to demonstrate the "formalistic adequacy" of stage 6.

unclear what he means by "more moral" (he dismisses some of the obvious interpretations) other than "providing a more adequate basis for moral decision-making."

It might be thought that our move through three stages is something like Kohlberg's move from stage 5 to stage 6. Certainly, the rabbis in the days before the formulation of the *middot* were behaving in a sort of Kohlberg-5 fashion, making decisions which involved the change (they would have said interpretation) of law in terms of rational considerations of social utility. The Stage Three rabbis might, superficially, be described as acting in Kohlberg-6 fashion; they probably thought they had developed a system both comprehensive and consistent for solving their problems, though they might have been troubled over the application of the word 'universal' to their system; they could certainly not have used it as Kohlberg does, for they were dealing with techniques of interpretation and not with universal moral values. Here, indeed, lies the weakness of the analogy with Kohlberg. We are not comparing like with like. Kohlberg is concerned with the development of moral decision-making by the individual; we are concerned with attempts to consolidate a legal system and to derive decisions from it. There is absolutely no reason to suppose that legal systems would or should develop in the same way as the individual human perception of moral values. Indeed, a virtue in one can very easily become a vice in the other. It may be good (I don't in fact believe it is) for the individual to make his decisions by reference to a 'universal principle of justice.' It would certainly be bad law, and almost certainly bad social policy, for a judge to decide in that way, other than in the rather rare circumstances in which he has to appeal to 'second-order' rules because the rule-system does not adequately cover his problem.[33]

Despite the evident superficiality of the comparison there is one significant *mis*conception shared by Kohlberg and the late rabbis. It is the seductive notion that because something is more logical, because it facilitates decision-making, it somehow rises superior to the less organised system, the system in which decisions are hard. Kohlberg is very careful indeed in claiming only greater "moral adequacy" for his stage 6, not

---

But in describing, as sensitively as he undoubtedly does, the ways of *sui generis* moral reasoning of the stage 6 decision-maker, he is surely not showing that the stage 6 individual has finer moral perceptions than people at earlier stages but only that he is better at reasoning out his decisions. H. L. A. Hart, in *The Concept of Law* (Oxford: Clarendon Law Series, 1961), chap. 7, has argued for a balance, in law, between formalism and rule-scepticism. But whereas law, as an instrument of social control, depends on the predictability which can only be ensured by a positive body of rules, it is by no means as clear that moral decision-making is enhanced by "formal adequacy," and it is a "naturalistic fallacy" to confuse morality with facility to reason about morals.

[33] See, for instance, R. Dworkin, *Taking Rights Seriously* (London: Duckworth, 1977), chap. 4.

objective moral superiority, a concept which he sensibly avoids handling. But why should he assume that a *formalistic* "meta-ethical conception" has greater "moral adequacy" than, say, an intuitive one? It may well be that ethical decision-making—unlike the application of law—is essentially an intuitive process, and it is clear that subjectively at least intuition yields greater certainty than rational decision in accordance with universal principles. Even as an objective procedure rational decision manifestly fails to achieve either agreement or certainty. The rabbis likewise erred in thinking that a self-contained system of legal interpretation would guarantee certainty, correctness or even widespread agreement in Torah-law, and the system was speedily abandoned by their successors. (In fact the system was never utilized significantly, for the very rabbis who devised it used it not for any important legislative activity of their own but pseudepigraphically in the elaboration of the traditions of their predecessors. At no time were the *middot* the actual determinants of development in Jewish law.)

One day, perhaps, it may be possible to construct a logically coherent system which will embrace our agreed moral judgments and perhaps another coherent system, related to the former in a simple fashion, which can articulate clearly the laws needed to govern society. Advances in philosophy, individual and social psychology, and certainly in neurophysiology will be necessary before this can be done. The danger is that in prematurely constructing a system we will oversimplify and distort the few clear moral perceptions we have. The fifth-century Babylonian rabbis fortunately did not in practice reach decisions of any importance by recourse to such contrived techniques as that of the *tsedadim*; such decisions as they made were subject to other checks. The more elevated Kohlberg-6 scheme of decision by reference to universal principle is, in practice, also constrained by cross-checks; only self-deception can lead a man to think that his decisions are reached by deduction from general, universal moral principles, for in practice he usually proceeds in precisely the opposite way, constructing general principles out of his specific intuitions, and being guided in their usually problematic application by those same intuitions.

Summary and Historical Question

Stage One—late tannaitic—the *middot* are listed in an attempt to describe the processes of inference used by earlier *tannaim*, whose *dicta* are reformulated in the new terminologies.

Stage Two—up to the fourth generation amoraic, both Palestinian and Babylonian—clearer definition of the *middot* raises problems of their mutual consistency. Hermeneutic rules rather than general ethical or religious principles have come to dominate exegesis.

Stage Three—late amoraic, Babylonian, perhaps seboraic—the grafting of the teaching on *tsedadim* (legally relevant aspects) into the *kelal uferat* and *ribbui umi'ut* systems in an attempt to afford the *middot* quantitative precision.

One would like to be able to relate these developments to developments in, say, Hellenistic rhetoric or Roman law, as Lieberman and Daube tried to do with regard to rabbinic hermeneutics in general. Lieberman, in fact, having led us to expect links between the *middot* and the methods of Hellenistic commentators and rhetoricians, says nothing about *kelal uferat*. Daube at least attempted to draw some analogies and suggest some tenuous links between Roman lawyers and *kelal uferat* rabbis. A lot has happened in Jewish scholarship since Daube wrote on this topic, however, and I expect he would nowadays readily admit that he was working on a faulty historical basis. His analogies are sound, but we cannot accept them as, for instance, evidence for Hillel's indebtedness for his ideas on *Kelal uferat* to the predecessors of Celsus;[34] we can no longer confidently associate Hillel with this *middah*. Experts in Roman legal history may likewise be circumspect about taking at their face value attributions in the '*Digest*'. When both Roman lawyers and rabbinic scholars have progressed in dating their sources it will become possible to ascertain whether there are actual points of contact, rather than mere analogies, between Roman and Jewish methods of legal argumentation. Indeed, it is already easier to envisage some influence, whether direct or not, of Celsus and other Roman lawyers on late tannaitic developments, which we have seen as a crucial period for rabbinic exegesis, than it was to envizage comparable influence in the days of Hillel. On the other hand, one does not expect to find links between Rome and fifth-century Babylonian developments.

[34] D. Daube, "Rabbinic Methods of Interpretation and Hellenistic Rhetoric," *Hebrew Union College Annual* 22 (1949), 253.

SOME STOCK ARGUMENTS FOR THE MAGNANIMITY OF THE LAW IN HELLENISTIC JEWISH APOLOGETICS

by

*ABRAHAM TERIAN**

The predominantly apologetic literature of Hellenistic Judaism developed as a response to anti-Jewish slander from without and disenchantment with traditional religion from within.[1] Further encounters with Hellenism and proselytising endeavours brought new dimensions in the understanding of the Law and underscored its importance for the self-consciousness of the Jewish communities—especially in the Diaspora.[2] Whether with an apologetic or a missionary thrust, Judaism was presented in a way that could be understood in terms of Greek rationality. Consequently, arguments for the magnanimity of the Mosaic Law and the high morality of the Jews were formulated in accordance with Greek jurisprudence and its attendant allegory, aimed at showing that the end of the Law is philanthropy.[3]

There were stock arguments in defense of Judaism as a philosophy, a political constitution, or a code given by a divinely inspired legislator. A major argument for the universal significance of the Jewish Law was that it has God for its starting point, or that it begins with creation—due emphasis being placed on its supernatural origin and superiority because of its antiquity.[4] As will be shown, however, when specific commandments were

---

*Professor of Intertestamental and Early Christian Literatures, Andrews University, Michigan.

[1] V. Tcherikover, "Jewish Apologetic Literature Reconsidered," *Eos* 48, fasc. 3 (1956), 169–93, attempts to show that the earlier writings were specifically directed at Jews. While his arguments make a good case for the inclusion of Jewish readers among the intended audience(s), they fail to negate the traditional understanding that the same literature was directed also at Gentiles (see *infra* n. 6). *Cf. idem*, ed., *Corpus Papyrorum Judaicarum* 1 (Cambridge, MA: Harvard University Press, 1957), 41–43.

[2] *Cf.* P. Dalpert, *Die Theologie der hellenistisch-jüdischen Missions-Literatur unter Ausschluss von Philo und Josephus* (Theologische Forschung 4; Hamburg: Reich, 1954).

[3] Typical of this development is Philo's tractate on philanthropy (*Virt.* 51–174), a virtue illustrated at its best through the legislation of Moses. *Cf.* the description of Wisdom as *philanthropos* in *Wisd. of Sol.* (1:6; 7:23) and "that the righteous man must be humane" (12:19).

[4] See, *e.g.*, *Aristeas* 31; Philo *Ios.* 31; *Vita Mos.* 2.51; *Dec.* 15–18; Josephus *Ap.* 2.154, 164–65, 184–85, 279–80; *Ant.* 3.286; etc.

cited to illustrate the excellence of the Law, those pertaining to dietary regulations were foremost among the examples given—especially those about unclean birds (*Lev.* 11:13; *cf. Deut.* 14:11-20) and, to a certain extent, that on the bird's nest (*Deut.* 22:6-7). The magnanimity of the Law was demonstrated through the lesser as well as "the least of the commandments"—as the rabbis later referred to *Deut.* 22:6-7.[5] To establish these early *topoi* or common and concise arguments, we shall begin with a pair of somewhat problematic passages in two particularly apologetic works, Philo's *Hypothetica* or *Apologia pro Iudaeis* and Josephus' *Contra Apionem*, and shall conclude with a central passage in *Aristeas to Philocrates*.[6]

A curious *halakhah* in Philo's *Hypothetica* reads as follows: "Do not render desolate the nest under your roof or make the appeals of creatures of none effect when they seem to fly to you for help as they sometimes do" (7.9).[7] He introduces it as the only example of "little things of casual occurrence" contained in the Law, and adds: "These things are of no worth at all, you may say, yet great is the Law which ordains them and ever watchful is the care which it demands" (*ibid.*). Similarly, Josephus' *Contra Apionem* has: "Creatures which take refuge in our houses like suppliants he has forbidden us to kill; he would not suffer us to take

---

[5] *Y. Kidd.* 1 (61b58); *Deut. R.* 6:2; *cf. Lam. R.* 1:9:37, all attributed to R. Abba b. Kahana (late third century); *cf.* also the earlier dicta ascribed to Tanna Judah Hanasi in *Hull.* 12:5b and *Ab.* 2:1. See the recent article by my colleague, R. M. Johnston, "'The Least of the Commandments': Deuteronomy 22:6-7 in Rabbinic Judaism and Early Christianity," *Andrews University Seminary Studies* 20 (1982), 205-15, which was a sequel to this paper at an earlier stage of the study.

[6] V. Tcherikover, "The Ideology of the Letter of Aristeas," *Harvard Theological Review* 51 (1958), 59-85, warns against bringing into the concerns of pseudo-Aristeas, who wrote for Jewish readers, the apologetics of Philo and Josephus, who wrote primarily for Gentile audiences; or, against reading into the favourable conditions for the Jews under the Ptolemies, in mid-second century B.C.E. Alexandria, the later defense of Judaism against the antisemitism that characterized the end of the Hellenistic and the beginning of the Roman period.

There are, however, anachronistic elements in *Aristeas* that reflect conditions subsequent to the Hasmonean revolt (*cf. infra* n. 22). Moreover, contrary to Tcherikover's assumption that the author's "attitude toward Greeks is full of respect and praise" (*ibid.*, 63) and that "no attempt is made to emphasize the moral and religious depravity of paganism" (*ibid.*, 69), one finds in the discourse attributed to Eleazar (128-71) criticism of the pagan religions (134-38, 152) and possible responses to charges of separatism (139-43) and misanthropy (148; *cf. infra* n. 25).

We therefore persist in the understanding that these apologists wrote for mixed audiences and that they stood in the mainstream of a certain halakhic and literary tradition. This is to be seen not only in the well known passages where Philo shows familiarity with the text of Aristeas and Josephus acknowledges his dependence on it (see *infra* n. 23), but also in the overwhelming theological influence of Aristeas on Philo and Josephus.

[7] *Apud* Eusebius, *Praeparatio Evangelica* 8.7.9.

the parent birds with their young" (2.213).[8] He introduces it as an example of a most thorough lesson in "gentleness and philanthropy," adding: "Thus in every detail, he [*i.e.*, our legislator] had an eye on mercy" (2.214).

Each of the above passages consists of two parts, the first part of the one corresponding with the second part of the other. In other words, the passages under consideration show a conflation of related *halakhot*, handed down in reversed order. Thus, the first part of the Philonic passage, "Do not render desolate the nest under your roof," corresponds with the second part of the passage in Josephus, "He would not suffer us to take the parent birds with their young." Commenting on the first part of the Philonic passage, Colson rightly observes: "The allusion is clearly to *Deut.* xxii. 6, where anyone who finds a bird's nest 'in the way or on a tree or on the ground' may take the eggs, but not the mother bird."[9] The parallel passage in Josephus leaves no doubt about the identification of the law with *Deut.* 22:6–7. As for the law alluded to in the other part of each of these passages, it is somewhat elusive. In a note to the second part of the Philonic passage, "[Do not] make the appeals of creatures of none effect when they seem to fly to you for help as they sometimes do," Colson invites attention to the parallel passage in Josephus, "Creatures which take refuge in our houses like suppliants he has forbidden us to kill," and admits: "I do not understand what is meant."[10] In an extended note in the "Appendix" Colson goes on to say: "The statement seems to me remarkable and I should like to meet with some illustration of it or a comment on it particularly in the form given it by Josephus. When is it that animals enter our houses as suppliants?"[11] Likewise, in a note to the passage in Josephus, Thackeray declares: "Not in the Law."[12]

The somewhat elusive law is to be identified with the legislation which proscribes the killing or slaughtering of unclean birds for food (*Lev.* 11:13–19; *cf. Deut.* 14:11–20). This is strongly suggested by the reference to birds in the second part of the passage in Philo ("creatures . . . fly") and more so by the statement which disallows killing in the parallel part of the passage in Josephus ("creatures . . . he has forbidden us to kill"). The identification of the law may be further substantiated by two passages found in Philo's

---

[8] Porphyry, following Josephus, states in *De Abstinentia* 4.14: "They were likewise forbidden not only to refrain from eating, but also from killing animals that fled to their houses as suppliants" (see 4.11, where he refers to Josephus); *cf.* 3.19: "sparrows and swallows who nest in the roofs of houses."

[9] F. H. Colson, ed. and trans., *Philo* 9 (The Loeb Classical Library; Cambridge, MA: Harvard University Press, 1941), 430, n. *a*.

[10] *Ibid.*, n. *b*.

[11] *Ibid.*, 540.

[12] H. St. J. Thackeray, ed. and trans., *Josephus* 1 (The Loeb Classical Library, Cambridge, MA: Harvard University Press, 1926), 379, n. *e*.

dialogues with Alexander, his renegade nephew. Alexander argues in *De Providentia* that Providence, if it existed, would not have allowed edible birds to flee to deserts and "swallows and crows which are of no profit to build their nests in human dwellings and cities" (2.92). To this Philo responds: "If swallows live with us there is nothing to be wondered at for we do not attempt to catch them.... But birds which we like to eat will have nothing to do with us because they fear our designs against them except in cases where the law forbids that their kind should be used as food" (2.106).[13] Again, in *De Animalibus*, speaking of the swallow or house martin, Alexander postulates: "Fleeing from the menace of vultures, it appeals to man first of all and seeks shelter like those who take refuge in temples" (22).[14]

Notwithstanding the inherent difficulties of the two passages, it may be noted that both parts of the passage in Josephus are more suggestive of the underlying laws than are the parallel parts in Philo. Also, in light of the supporting passages from Philo's dialogues, we may be able to narrow down *Lev.* 11:13–19 to v. 15 (*cf.* v. 14 in *Deut.* 14:11–20).

The combination of the law of the nest with the law of the unclean birds and the resultant halakhic conflation may be explained by the fact that *Deut.* 22:6–7 is a kind of dietary law concerning birds and, as such, it is invariably related to the dietary laws pertaining to birds in *Lev.* 11:13–19 and *Deut.* 14:11–20. Moreover, other dietary laws in *Leviticus* 11 and *Deuteronomy* 14 and several of the remaining laws in *Deuteronomy* 22 have likewise acquired moral, ethical, or humanitarian—if not anthropocentric—dimensions in the more apologetic realms of interpretation.[15] While it will be worth considering the various interpretations of these other laws, and this seems to be a promising line of investigation to enhance the discussion, we shall refer to some of them only in passing. For unlike these other laws, the law of the nest and that of the birds of prey appear to have acquired greater significance in arguments for the magnanimity of the Law.

The shift from dietary laws to ethical concerns is reminiscent of the parenesis *a minori ad maius*, "from the lesser to the greater," better known as R. Hillel's *ḳal vaḥomer*, "light and heavy," as one of the seven

---

[13] The swallow or house martin is considered unclean; in addition to the Pentateuchal passages cited above, see *Hull.* 63a–b, 65a.

[14] The thought is based on the universal right of asylum granted to suppliants in a temple. Much of the description of the swallow in *De Animalibus* 22 is indebted to Aristotle; see the ancient authorities cited by D'Arcy W. Thompson, *A Glossary of Greek Birds* (rev. ed.; Oxford: Oxford University Press, 1936), 314–25; also, Plutarch, *Moralia* 984d, on swallows taking to houses for security, and Plato *Leges* 814b, on birds taking refuge in temples.

[15] See, in particular, *Spec. Leg.* 4.100–131, on *Lev.* 11 and *Deut.* 14; and 4.203–18 and *Virt.* 125–47. on *Deut.* 22.

middot or hermeneutical rules for the Torah.[16] Philo and Josephus use this hermeneutical principle, which is based on the presupposition that upon careful search nothing base or unworthy of the oracles of God could be found in them. Philo refers to this principle as "forbidding from afar" or "teaching by implication" (*makrōthen* or *porrōthen*; e.g., *Spec. Leg.* 3.48, 63, 117; 4.104, 203, 218; *Virt.* 21, 116, 137, 160).[17] The extent of the usefulness of the method in allegorical interpretations of some parts of the Mosaic legislation may be demonstrated by the following example: To the injunction in *Ex.* 22:26-27, "If ever you take your neighbour's garment in pledge, you shall restore it to him before the sun goes down; for that is his only covering, it is his mantle for his body," Philo posits the interpretive question: "Does the Creator and Ruler of the universe speak of himself as compassionate in regard to so trivial a matter, a garment not returned to a debtor by a lender of money?" (*Somn.* 1.93).[18]

Such anthropocentric teleology is commonplace in the allegorical interpretation of commandments concerning animals. The special injunctions of kindness to them (and to plants) are interpreted to mean that through kindness to the irrational creation one learns to be kind to rational beings (*Virt.* 81, 116, 123-60; *cf. Spec. Leg.* 2.69; 4.205-6, 226-29). The commandment forbidding the mating of the different species (*Lev.* 19:19) is to admonish men and women against unlawful intercourse (*Spec. Leg.* 3.46-48; 4.203). It was to train his people in frugality and against the sin of covetousness that Moses forbids the enjoyment of pork, scaleless aquatic species, and the fat of sacrificial animals (*Spec. Leg.* 4.101, 124). The reason for the law forbidding the eating of carnivorous animals is to save men from beastly behaviour (4.103-4). Likewise, the legislation against eating animals that have been torn by wild beasts (*Deut.* 14:21) teaches that "a man ought not to have table fellowship with savage brutes" (*Spec. Leg.* 4.119); the same prohibition is extended to "what one should feel with regard to human enemies" (4.121). The prohibition against sacrificing a mother animal and her young on the same day (*Lev.* 22:28) leads to outlawing the sacrifice of pregnant

---

[16] The origin of the concept may be traced to Hellenistic jurisprudence, as suggested by I. Heinemann, *Philons griechische und jüdische Bildung* (Breslau: M. & H. Marcus, 1932), 493 with n. 6, and D. Daube, "Rabbinic Methods of Interpretation and Hellenistic Rhetoric," *Hebrew Union College Annual* 22 (1949), 239-64.

[17] On Philo's use of these categories, see Colson, *supra* n. 9, at 8:432-34. *Cf.* the use of *posō mallon*, *pollō mallon*, and *polu mallon* in the New Testament, e.g., Mt. 6:26 (par. Lk. 12:24); 6:30 (par. Lk. 12:28); 7:11 (par. Lk. 11:13); Heb. 9:13-14; 12:9, 25; etc.

[18] Note the similarity with Paul's treatment of *Deut.* 22:10 in *2 Cor.* 6:14-15 and *Deut.* 25:4 in *1 Cor.* 9:9-10. In later Talmudic tradition there is a protest against this allegorizing of laws which deal with seeming trivialities. In reference to *Deut.* 22:6, *Ber.* 33a reads: "Whoever says, 'Do God's mercies extend to the bird's nest? Can God concern himself with such trivial things?' is to be silenced."

animals and finally to proscribing the execution of pregnant women (*Virt.* 134:139; it may be noted that *Deut.* 22:6-7 is also related to the law of prohibiting the slaughter of a mother animal and her young on the same day).

Along with the nest law, Josephus has a whole cluster of similarly expounded *halakhot* whereby he endeavours to emphasize the humanity of the Law (*Ap.* 2.259–260). In the *Antiquities* he promises to explain in a proposed future work why certain animals are forbidden for food and certain others permitted (3.259). Unfortunately, he fails to fulfill this promise. From what can be gathered from elsewhere in his writings and the commonplaces of Hellenistic Judaism, however, it seems likely that he would have interpreted the dietary laws as more than a mere discipline of temperance. The social implications of the dietary laws may be sensed in the following lines:

> Starting from the very beginning with the food of which we partake from infancy and the private life of the home, he left nothing, however insignificant, to the discretion and caprice of the individual. What meats a man should abstain from, and what he may enjoy; with what persons he may associate . . . for all this our leader made the Law the standard and rule. (*Ap.* 2.173–174)

Inevitably, observance of the dietary laws became a determining factor in communal association.[19] The resultant separatism intensified with the historical situation of foreign domination and the concerns of the Diaspora Jews with those parts of the Law which differentiated them as a people, for example, the Sabbath, circumcision, and the rules governing foods. The daily observance of these latter laws of purity, more than other peculiar observances of everyday life, became the hallmark of Jewish religious identity during the Second Temple period. Even in the rabbinic traditions before 70 C.E., as Neusner observes, "approximately 67% of all legal pericopae deal with dietary laws: ritual purity for meals and agricultural rules governing the fitness of food for Pharisaic consumption. Observance of Sabbaths and festivals is a distant third."[20] Neusner bases his understanding of the early history of the Pharisees on this observation,[21] which seems to suggest the initial reason for Pharisaic separatism—though certainly they were not alone to see food laws in terms of separation from others.

---

[19] The connection between dietary laws and interpersonal relationships may be seen in the broader concept that observance of the commandments is directly connected with social justice; see, *e.g.*, *Aristeas* 168–69; *Sirach* 19:20–24; etc.

[20] J. Neusner, *The Rabbinic Traditions About the Pharisees Before 70, Part III* (Leiden: E. J. Brill, 1971), 303–6.

[21] *Ibid.*; *idem*, *The Idea of Purity in Ancient Judaism* (Studies in Judaism in Late Antiquity 1; Leiden: E. J. Brill, 1973), 64–71; *idem*, *From Politics to Piety: The Emergence of Pharisaic Judaism* (Englewood Cliffs, N.J.: Prentice-Hall, 1973), *passim*, especially 80, 90.

Important for our consideration is *Aristeas to Philocrates*, to which a date ca. 150–100 B.C.E. is generally given and the Alexandrian provenance of which cannot be doubted.[22] Moreover, at various places Philo shows familiarity with the text and Josephus acknowledges his dependence on it.[23] The central part of the document, Eleazar's apology for the Mosaic Law (128–71), is often eclipsed by the overall account dealing with the translation of the Septuagint. The main argument, however, centers around dietary laws and is developed as an answer to what pseudo-Aristeas considers a pressing issue, expressing what seems to have been a most common question addressed to Jews and a usual objection given to their faith: "For I believe that most men feel some curiosity concerning passages in the Law dealing with food and drink and animals regarded as unclean," and "Why was it that, creation being one, some things are regarded as unclean for food and some even to the touch?" (128–29).[24] Eleazar's purported answer contains several of the apologetic elements hitherto observed in Philo and Josephus. After a general statement on the distinctiveness of Jewish piety, the reply to the above inquiries and to implied slanders[25] begins as follows:

> When therefore the lawgiver, who had been endowed by God with insight into all things, had considered all these matters, he fenced us about with inpregnable palisades and iron walls, in order that we might not in any way mix with the other nations, remaining pure in body and soul, free of vain opinions, revering the one and almighty God above the whole of creation. Hence the priests, who are the guides of the Egyptians, having looked

[22] For the upper limit, see E. Bickermann, "Zur Datierung des Pseudo-Aristeas," *Zeitschrift für die neutestamentliche Wissenschaft* 29 (1930), 280–96; favoured by Tcherikover, *supra* n. 1, at 60, n. 9; an earlier date in the second century B.C.E. is maintained by E. Van 't Dack, "La date de la lettre d'Aristée," in *Antidorum W. Peremans sexagenario ab alumnis oblatum*, ed. L. Gerfaux et al. (Studia Hellenistica 16; Louvain: Publications Universitaires, 1968), 263–78. For the lower limit, see H. G. Meecham, *The Letter of Aristeas: A Linguistic Study with Special Reference to the Greek Bible* (Manchester: Manchester University Press, 1935); *cf.* A. Momigliano, "Per la data e la caratteristica della lettera di Aristea," *Aegyptus* 12 (1932), 161–72. M. Hadas, *Aristeas to Philocrates* (New York: Harper and Brothers, 1951), 9–54, favours 130 B.C.E. as a hypothetical date, though he seems to be overwhelmed by the major arguments for a later date.

[23] Besides Philo's enormous theological indebtedness to *Aristeas* (*e.g., infra* n. 28), see his account of the translation of the LXX in *Vita Mos.* 2.25–44. M. Hadas (*supra* n. 22, at 22) thinks "it is altogether possible that Philo used an independent tradition, perhaps indeed the same tradition which Aristeas himself used." As for Josephus, see *Ant.* 12.11–118. *Cf. Aristeas* 9:46, 51–81, 172–87, 292–305, 308–21.

[24] Such was the argument of the Cynic teacher Diogenes, according to Diogenes Laertius (6.73; *cf.* Porphyry *De Abstinentia* 1.42). *Cf.* also the Stoic-Middle Platonic doctrine in the first century C.E. writer Musonius Rufus, who argues that food restrictions are for ascetic reasons; C. E. Lutz, "Musonius Rufus, 'The Roman Socrates,'" *Yale Classical Studies* 10 (1947), 115–19.

[25] See the notes of M. Hadas, *supra* n. 22, at 157–59, on sections 142, 144, 148.

closely into many things and being conversant with such matters, have called us "men of God.". . . The rest are men of food and drink and raiment. . . .[26] Among our people, however, these things are reckoned as nothing, but throughout the whole of life their meditation is on the lordship of God. And lest we should be polluted by anyone or be perverted by associating with worthless persons, he fenced us about on all sides with prescribed purifications in matters of food and drink. . . . There is a profound logic for our abstinence from the use of some things and our participation in the use of others. For the sake of illustration I will run over one or two details and provide you an explanation. (139-43)

It is significant that the "one or two" detailed illustrations which Eleazar wishes to give as examples of the magnanimity of the Law, as the immediately following sections indicate (147-50), begin with the legislation forbidding the eating of birds of prey (*Lev.* 11:13-19; *cf. Deut.* 14:11-20), which is interpreted to mean "that those for whom the legislation was drawn up must practice righteousness in spirit and oppress no one, trusting in their own strength, nor rob anyone of anything, but must guide their lives in accordance with justice, just like the gentle creatures among the birds" (147). Eleazar concludes his exposition of the passage on the birds of prey, which could well be the earliest extant example of what had become commonplace argumentation from *a minori ad maius* in Hellenistic-Jewish apologetics, with these words: "Wherefore all the rules which he had laid down with regard to what is permitted in the case of these [birds] and other animals, he has enacted with the object of teaching us a moral lesson" (150).[27]

The High Priest goes on to talk about "the other animals" and the allegorical meaning of "the parting of the hoof and the chewing of the cud" (*Lev.* 11:3-7; *cf. Deut.* 14:6-8) as separation from the rest of mankind and the processes of memory that lead to right reason and justice (150-62). In his explanation of these "symbols" he refers to the precepts on *tefillin* and *mezuzot* (*Num.* 15:38; *Deut.* 22:12 and 6:4-9, 11:13-21), since they too represent the same meaning: "remembrance of God" and "that every action must be carried out with justice and that we must retain remembrance of our composition and above all fear of God. He [*i.e.*, our legislator] bids us to meditate upon God" (158:160).[28] This

---

[26] *Cf. Mt.* 6:31-33: "Therefore take no thought, saying, What shall we eat? or, What shall we drink? or, Wherewithal shall we be clothed? For after all these things do the Gentiles seek. . . . But seek first the kingdom of God and his righteousness. . . ."

[27] The translation of this section is by T. H. Andrews, "The Letter of Aristeas," *The Apocrypha and Pseudepigrapha of the Old Testament*, ed. R. H. Charles, 2 (Oxford: The Clarendon Press, 1913), 108; the translation of the previously quoted sections from *Aristeas* is, with some modifications, by M. Hadas, *supra* n. 22.

[28] The allegorical meaning of these "symbols" is reverberated by Philo in *Agr.* 131-45; *Spec. Leg.* 4.106-8, 136-42.

explains why in the above excerpt Eleazar interjects his remarks on the observance of the dietary laws with the statement (introduced by an adversative correlator) that "throughout the whole of life their [*i.e.*, his countrymen's] meditation is on the lordship of God" (141).

It is noteworthy that in conjunction with the dietary laws in the panegyric of the Law, the High Priest in *Aristeas* refers only to the precepts on *tefillin* and *mezuzot*. These laws together seem to constitute the two extremes of the continuum of Jewish Law—at least in Hellenistic Jewish thought: from the least of the commandments (on what to do with birds) to the greatest (on divine meditation), both of which are encompassed in *Deut.* 22:6–12. Moreover, among the commandments concerning animals, particularly the dietary regulations, are found the enactments that may rightly be termed "the least of the commandments," and in the apologetic aspect of their allegorical meanings are seen "the weightier matters of the Law"—to use the language of the New Testament.[29] An overwhelming burden of Hellenistic Jewish apologetics is to show that there is no difference between the vastly dissimilar categories of the Mosaic Law: the least are as significant as the greatest. They all are intended to teach justice and humanity.

[29] *Mt.* 5:19; 23:23; cf. Philo, *Gaium* 211.

ABSTRACTS

PROBLEMS OF ESTABLISHING CRITERIA OF HALAKHAH IN REFORM JUDAISM

by

D. COHN-SHERBOK*

Recently a number of leading Reform Rabbis have criticised Reform Judaism of the past for its emphasis on individual decision making, and they strongly advocate formulating a new approach to the legal system. What is needed, they argue, is a modern code of law for Reform Jews which is rooted in our heritage. Such a code would require explicit criteria for deciding which traditional laws should be eliminated and which retained. Thus, in a variety of publications, Reform Rabbis have been giving a great deal of thought to the principles they believe could be employed.

On the basis of an analysis of these arguments it can be seen that there is no way to decide which traditional laws ought to be included in a contemporary system of law for Reform Judaism. Revelation, conscience, relevance, contemporary appeal, ethical propriety, justice, aesthetic value, psychological considerations, common sense, reasonableness, the good of the Reform Jewish community, the peoplehood of Israel—all these criteria which have been prescribed by numerous leaders of our movement are so nebulous and contentious as to be of little if any use. All that we can say is that as Reform Jews we are heirs to a vast legal tradition, yet we lack any well-defined, coherent, and consistent method for sorting out those traditional laws we should adopt for ourselves. This is not a temporary difficulty which we can resolve in the future; it is rather an inevitable consequence of our rejection of the Divine authority of the legal system.

An expanded version of the conference paper appears as "Freedom and Law in Reform Judaism," *Journal of Reform Judaism* (Winter, 1983), 88–97.

---

*Director, Centre for the Study of Religion and Society, University of Kent, Canterbury, England.

THE JEWISH LAW OF USURY AS SEEN IN ELIZABETHAN LITERATURE

by

*JEAN JOFEN**

Ari Ibn-Zahav, a Hebrew writer, wrote a novel based on *The Merchant of Venice*. In this novel, the author reverses the condition of the bond. The pound of flesh is demanded not by Shylock but Antonio out of contempt for the Jew who lends money at interest. This novel was adapted into a play by the Yiddish writer–actor, Maurice Schwartz.

On Nov. 30, 1947, Brooks Atkinson, the Drama Editor of the N. Y. Times, published his review of this new play, *Shylock and his Daughter*. He ends with these words: "It is impossible to motivate the pound-of-flesh bond to the point of making it palatable or creditable. That is the one thing that cannot be argued away. It is the chief stumbling-block to Ibn-Zahav's new version. His Shylock may be a finer character, but the horrific bond device traps him in the mare's nest at the end." Every Jew and every sympathizer of Jews has had a feeling of shame and anger that a Jew was portrayed by Shakespeare as demanding a pound of flesh from a Christian as penalty for non-payment of a debt.

It will be shown that the bond in *The Merchant of Venice* is a covert attack on the Pope.

---

*Chairperson, Dept. of Modern Languages, Baruch College, CUNY; President, Marlow Society, USA.

THE *MOREDET*: A STUDY OF THE REBELLIOUS WIFE AND HER STATUS IN INITIATING DIVORCE IN JEWISH LAW

by

SHLOMO RISKIN

In Mishnaic and early Talmudic times, a *moredet* was a woman who denied sexual relations to her husband as a punishment for some offense he had committed against her—real or imagined. Since she wished to remain his wife, the earliest halakhic approach was to legislate successively harsher decrees against her, designed to coerce her into resuming marital relations.

But what about the woman who "merely" found her husband distasteful, although she had no objective, legally justifiable grounds for divorce? The legal authorities are divided over this issue, presumably on the basis of the relative importance they placed on the feelings of the woman versus the stability of the family.

The Jerusalem Talmud and ancient marriage contracts found in the Cairo *Geniza* seem to prove that in early Amoraic times (third and fourth centuries of the Common Era) the dilemma was resolved in favor of the woman's sensitivity. A stipulation in the *ketubah* ensured that if either party found the other distasteful, the court could impose a divorce. Later, the *geonim* (800–1000 C.E.) went a step further by eliminating the twelve-month waiting period and re-instituting the alimony payment. The scholars Alfasi (1013–1103 C.E.), Rashbam (ca. 1080/85–1174 C.E.), and Maimonides (1135–1200 C.E.) likewise followed the Geonic precedent of coercing the husband to grant a divorce, although different traditions existed regarding monetary compensation.

The entire picture changed radically in later generations, due largely to Rabbenu Tam (ca. 1100–1171 C.E.). His chief concern was preserving the institution of marriage and minimizing the number of divorces. Insisting that there was no Talmudic precedent for coercing a husband to divorce his wife, on the basis of her subjective claim that he was repulsive to her, he rejected the earlier Geonic decrees. So overwhelming was his personality, and so cogent his legal reasoning, that his ruling influenced all subsequent halakhic authorities. To this day the law is such that a woman who finds her husband distasteful has no legal recourse, and must remain tied to a husband she abhors. In this work I hope to prove that Rabbenu Tam's was a minority opinion, and that there is no reason not to enable the woman to free herself from an intolerable marriage.

THE OCHNAI OVEN AND THE LAW: TALMUDIC JUDAISM'S RESPONSE TO NATURAL LAW

by

A. YUTER*

The Ochnai Oven Legend (*B.M.* 59b) has often been quoted by various Jewish thinkers to justify their positions. In this paper, it will be argued that the story's *literary* structure embodies a consistent polemic in favor of positive law and against natural law.

Ultimately, the debate between natural and positive legal thinkers rests on two opposing views of the nature of law. For the positivist, the science of law examines the statutes and norms of the legal order; while the natural lawyer believes that legal norms necessarily hint to a higher ethic, *telos*, or to the mind of God.

In the Ochnai oven account, R. Eliezer argues that his lenient ruling is in conformity with the ancient law. Indeed, it can be demonstrated that his opinion (that the oven is indeed pure after having been broken) concurs with the old Mishnah in *Kelim*. But the positive legal order invests the court with the authority to reformulate the positive norms of the legal order. Unable to refute the implied claim of the court, R. Eliezer appeals to nature and ultimately to God, the creator of nature. But according to Jewish law, once the legal order is in the hands of mankind, there is no positive legal provision for what Divine intention happens to be, any more than legal norms can be derived from nature. Jewish legal "oughts" are derived from norms, not from Nature or the Deity.

By having the Almighty concede that the law is not in heaven, but in the hands of the legally ordained juridic organ, Talmudic Judaism affirms that Jewish legal procedures recognize legal criteria alone and that appeals to reason, nature, or God Himself fall outside the universe of legal discourse.

*Rabbi, Congregation Ohr Yisrael, Jewish Community Center of Spring Valley; Adjunct Faculty, Rockland Community College.